Transcendence ⌣ ⌐.

The Queen Mother
of the West
in Medieval China

Transcendence & Divine Passion

The Queen Mother of the West in Medieval China

Suzanne E. Cahill

Stanford University Press
Stanford, California

Stanford University Press
Stanford, California
© 1993 by the Board of Trustees of the
Leland Stanford Junior University
Printed in the United States of America

CIP data appear at the end of the book

Published with the assistance of the
Chiang Ching-kuo Foundation

Original printing 1993
Last figure below indicates year of this printing:
04 03 02 01 00 99 98 97 96 95

Stanford University Press publications are
distributed exclusively by Stanford University
Press within the United States, Canada, Mexico,
and Central America; they are distributed exclusively by Cambridge University Press throughout the rest of the world.

To Edward H. Schafer
1913–1991

Acknowledgments

My thanks are due to many teachers, colleagues, and friends who have given me guidance and encouragement. I owe a debt of gratitude to those who introduced me to Chinese poetic texts: Peter Boodberg, Cheng Ch'ing-mao, and Edward Schafer. The research for this book began with my doctoral dissertation at the University of California, Berkeley, directed by Edward Schafer, Chang Kun, and Frederic Wakeman, all of whom made valuable suggestions. During two years at Peking University, I had lively discussions with Professor Ch'en I-hsin and others concerning interpretations of T'ang poetry and Taoist texts. In addition, several people have read and criticized various parts and versions of this manuscript or helped with specific problems, including Steve Bokencamp, Ch'en Kuo-fu, Chang Ming-fei, David Noel Freedman, Barbara Kandel Hendrischke, Thomas A. Hessling, David Keightley, Ko Shao-yin, Paul Kroll, Daniel Overmyer, Anna Seidel, Christena Turner, Victoria Vernon, Wang Shih-lun, and Angela Zito. Audrey Spiro and Ann Waltner read numerous recensions and patiently contributed their wisdom. I have benefited from the advice of all these scholars; the mistakes that remain are my own.

I am grateful to the Committee for Scholarly Communication with the People's Republic of China for grants that enabled me to study in Peking from 1980 to 1982 and to the Smithsonian Institution in Washington, D.C., for a postdoctoral fellowship at the Freer Gallery of Art (1982–83), where I did the research on the Queen Mother of the West in early Chinese art. A postdoctoral teaching fellowship from the Mellon Foundation allowed me to spend a year at Emory University (1983–84) revising my manuscript and exploring women's studies; a further postdoctoral appointment at the Center for Chinese Studies at the University of California, Berkeley (1984–86), gave me access to many colleagues as well as the East Asian Library and its fine staff. I also express my gratitude to Muriel Bell, senior editor at Stanford University Press, for her perceptive handling of both author and manuscript. As always, I thank my husband, friends, and family for their support and encouragement.

An earlier form of Chapter 6 appeared in the *Journal of the American Oriental Society* (1986). A few poems and other texts translated in Chapters 1, 3, and 4 were published in short essays in the *Journal of Chinese Religions* (1984, 1985–86, and 1988) and *T'ang Studies* (1986, 1987).

S.E.C.

Contents

Figures

Preface

This book is about love, death, and immortality. It examines the greatest goddess of medieval Taoism, the Queen Mother of the West (Hsi Wang Mu), through the eyes of medieval Chinese people. My main sources are a religious biography of the goddess written by the Taoist master Tu Kuang-t'ing (850–933), and the works of numerous poets of the T'ang dynasty (618–907). Both Taoism, the native higher religion of China, and poetry flourished during this era. The main body of this book interweaves information from Tu's account with T'ang poems to reveal what T'ang people thought about the Queen Mother's identity and about her acts among humans.

My own interest in this subject arises from a fascination with Taoist religion, T'ang poetry, and women. The Queen Mother of the West joins all three. Medieval Taoists considered her the embodiment of the ultimate yin, the dark female force. Taoist texts claim that, along with the other high deities, she created the world and continues to maintain cosmic harmony. Her followers associated the Queen Mother of the West with transcendence and divine passion. Transcendence implies overcoming human limitations such as mortality and ignorance. Divine passion suggests the communication between humans and deities that was one means to achieve transcendence. Divine passion mirrors the bliss of the immortals in the human metaphor of sexual love. The Queen Mother of the West governed both immortality and the means through which it might be achieved. Her image in T'ang Taoist texts and poetry embodies universal human concerns of love and death at a specific time and place.

I am not the first person to study Chinese goddesses. I am indebted to David Hawkes for his identification of the quest theme in early Chinese poetic texts and to Edward Schafer for his work in *The Divine Woman* on the treatment of other ancient Chinese goddesses in T'ang literature. Scholars before me have taken an interest in the Queen Mother of the West during the Han and Six Dynasties periods: I have made grateful use of Homer Dubs's early article on a Han dynasty peasant cult devoted to that deity, of Kominami Ichirō's research linking her with the festival of Double Seven, and of Michael Loewe's careful survey of the early sources in his *Ways to Paradise*. I have also benefited profoundly from work done by others in Taoist studies, most notably Ch'en Kuo-fu, Isabelle Robinet, Edward Schafer, Kristopher Schipper, Anna Seidel, and Michel Strickmann. The research of Joseph Needham and Nathan Sivin in Chinese alchemy has also helped me. Some fine related work reached publication too late to assist in my own research, but welcome all the same, including Wu Hung's book on the Wu Liang shrine of the Han and Franciscus Verellen's study of the life and works of Tu Kuang-t'ing.

The special contributions of the present study are its focus on a single great goddess, the Queen Mother of the West, during the period when her Taoist cult and literary image were most fully developed, the T'ang dynasty, as well as the questions it raises about that goddess and the society that revered her. What kind of a goddess was she, and how does she compare with other deities in China and elsewhere? What does her worship tell us about religion and the state, about religion and the lives of men and women, courtiers and peasants, during T'ang China? What can we say after studying her about the relation of Taoism and T'ang poetry? My goal has been to present an integrated picture of the goddess, as portrayed in both religious and literary texts, in her social and historical context. I also hope to bring rarely studied texts and beliefs into the light they deserve.

Note on Citation
and Abbreviations

Unless otherwise noted, T'ang poems are cited by page number in the edition of the *Ch'üan T'ang shih* published by the Fu hsing Bookstore (Taipei, 1967). Texts in the Taoist canon (*Tao tsang*) are cited by their serial number in Weng Tu-chien, *Tao tsang tzu mu yin te*, Harvard-Yenching Sinological Index Series 25 (Peking, 1935). Volume numbers are followed by a colon; *chüan* numbers by a period. Except as noted, all translations are my own.

The following abbreviations are used throughout the book; see the Bibliography, pp. 263–80, for complete references.

ch.	*chüan*
CMYC	Tu Kuang-t'ing, *Chin mu yüan chün* (The primordial ruler, metal mother), in *YCCHL*, 24158–64
CTS	*Ch'üan T'ang shih*
FSTI	Ying Shao, *Feng su t'ung i*
HHS	Fan Yeh et al., *Hou Han shu*
HNT	*Huai nan-tzu hung lieh chi chieh*
HS	Pan Ku et al., *Han shu*
HWTNC	*Han Wu-ti nei chuan*
HY	Weng Tu-chien, *Tao tsang tzu mu yin te*
MTTC	*Mu T'ien-tzu chuan*
PWC	Chang Hua, *Po wu chih*
SC	Ssu-ma Ch'ien, *Shih chi*
SHC	*Shan hai ching chiao chu*

TSCC   T'u shu chi ch'eng
TSYT   Tu Fu, *Tu shih yin te*
WH   Hsiao T'ung, *Wen hsüan*
WSPY   *Wu shang pi yao*
YCCHL   Tu Kuang-t'ing, *Yung ch'eng chi hsien lu*

Chronologies

Major Chinese Dynasties and Periods

Hsia	ca. 2100–ca. 1600 B.C.
Shang	ca. 1600–ca. 1028 B.C.
Chou	ca. 1027–256 B.C.
Western Chou	ca. 1027–771 B.C.
Eastern Chou	ca. 770–256 B.C.
Spring and Autumn	722–468 B.C.
Warring States	403–221 B.C.
Ch'in	221–207 B.C.
Han	206 B.C.–A.D. 220
Former Han	206 B.C.–A.D. 8
Hsin	A.D. 9–25
Latter Han	A.D. 25–220
Three Kingdoms	220–265
Wei	220–265
Shu	221–263
Wu	222–280
Six Dynasties (Wu, Eastern Chin, Liu Sung, Southern Ch'i, Southern Liang, and Southern Ch'en)	222–589
Chin	265–420
Western Chin	265–317
Eastern Chin	317–420

Southern Dynasties	420–589
Former (Liu) Sung	420–479
Southern Ch'i	479–502
Southern Liang	502–557
Southern Ch'en	557–589
Northern Dynasties	386–581
Northern Wei	386–534
Eastern Wei	534–550
Western Wei	535–577
Northern Ch'i	550–577
Northern Chou	557–581
Sui	581–618
T'ang	618–907
Chou	690–705
Five Dynasties	907–60
Liao	916–1125
Sung	960–1279
Northern Sung	960–1126
Southern Sung	1127–1279
Chin (Jurchen)	1115–1234
Yüan	1260–1368
Ming	1368–1644
Ch'ing	1644–1911

T'ang Dynasty Emperors and Reign Periods

Emperors

Posthumous title	Personal name	Accession date
Kao tsu	Li Yüan	18 June 618
T'ai tsung	Li Shih-min	4 Sept. 626
Kao tsung	Li Chih	15 July 649
Chung tsung	Li Hsien	3 Jan. 684
Jui tsung	Li Tan	27 Feb. 684
Tse-t'ien huang hou	Wu Chao	16 Oct. 690
Chung tsung	Li Hsien	23 Feb. 705
Shao ti	Li Ch'ung-mao	5 July 710

Posthumous title	Personal name	Accession date
Jui tsung	Li Tan	25 July 710
Hsüan tsung	Li Lung-chi	8 Sept. 712
Su tsung	Li Heng	12 Aug. 756
Tai tsung	Li Yü	18 May 762
Te tsung	Li Kua	12 June 779
Shun tsung	Li Sung	28 Feb. 805
Hsien tsung	Li Ch'un	5 Sept. 805
Mu tsung	Li Heng	20 Feb. 820
Ching tsung	Li Chan	29 Feb. 824
Wen tsung	Li Ang	13 Jan. 827
Wu tsung	Li Yen	20 Feb. 840
Hsüan tsung	Li Ch'en	25 Apr. 846
I tsung	Li Ts'ui	13 Sept. 859
Hsi tsung	Li Hsüan	15 Aug. 873
Chao tsung	Li Yeh	22 Apr. 888
Ai ti	Li Chu	26 Sept. 904

Reign Periods

Reign name	Translation	Inaugural date
Wu te	Martial Virtue	18 June 618
Chen kuan	Honorable Outlook	23 Jan. 627
Yung hui	Eternal Beauty	7 Feb. 650
Hsien ch'ing	Manifest Felicitation	7 Feb. 656
Lung shuo	Dragon Conjunction	4 Apr. 661
Lin te	Unicorn Virtue	2 Feb. 664
Ch'ien feng	Supernal *feng* (Sacrifice)	14 Feb. 666
Tsung chang	Consolidating Design	22 Apr. 668
Hsien heng	Total Efficacy	27 Mar. 670
Shang yüan	Supreme Prime	20 Sept. 674
I feng	Exemplary Phoenix	18 Dec. 676
T'iao lu	Harmonious Dew	15 July 679
Yung lung	Eternal Ascendancy	22 Sept. 680
K'ai yao	Opened Coruscation	15 Nov. 681
Yung ch'un	Eternal Purity	2 Apr. 682
Hung tao	Accrescent Tao	27 Dec. 683
Ssu sheng	Heritor Sage	23 Jan. 684

Reign name	Translation	Inaugural date
Wen ming	Cultured Illumination	27 Feb. 684
Kuang chai	Radiant Residence	19 Oct. 684
Ch'ui kung	Hanging (Robes) and Folded (Hands)	9 Feb. 685
Yung ch'ang	Eternal Glory	27 Feb. 689
Ts'ai chu	Beginning of the Era	18 Dec. 689
T'ien shou	Heaven Given	16 Oct. 690
Ju i	As You Wish	22 Apr. 692
Ch'ang shou	Prolonged Longevity	23 Oct. 692
Yen tsai	Extended Era	9 June 694
Cheng sheng	Proven Sage	23 Nov. 694
T'ien tse wan sui	A Myriad Years on Heaven's Tablatures	22 Oct. 695
Wan sui teng feng	A Myriad Years' Ascent for the feng (Sacrifice)	20 Jan. 696
Wan sui t'ung tien	A Myriad Years' Communication with Heaven	22 Apr. 696
Shen kung	Divine Exploit	29 Sept. 697
Sheng li	Sage Calendar	20 Dec. 697
Chiu shih	Enduring Vision	27 May 700
Ta tsu	Great Footstep	15 Feb. 701
Ch'ang an	Prolonged Stability	26 Nov. 701
Shen lung	Divine Dragon	30 Jan. 705
Ching lung	Spectacular Dragon	5 Oct. 707
T'ang lung	T'ang Ascendant	5 July 710
Ching yün	Spectacular Cloud	19 Aug. 710
T'ai chi	Grand Culmination	1 Mar. 712
Yen ho	Extensive Accord	21 June 712
Hsien t'ien	Preceding Heaven	12 Sept. 712
K'ai yüan	Opened Prime	22 Dec. 713
T'ien pao	Heavenly Treasure	10 Feb. 742
Chih te	Ultimate Virtue	12 Aug. 756
Ch'ien yüan	Supernal Prime	18 Mar. 758
Shang yüan	Supreme Prime	7 June 760
Pao ying	Treasure Response	13 May 762

Reign name	Translation	Inaugural date
Kuang te	Ample Virtue	24 Aug. 763
Yung t'ai	Eternal Majesty	26 Jan. 765
Ta li	Great Calendar	18 Dec. 766
Chien chung	Established Center	11 Feb. 780
Hsing yüan	Exalted Prime	27 Jan. 784
Chen yüan	Honorable Prime	14 Feb. 785
Yung chen	Eternal Probity	1 Sept. 805
Yüan ho	Primal Accord	25 Jan. 806
Ch'ang ch'ing	Prolonged Felicitation	9 Feb. 821
Pao li	Precious Calendar	29 Jan. 825
T'ai ho	Grand Accord	14 Mar. 827
K'ai ch'eng	Opened Perfection	22 Jan. 836
Hui ch'ang	Assembled Glories	4 Feb. 841
Ta chung	Great Center	6 Feb. 847
Hsien t'ung	Total Comprehension	17 Dec. 860
Ch'ien fu	Supernal Talisman	17 Dec. 874
Kuang ming	Broad Illumination	14 Feb. 880
Chung ho	Centered Accord	9 Aug. 881
Kuang ch'i	Radiant Disclosure	2 Apr. 885
Wen te	Cultured Virtue	7 Apr. 888
Lung chi	Dragon Cycle	4 Feb. 889
Ta hsun	Great Compliance	22 Jan. 890
Ching fu	Spectacular Fortune	22 Feb. 892
Ch'ien ning	Supernal Peace	10 Feb. 894
Kuang hua	Radiant Transformation	16 Sept. 898
T'ien fu	Heavenly Restoration	16 May 901
T'ien yu	Heavenly Safekeeping	28 May 904

(End of T'ang: 5 June 907)

(SOURCES: Nienhauser, *Indiana Companion*, xli–xlii; Kroll, "True Dates.")

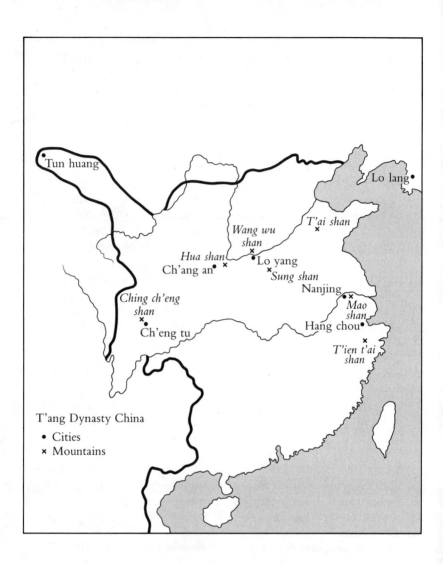

Tun huang

Lo lang

T'ai shan

Wang wu
shan

Hua shan
Ch'ang an   Lo yang

Sung shan

Nanjing

Ching ch'eng
shan

Mao
shan

Ch'eng tu

Hang chou

T'ien t'ai
shan

T'ang Dynasty China

• Cities
× Mountains

Transcendence & Divine Passion

The Queen Mother
of the West
in Medieval China

※ *Introduction*

The Goddess

This book examines the greatest Taoist goddess of the T'ang dynasty (618–907), the Queen Mother of the West (Hsi Wang Mu), through the eyes of medieval Chinese people. We begin our quest of the goddess with a work by the poet Li Po (701–62) celebrating his ascent of Mount T'ai in 742:

> In the morning I drink from the Queen Mother's Pond;
> At dark, I seek Heavenly Gate Pass.
> Alone, I carry in my arms the zither "Wrapped in Green Damask";
> At night I go along between blue mountains.
> The mountains are brilliant, moon and dew white.
> Night grows quiet; the pine wind stops.
> Transcendent people wander to cyan peaks;
> Everywhere their mouth organ sounds arise.
> In isolation, I enjoy pure brightness;
> Jade Realized Ones join together with faint blue of distant hills.
> I imagine phoenix and simurgh dancing;
> Whirling and twirling: dragon and tiger clothes.
> Touching heaven, I pluck the Calabash Gourd;
> Confused and uncertain, I don't remember how to go home.
> Lifting my hands, I play with clear and shallow water;
> Mistakenly I seize the Weaver Girl's loom.
> At bright dawn, as I sit, stars becoming lost in relation to each other,
> I can only see five-colored clouds flying.
>
> (*CTS*, 1003)

This poem, the last of six on Li Po's climb of Mount T'ai, embodies the two main elements of our quest: Taoism and poetry.[1] By the T'ang dynasty, Taoism, the native major religion of China, had absorbed both ancient goddesses such as the Queen Mother and ancient holy places such as Marchmount T'ai (T'ai yüeh), the sacred mountain of the east (located in present-day Shantung province). Li Po, a poet deeply influenced by Taoism, makes a pilgrimage to the mountain. Nestled into its foothills was a temple to the Queen Mother, where both state and Taoist rituals were performed. Inspired by the numinous landscape, Li models his verses on songs about the Taoist adept's ecstatic flight through the heavens. His ascent begins with a ceremonial drink of holy water from the goddess's Turquoise Pond. "Wrapped in Green Damask" was the name of the zither belonging to Ssu-ma Hsiang-ju, a great Han dynasty poet who wrote of the Queen Mother's visits. Cyan (*pi*) is a dark blue-green color. Transcendent people (*hsien jen*) and realized ones (*chen jen*) are the immortals of medieval Taoism. Li Po sees the phoenix (*feng*) and simurgh (*luan*), two auspicious mythical birds of ancient China (the English names of these birds are borrowed from Greek and Persian legend). The Calabash Gourd and Weaver Girl are constellations; the water he plays with flows in the Milky Way. The company of goddesses and transcendents has left him dazed and wondering. Li Po's poem testifies to worship of the Queen Mother among T'ang intelligentsia, her connection with an ancient holy mountain, and her link to the Taoist pursuit of immortality.

The Queen Mother of the West appears frequently in sacred and secular literature of the T'ang dynasty. Her medieval definition reflects beliefs of the Shang ch'ing (Realm of Supreme Clarity) school of Taoism, the tradition favored by T'ang emperors and literati. The Shang ch'ing tradition is also called Mao shan Taoism after the holy mountain of that name near Nanjing. This form of Taoism began in the fourth century with revelations from deities in the three highest heavens, known as Realms of Clarity, to the young visionary Yang Hsi. The texts, later compiled by the great fifth-century editor T'ao Hung-ching, explicate a rich and complex religious system combining various older elements from both north and south. The Shang ch'ing school emphasized individual religious practices, such as alchemy and meditation, that led to immortality in the Realms of Clarity. This school appealed to the court and official class, the educated elite of early China. In contrast, the other main tradition of medieval Taoism, the Ling pao (Numinous Treasure) school, which arose slightly later, emphasized public ritual or liturgy and tended to have a broader popular appeal.[2] The two schools grew up side by side during the Chinese Middle Ages, rivals with a great deal of mutual influence.

Medieval Taoists considered the Queen Mother of the West the embodiment of the ultimate yin, the dark female force. They believed that, along with other high deities of Taoism, she created the world and continued to maintain cosmic harmony. The goddess's name, Queen Mother of the West, reveals three essential components of her character: she was regal, female, and associated with the west. As a ruler, she controlled creation, transcendence, and divine passion. As a woman, she was mother, teacher, and lover. Her western association links her in traditional Chinese cosmology with autumn, death, the afterlife, and paradise. Further connections with the west, important in poetry, include the color white, the element metal, and the emotion of melancholy.

It may startle Western readers to learn that the Queen Mother's followers pass over her role in creation, which they see as an automatic and inevitable natural process, to emphasize two other themes: transcendence and divine passion. Transcendence implies overcoming human limitations such as mortality and ignorance. The goal of the Taoist adept was to transcend the human condition and become a perfected, immortal being. Divine passion is the desire of deities and humans for mutual union and communication. One means to transcendence was marriage with a deity of the opposite sex. The marriage, often described in the most sensual of metaphors, was meant to leave sexuality behind and concentrate on the spiritual advancement of both parties. Perfection might also be attained by means of meditation or ingestion of elixirs, always under the tutelage of a divine master of the opposite sex. The Queen Mother of the West governed both immortality and the holy marriage or discipleship through which it might be achieved. No matter what other meanings are present, representations of the goddess throughout Chinese history have always evoked the two themes of transcendence and divine passion.

Sources

The T'ang dynasty image of the Queen Mother survives today in archaeological remains and in texts. Inscriptions and traces of shrines constitute the archaeological record. The much more extensive textual heritage includes two principal sources: scriptures compiled in the Taoist canon *Tao tsang* (The treasure house of the Way) and poems collected in the *Ch'üan T'ang shih* (Complete T'ang poetry) anthology. This book relies principally on the written record to reconstruct the medieval Chinese view of the goddess, her worship, and her world.

Taoist Canon

Accounts of her life and acts, along with descriptions of her appearance, character, and functions are found in numerous texts preserved in the *Tao tsang*. Although this collection of scriptures did not close until centuries later, the T'ang Taoist canon was already divided into three sections, one of which was devoted to works of the Shang ch'ing school. Partly in order to keep themselves distinct from the ever-growing foreign religion of Buddhism, Taoists of all schools were actively publishing texts during this era. The imperium also sponsored Taoist compendia and commentaries. Some commentaries in the canon are even attributed to imperial authors.[3]

Canonical works on sacred geography, hagiography, ritual, meditation, and nourishing the vital essence mention the Queen Mother and her worship. The most important of canonical works for our purposes is the lengthy hagiographical account of the goddess found in the *Yung ch'eng chi hsien lu* (Records of the assembled transcendents of the Fortified Walled City), a collection of lives of female deities and saints by the Shang ch'ing Taoist master Tu Kuang-t'ing (850–933).[4] Tu's record, the fullest account of the goddess according to Shang ch'ing Taoism, presents the Queen Mother as T'ang people imagined her. The main body of this book draws on his biography together with works of T'ang poets.

Since Tu Kuang-t'ing's account is central to this study, we should understand something about both author and text. Tu was unquestionably the most important Taoist writer and editor of his time. A member of the literati or educated official class, he lived and worked during a tumultuous time for the Chinese nation and for the Taoist religion. He survived the fall of the T'ang dynasty with its attendant chaos and loss of lives and texts and saw the establishment of the Former Shu (891–925). He served under both dynasties before establishing a monastery at Blue Walled-City Mountain outside Ch'eng tu in present-day Szechwan and retiring there to devote himself exclusively to religious studies. Tu wrote at the end of the long creative period of Shang ch'ing Taoism, during a period when he could survey and sum up the great teachings of his school. As Taoist master as well as a Chinese official honored under two dynasties, Tu was interested in both religion and the state: his work on the Queen Mother reflects these concerns.

Tu Kuang-t'ing had several purposes in compiling the *Records of the Assembled Transcendents of the Fortified Walled City*. Some of these are stated; others implied. One explicit purpose was to save as much of the Shang ch'ing scriptural heritage as possible, while establishing orthodox versions of the texts he preserved. He also wanted to glorify the ruling dynasty by recording auspicious omens of heaven's favor as signs of the approval and assistance of important Taoist deities. He hoped to recommend Taoism to his royal patrons as a faith eminently worthy of support and to show the efficacy of the faith as a means of salvation and consolation in troubled times. He wished to present his subjects as powerful divinities for the faithful to revere and models to emulate. Tu also clearly states his goal of preserving records of female deities and immortals: his is the only Taoist hagiographical work up to that time devoted exclusively to female subjects. Implicit in the text is his strong desire to integrate his own school of Shang ch'ing Taoism with the other major school of T'ang and earlier times, the Ling pao school. The Ling pao school had concentrated on developing great popular liturgies, whereas the Shang ch'ing school had devoted itself to perfecting techniques of individual practice leading to immortality. Together they would form a more complete teaching, satisfying both to the community and to the individual practitioner, and capable of long survival. At the same time, Tu placed his own lineage first and constantly used his biography to teach the basic lessons of Shang ch'ing Taoism through the example of the Queen Mother and her interaction with humans. Tu Kuang-t'ing's beliefs and purposes sometimes place him in agreement and sometimes in conflict with our other major source for the Queen Mother during the T'ang dynasty, which we take up next.

T'ang Poetry

The T'ang dynasty was the golden age of Chinese poetry. Poems were mostly four, eight, or other multiples of four lines long, with five or seven words per line and rhyme words at the end of even-numbered lines. Some poems, in the style known as regulated, also featured strict tonal patterning. The ability to compose poetry formed part of the repertory of skills that every educated person of this era was expected to display; poetry was a subject on the official examinations leading to employment in the imperial bureaucracy. Poems were written on every theme: love and friendship, politics and war, careers and domestic life. Composed on every occasion, serious or trivial, they form one of our best records of medieval life. Everyone who was literate, from emperor to courtesan and from monk to official, was expected to write poetry. Nearly fifty thousand poems by over two thousand authors from the seventh through tenth centuries are preserved in the Ch'ing dynasty compilation known as the *Complete T'ang Poetry*. This greatest of all compendia of medieval Chinese verse provides us with a major source of information about how people of the time thought about the Queen Mother.

T'ang dynasty poets refer frequently to the Queen Mother of the West. More than five hundred poems in the *Complete T'ang Poetry* mention her. She appears in a wide range of poetry, in works of every style from regulated quatrains to informal songs, in every genre from diary to hymn, composed for every purpose from amorous flattery to Taoist liturgy. The ideologies of authors vary as well: devout Taoists as well as Buddhists or nonbelievers might invoke her. In making my selection here, I have tried to choose poems that tell her story well, represent various points of view, and show originality of language.

In the works of medieval poets, the goddess received her fullest and most detailed literary definition. Seen cumulatively in the poetry of many authors, her image comes together and the focus sharpens. Despite a multiplicity of appearances, her image is unified. When they allude to the goddess, medieval writers draw on her authoritative Shang ch'ing Taoist definition: an image of creativity, femaleness, transcendence, and divine communion. This image provides the basic framework on which they elaborate, devising a baroque multiplication of detail in their descriptions of her heavens, appearance, arts, and meetings. The Queen Mother's complex and many-layered image provides a vocabulary of extreme flexibility and breadth, giving meaning to the individual poet's purposes and talents. The poetic transformations of the goddess are as varied as the poets who evoke her. In turn the poets provide a rich and full picture of the goddess as perceived by people of the T'ang.

Structure and Issues

Chapter 1 investigates worship of the Queen Mother and her meetings with humans up to the T'ang dynasty in order to show the historical development of her form and functions. The reader who wants to get right to the T'ang material might skip this chapter. The rest of the book follows the order of Tu Kuang-t'ing's narrative of the goddess's life. In each section, I translate what Tu tells us and then discuss various T'ang poems dealing with the same subject. Juxtaposing Tu's text with the words of contemporary poets, I attempt to define the goddess as a religious and literary figure during the seventh through the tenth centuries. I also use inscriptions, historical references, and images from the pictorial arts to fill out the picture.

Chapter 2 defines the goddess's names, birth, appearance, companions, and home, setting the stage for her acts among humans. Tu explains the Queen Mother's nature and functions; next he will tell us what she does. Poets draw on the same material in different ways.

Chapter 3 considers her meetings with legendary rulers and sages of antiquity. She first meets the Yellow Thearch. (Thearch is a literal translation of *ti*, a divine king; the Yellow Thearch or Huang ti is more commonly known as the Yellow Emperor.) Stories of the Yellow Thearch and Lao tzu lead up to the centerpiece of this series: the Queen Mother's love affair with King Mu of the Chou dynasty. King Mu travels to her paradise on Mount K'un-lun as part of a great questing journey. The themes are love and loss, immortality and death, politics and the power of religion. The Yellow Thearch's success in achieving eternal life is balanced against King Mu's tragic failure.

Chapter 4 finds the goddess saluting a Taoist immortal, then rejecting the first emperor of all of China, Ch'in Shih huang ti (literally, the First Illustrious Thearch of the Ch'in Dynasty). In the central tale of this chapter, she visits Emperor Wu of the Han dynasty to teach him the secrets of Taoism, but in the end he proves unworthy and perishes. She next descends to the mountain dwelling of Lord Mao, founder of Shang ch'ing Taoism, and presents him with a divine bride along with the texts and teachings of his school. This series of encounters continues the themes of transcendence and divine passion, religion and the Chinese state. Again a tragic hero, Emperor Wu, is contrasted with a model adept, Mao Ying. The Shang ch'ing Taoist content of these stories becomes more explicit and detailed.

Finally, Chapters 5 and 6 feature the goddess's encounters with men and women of the T'ang, showing her role in the lives of people contemporary with our sources. She tends to grant gifts of wisdom or legitimacy to men and to serve as patron or protector as well as teacher of women.

The constant interweaving of the hagiographical text with roughly contemporary poems provides a complex and richly textured picture of the deity. Neither source would seem as complete without the other. Tu Kuang-t'ing's account and the T'ang poems illuminate one another; they also have important differences that will emerge in detail as the story progresses. The hagiography is the work of one man in one place at one time. The poems are written by many people in all parts of the empire over a span of three centuries. Tu's record is a long piece of historical prose, with plenty of opportunity for discourse or narrative; the poems are short, condensed, and often allusive. One challenge has been to treat all of T'ang poetry on the Queen Mother as one giant text while preserving the individual nature of each poem. I have considered any T'ang poem as a legitimate piece of evidence for my story, as all coming from one cultural whole. But I have also tried to respect the very different authors and contexts of the individual works.

Once we acknowledge the inevitable influence of differences in time, place, and medium, there are still other significant contradictions to explain between Tu's hagiography and the works of T'ang poets. Although Tu and the poets tell essentially the same stories, the poets tend to write works that are emotionally charged and informal, whereas Tu's writing is more cool and formal. The picture of the Queen Mother that emerges in the poetry can be more playful or sensual than Tu's depiction, which always seems serious and awe-inspiring. Relations between humans and the goddess portrayed by the poets can be intimate and even sexual; Tu's people are more reverent and subservient.

Most such conflicts result from the different tasks of the religious writer and the poet: the religious writer concentrates on presenting the correct teachings of his faith as clearly as possible; the poet tries to write as well as possible. The poet may and often does share the religious writer's convictions, the Taoist author (Tu wrote poetry, after all) is not indifferent to good literature, but the priorities of each are arranged differently. In the end, the similarities between the two in conception of the Queen Mother and her role in people's lives are truly startling.

In the religions of the world, there are many possible roles for goddesses, including such types as great mother, ruler, savior, teacher, lover, servant, or destroyer. By medieval times, any role the Queen Mother may have played as primal mother goddess is lost in the mists of distant antiquity. Our sources agree in depicting her as a great teacher who stands at the origin of a lineage of powerful texts and practices in the Taoist religion explaining techniques leading to immortality, and who may grant dynastic legitimacy or the right to rule. Thus her central identity is involved in matters of Taoist religion and the Chinese state. She also appears as the lover of royal heroes, as well as the divine matchmaker who provides heavenly spouses to humbler souls. The roles she plays in our texts in an almost infinite variety of specific human times and places always give expression to two main themes: eternal life and communication between the divine and human realms.

One of my interests has been to see how images of the Queen Mother reflect or contradict traditional Chinese ideas about the family and women's roles. In premodern Chinese society, the family was one of the great models of order, and women especially were defined by and confined to the family. Medieval thinkers had to reconcile the individual power of the goddess with the collective power of the Chinese family, and harmonize her female or yin nature with the predominantly male or yang face of potency in traditional Chinese society. The conflicts and tensions themselves, as well as their resolutions, shed light on medieval Chinese thought and society.

The book that follows weaves together Taoist texts and T'ang poetry to present an integrated picture of the Queen Mother of the West in her social and historical context. The full image of the goddess visible in T'ang literature is a rich pattern, composed of many separate threads, that developed over the course of centuries. That historical process is the subject of Chapter 1.

❖ *The Most Honored One*

Before turning to her image during the T'ang, we will first survey the Queen Mother's early history. Her medieval image draws on a long past in Chinese myth and cult. By the T'ang dynasty, she had already undergone many transformations corresponding to the ways people worshiped her. During the course of development, components of her image gradually emerged. Specifics of her character, appearance, and acts received definition. She became the dominant deity who presides over immortality and communication between heaven and earth.

This chapter surveys the history of the Queen Mother of the West. First we trace her worship from the Bronze Age through the Six Dynasties (from around 1400 B.C. to A.D. 600), describing her nature, paradise, and deeds. Next we read stories about her meetings with humans from the era of Confucius (551–479 B.C.) on that were familiar to medieval writers. Finally we study her shrine during the T'ang as an embodiment of her cult and a subject of poetry.

During a period of over two thousand years, the Queen Mother of the West goes through several transformations. She may begin as the Western Mother, an archaic directional deity who received sacrifices during the Bronze Age; a few centuries later we find references to cults to several Queen Mothers, who may be different goddesses with the same name. Records of the first century B.C. show her as the maternal savior of a messianic peasant cult as well as an object of worship among the elites. By the fifth or sixth century A.D., she reaches her mature form as a divine matriarch and teacher, the most honored goddess of the school of Taoism dominant among medieval literati. Her fully developed form absorbs all the earlier stages. This chapter treats that process of development. The rest of the book will be concerned with her mature form.

Worship

Oracle Bones: The Shang Dynasty

No traces remain in China of a neolithic Great Mother goddess of the kind found in Europe and Japan. Only the word "mother" in the Queen Mother's name hints at prehistoric connections with fertility and Great Mother cults. The earliest possible mention of the Queen Mother of the West occurs in oracle bone inscriptions of the Shang dynasty (traditional dates 1766–1122 B.C.), which record prognostications carried out by priests on behalf of the Shang rulers. One inscription reads: "Crack-making on IX.9 day; we divined: If we make offering to the Eastern Mother and Western Mother, there will be approval."[1]

The term hsi mu (Western Mother) refers to an archaic divinity residing in the west. Her eastern counterpart in oracle bone inscriptions is tung mu (Eastern Mother). The exact nature of the mu divinities is unclear. They figured among a host of directional deities to whom people of the Shang dynasty performed sacrifices, of whom the most important were the Four Quadrants. Mu divinities are linked to the sun and moon, perhaps to their celestial paths, and may also have controlled successful harvests. Shang people saw mu divinities as powerful religious forces to be honored in ritual.[2]

We do not really know much about Shang deities. On the basis of oracle bone inscriptions and bronze sacrificial vessels, we can identify two types: personifications of natural forces and deified royal ancestors. The highest god of the Shang people, for example, known as Shang ti (Lord on High), may have been an imperial progenitor who became supreme ancestor of the whole nation. The Western Mother may be an archaic combination of the two types: royal mother of all Chinese people and embodiment of the west.

Elements already present in the Shang dynasty mu divinity appear over two thousand years later in T'ang descriptions of the Queen

Mother of the West. The directional identification implicit in her name continues. To Shang people, directions were both locations of gods and the divinities themselves. Readers of early texts argue over whether Hsi Wang Mu was originally the name of a place or a being. Perhaps, like the Shang dynasty *mu* divinity, she was originally both. Another constant feature is the goddess's eastern counterpart. After the Shang dynasty, her counterpart is no longer female; various male personages, human and divine, play the ever-diminishing role of the goddess's consort. The Queen Mother's connection with the heavens, as well as her control over crops, remains important. The word "mother" in her name suggests a lineage function, perhaps as the ancestress of us all, which becomes explicit later. Images on sacrificial bronze vessels hint that Shang people already associated their *mu* deity with the tiger, a symbol of the west since neolithic times, an agent of death and transportation to the spirit world. Later the tiger is explicitly linked to the Queen Mother. Despite so many suggestive similarities, the identifications of the Shang dynasty deity known as *hsi mu* both with the later goddess called Hsi Wang Mu and with the tiger depicted on Shang and Chou bronzes remain tantalizing but unproved theories.[3]

Taoists, Confucians, and Exotic Geographers: The Warring States Period

When we reach the Warring States period (403–221 B.C.), also known as the period of a hundred schools of philosophy, we leave the realm of wild speculation to stand on firmer textual ground. We must make a leap of over a thousand years—an intriguing but so far unexplained gap—from the Shang oracle bones to the next mention of the Queen Mother of the West. During this era, several traditions about a goddess worshiped as the Queen Mother of the West emerge. They tell us more about her character and function than about actual cult practice. Various texts seem to describe several different goddesses, each called Hsi Wang Mu. Perhaps these deities represent different local cults and social strata. They include a teacher, a directional deity, spirits of holy mountains, a divine weaver, a shaman, and a star goddess. The texts in question have been claimed by early Taoism, Confucianism, and Legalism. By the end of the Warring States period, this constellation of different goddesses combines to form one being.

Chuang-tzu. The first reference to the Queen Mother after the oracle bones, and the first secure mention of her in any text, appears in an early classic of natural mysticism known as the *Chuang-tzu.* This work, dating to perhaps the third century B.C., was later incorporated into their canon by the Taoists, who revered it as a primary source of their beliefs. In a chapter entitled "Great Instructors," the author of the *Chuang-tzu* lists beings who had attained the Tao or the Way. He characterizes the Way as invisible and immanent, preceding and outlasting heaven and earth, underlying yet extending beyond the cosmos. The author's list includes the sun, moon, and the Yellow Emperor. The passage that concerns us reads: "The Queen Mother of the West obtained it and took up her seat at Shao kuang. No one knows her beginning; no one knows her end."⁴ The goddess sits in isolation on a mythical western mountain called Shao kuang. Shao kuang is also the western region of the sky. This passage emphasizes her connection with the west and with the heavens. The author of the *Chuang-tzu* ranks her with the high gods of antiquity who possess divine powers and immortality conferred by the Way. Aside from listing her as a teacher, the passage gives no indication that she communicates with humans. Perhaps she is a silent model who instructs by example, like the sun and the moon.

Hsün-tzu. Another Warring States writer provides our first reference to the Queen Mother of the West acting in the lives of men. She does so as teacher of an emperor. According to Scroll 27 of the *Hsün-tzu*, a classic of statecraft of the third century B.C. by a follower of Confucius who became in turn a founder of Legalist thought, the legendary early emperor "Yü studied with the Queen Mother of the West."⁵ Yü was the ancient ruler who saved the world from universal deluge in China's version of the ancient flood myth that appears in many cultures. A folk saying attributed to Confucius runs: "If it were not for Yü, we would all be fishes." The statement about Yü appears in a list of masters of the great sage-emperors of antiquity. Both the heroic emperor and the Queen Mother are made to look like historical people rather than deities. This is a fine example of the Chinese practice of euhemerization (turning mythical people and events into apparently historical ones). Ancient culture heroes who would be considered gods in another tradition are first turned into human ancestors and only then deified by worship in the ancestral cult.[6]

Warring States rhetoricians such as Hsün-tzu referred to the ancient emperors as models of virtuous and effective rule. Depicting the Queen Mother as teacher of Yü the Great grants her enormous power, since according to Chinese thinking the teacher automatically surpassed the disciple in generation and wisdom. She confers both legitimacy or the right to rule and the power necessary for ruling on Yü. Both the *Chuang-tzu* and the *Hsün-tzu*, contemporary works otherwise rather far apart in content, stress the goddess's role as master. She is worshiped in the sacred, superior, and legitimizing role of the teacher for centuries to come.

Classic of Mountains and Seas. The oldest sections of a geographical encyclopedia called the *Shan hai ching* (Classic of mountains and seas), dating to perhaps the fourth century B.C., contain material rather different from that found in the *Chuang-tzu* or *Hsün-tzu*.[7] This classic—a fantastic combination of geography, ethnography, and myth—presents a map of the world based on traditional Chinese cosmology. The world is divided into four directions (north, south, east, and west) and a center. The four directions are further subdivided to obtain eight. All materials are classified according to the direction in which they are found, and within the direction, by their distance from the center. The text, which contains numerous passages mentioning the Queen Mother, is included in its entirety in the Taoist canon.

The *Classic of Mountains and Seas* is an early example of a type of text joining verbal description with pictures that became important later in Taoism. Although the illustrations accompanying the text have been lost, both visual and verbal descriptions of the Queen Mother recounted here remained important in later centuries. The earliest passage in the *Classic of Mountains and Seas* that mentions the Queen Mother occurs in a section called the "Classic of Western Mountains."

Another 350 *li* to the west is a mountain called Jade Mountain. This is the place where the Queen Mother of the West dwells. As for the Queen Mother of the West, her appearance is like that of a human, with a leopard's tail and tiger's teeth. Moreover she is skilled at whistling. In her disheveled hair she wears a *sheng* headdress. She is controller of the Grindstone and the Five Shards Constellations of the heavens.   (*SHC*, 2.19a)

This spare account fits into the early cult of five holy mountains (one for each compass direction plus the center) and of paradises in the east and west where immortals were believed to dwell. It associates the Queen Mother with the west, jade (that symbol of incorruptibility and eternal life), and mythical mountains. The classic also describes her bizarre and frightening form—part human and part ferocious beast. The author refers to the tiger, later the goddess's familiar, as a physical part of her. Like many archaic Chinese deities, the Queen Mother assumes therianthropic form. Skill at whistling signifies to later Taoists a realized person who has achieved breath control and communication with spirits. Command of constellations indicates her power in maintaining cosmic balance and her membership in the group of high deities controlling human fate. In her wild hair she wears the ornament associated with her in iconography ever after.

The *sheng* headdress remains one of the goddess's most fixed attributes, although its shape alters over time. The headdress has received various interpretations. One plausible theory identifies it with the brake mechanism of the loom, connecting the goddess with the creation and maintenance of the universe through literally weaving its fabric. The *sheng* also occurs independently of the Queen Mother, as an auspicious symbol, in art from the Han dynasty on (see Fig. 1). The *sheng* as portrayed in Chinese pictorial art resembles an axle with two wheels attached, one at either end. They were depicted in tombs and exchanged as gifts on festivals such as Double Seven, which also involved demonstrations of women's skill in weaving.[8] The picture of the goddess as weaver or creator contrasts with her image as tiger or destroyer. Both seem essential parts of her identity.

The *sheng* headdress may have also been a crown of stars originally. Commentators gloss the word *sheng* as related to "overcoming" and "height."[9] That interpretation suits the definition of the term in early commentaries, the custom of giving it as a gift on stellar festivals, and the Queen Mother's role as ruler of stars. The *sheng* represented in Han art resembles conventional Chinese depictions of constellations from the same period, which show circles usually in groups of two or three, connected by straight lines. And later Taoists pictured the Queen Mother and Taoist nuns wearing stellar crowns. The interpretation of her headdress as a star crown does not exclude its reading as part of a loom: the Queen Mother is connected with the Weaver Girl Star and with weaving in other contexts.

The description of the Queen Mother of the West in the *Classic of Mountains and Seas* suggests a shamanistic deity. The shaman was a person the community accepted as designated by the gods through an initiation rite to be the spokesperson for that community with their deities. This intermediary might receive messages from the gods and relay messages of the faithful to heaven through possession or through astral travel. The Queen Mother is linked with the native southern shamanism of early China in the songs of the *Ch'u tz'u* (Elegies of Ch'u) anthology in which she also figures. Her special headdress, leopard's tail, and tiger's teeth are reminiscent of costumes worn by Chinese shamans. The shaman's hair becomes disheveled in ecstatic communion. The connection with a world mountain and with stars is likewise shamanistic. Shamans travel back and forth to the heavens by climbing up and down world mountains and other pillars of heaven such as divine trees (both linked with the Queen Mother). They may summon deities by whistling or by roaring like a tiger. The shaman flies through the heavens on a quest for deities, often traveling to stars, where deities reside. The goddess's cult in medieval and modern times definitely has strong shamanistic overtones.[10]

During the Warring States period, works by philosophers and geographers show familiarity with the Queen Mother of the West as a mountain deity who dwelt in the exotic west, where she controlled immortality and heavenly asterisms. She was a revered teacher who occasionally taught special human men, such as sage-emperors or shamans. As a powerful shaman, she joined human and divine realms in communication.

Paradise, Peasant Cults, and Bronze Mirrors: The Han Dynasty

During the Han dynasty (202 B.C.–A.D. 220), our sources for the cult of the Queen Mother increase. Evidence of her worship by both peasants and the elite appears in dictionaries, geographies, histories, art, and literature. The greatest influence on her image toward the end of this period is the development of the Taoist religion out of earlier traditions. The earliest forms of Taoism as an organized religion date to the end of the Han, when the T'ien shih tao and T'ai p'ing tao, the Celestial Masters and Great Peace Ways, in competition with the imported faith of Buddhism and under the stress of dynastic decline, pull together many earlier strands of Chinese worship. At the same time numerous local cults to the Queen Mother merge to create a single great goddess. Her importance continually grows during the Han as she absorbs attributes and functions of many deities of diverse nature and origin. During the course of these four centuries, the goddess's main attributes and associations receive definition as a female deity of human shape who controls immortality and the stars. She lives on a world mountain in the far west that is a perfect and heavenly microcosm. She appears to human men. Han cosmologists associate her with yin in yin-yang dualism and with metal in the five-phases theories of cosmogony. She captures the imagination of writers, who elaborate old myths and legends or relate new stories.

   Name. Han dynasty dictionaries provide conclusive evidence that Hsi Wang Mu was understood as female. Authors of the *Erh ya*, a glossary for reading the classics, in a section on kinship terms, define the expression *wang mu*, "queen mother," as one's father's deceased mother. *Wang mu* was an honorific posthumous title conferred on female ancestors in the father's line, used in the ancestral cult. The counterpart of *wang mu* is *wang fu*, "king father," applied to one's deceased paternal grandfather and also a name for the goddess's consort.[11]

   The patrilineal ancestral cult was one of the primary reflections in early religion of the Chinese tendency to order the world in terms of kinship. Defining the Queen Mother in kinship terms in the context of the ancestral cult shows an attempt to incorporate her into the predominating view of the structure of the world. Her connection with lineages remains essential to her cult: in medieval times she is worshiped as high ancestress in Taoist sect and teaching lineages.

   Paradise. Han authors show great interest in locating the goddess. Historians make vague references to her western home, which none claims to have visited, locating it on Mount K'un-lun in the far northwest, beyond the desert of Flowing Sands, near where the sun sets. Rivers known as Black Waters, Red Waters, and Weak Waters surround her mountain, which Han geographers believed was the source of the Yellow River. They try to pin down her paradise with a geographical designation. But writers in all cases locate her realm outside the space surveyed, mapped, traveled, and controlled by men of the Han. They associate the Queen Mother's kingdom with the exotic occident: bizarre people, horrible dangers, fantastic creatures, magical plants, and amazing minerals; these became part of her legend. Specific details of western exoticism, connected to the lore of the newly opening west, show the influence on Han imagination of trade and exploration along the Silk Route. The unknown west and its inhabitants represent romance and mystery to Han people. As Chinese geographical knowledge and political power extend, writers move the goddess's territory ever westward, always locating it outside the known sphere.[12]

Now let us look closely at her dwelling place. A section of the *Classic of Mountains and Seas* called "Classic on Northern Regions Within the Seas," which dates from the Former (Western) Han dynasty (206 B.C.–A.D. 8), begins: "As for the mountain of the serpent shamans, on top of it is a person brandishing a cup as she stands facing east. One source calls it the Tortoise Mountain. The Queen Mother of the West leans on a stool; moreover, she wears a *sheng* and carries a staff. To the south are three blue birds who take food for the Queen Mother of the West, north of the K'un-lun barrens" (*SHC*, 12.1a).

This passage places the Queen Mother in the northwest, explicitly associating her with Mount K'un-lun and Tortoise Mountain, her homes in medieval times. (Although most closely associated with these mountains, she may appear at any holy mountain because of her ability to move freely through space.) The tortoise, legendary support of the world pillar, identifies her mountain as an *axis mundi*. The stool, headdress, and staff—still part of the shaman's paraphernalia in Taiwan today—reflect her shamanistic side. The three bird-envoys who bring her food and the attendant holding a cup for elixir become permanent parts of her entourage. The hint of a divine feast anticipates elixirs and transcendent banquets given by the goddess in later Taoist texts.

By the Western Han dynasty, Mount K'un-lun was considered a world mountain. It was a Chinese version of a type of religious geography that appears all over the ancient world: the *axis mundi*, or column joining heaven and earth, where humans and deities could ascend and descend. It was a place where the primal link between this world and heaven was not yet broken, a Garden of Eden where gods and men could still communicate freely. The *Classic of Mountains and Seas* emphasizes K'un-lun's extreme height. As cosmic mountain, it stood at the center of the world in sacred space and eternal time. K'un-lun was also a cosmogonic center. The name is a rhyming binom, a term made of two independent rhyming monosyllables, related to the rhyming binom *hun-t'un* ("primordial chaos," the undifferentiated state of the world before creation). The Queen Mother is thus linked to the universe prior to creation, a temporal primacy that raises her status among deities. She is also joined to the state of the world before the arising of Chinese order, distinctions, and categories—to something primitive, creative, and frightening.[13]

K'un-lun was also the dwelling place of all divinities. The *Classic of Mountains and Seas* calls K'un-lun the "lower capital of the Thearch" (*SHC*, 2.17b): the residence on earth of the highest god, ruler of the nine heavens. People of the Western Han conceived of K'un-lun as a paradise perfect and complete in all respects, a microcosm of the macrocosm, where pleasures of every kind abounded and suffering was eliminated.[14] Han dynasty references to the Queen Mother's house as a mountain cave or stone apartment reflect the same conception.[15] The expression "stone apartment" refers to the tomb, another structure supposed to embody the universe on a small scale. Slightly later the goddess's shrine, another microcosm, was called "stone apartment." Her cave foreshadows the grotto-heavens (*tung t'ien*) that appear in medieval Taoist texts. Grotto-heavens, numinous places for medieval Taoists, were underground microcosms: perfect worlds in miniature, parallel and superior to the everyday universe. Counterpart to the holy mountains above, these were subterranean paradises where adepts might travel for pleasure and the faithful could seek shelter when the world descended into chaos. Located beneath ancient sacred mountains and other auspicious places, these caverns were believed to be interconnected by underground tunnels.

Peasant cult. Just before the fall of the Former Han, a soteriological peasant cult dedicated to the Queen Mother of the West swept across China's northeastern provinces, reaching its height in 3 B.C. Activities of this cult received three separate entries in the official dynastic history known as the *Han shu* (Book of Han): in the imperial annals of Thearch Ai (r. 7–1 B.C.), in the essay on astronomy entitled "Monograph of Celestial Patterns," and in the essay on omens called "Monograph on Strange Phenomena" (*HS*, 11.6b, 26.59a, 27C(A).22a).[16]

The accounts in the *Book of Han* suggest that historians interpreted her cult as an abnormal occurrence that corresponded to heavenly patterns and as an ominous portent for the royal house. Official historians rarely noted peasant religious behavior: usually they ignored or suppressed such incidents. The authors' inclusion of material detracting from the emperor's prestige derives from a special context. The cult activity broke out at a time of great political strain and disorder. A severe drought blighted the northeastern provinces, rebellions rose up everywhere, and the Western Han dynasty found itself on the brink of collapse. Writers of the officially sponsored history, working a century or so later with hindsight to aid them, viewed the Queen Mother's cult as a sign of the imminent fall of the Han rulers. One passage in the *Book of Han* interprets the disorder as a response to an asterism called the Hound of Heaven that appeared in the sky on March 4 in 6 B.C. and that traditionally presaged drought, famine, and revolt (*HS*, 26.59a). Another passage juxtaposes the peasants' unruly behavior with a chronicle of the rise of Empress Dowager Fu's relations to prominent positions in the imperial court (*HS*, 11.6b). Tu Yeh interpreted the cultic activity as a sign of weakness in government, arising because Empress Fu exercised too much influence, and resulting in an imbalance of yin forces (*HS*, 25B.17b). Apparently Han historians viewed the cult as an indication of a rise in the power of yin, which they believed to have come to its apex in the rule of Wang Mang (A.D. 9–25).[17]

The account in the "Monograph on Strange Phenomena" captures the hysteria of the movement:

In the first month of the fourth year of the Establishing Peace reign period [3 B.C.], the population was running around in a state of alarm, each person carrying a manikin of straw or hemp. People exchanged these emblems with one another, saying that they were carrying out the advent procession. Large numbers of persons, amounting to thousands, met in this way on the roadsides, some with disheveled hair or going barefoot. Some of them broke down the barriers of gates by night: some clambered over walls to make their way into houses; some harnessed teams of horses to carriages and rode at full gallop, setting up relay stations so as to convey the tokens. They passed through twenty-six commanderies and kingdoms until they reached the capital city.

That summer the people came together in meetings in the capital city and in the commanderies and kingdoms. In the village settlements, the lanes, and paths across the fields, they held services and set up gaming boards for a lucky throw; and they sang and danced in worship of the Queen Mother of the West. They also passed around a written message, saying: "The Mother tells the people that those who wear this talisman will not die; let those who do not believe her words look below the pivots of their gates, and there will be white hairs there to show that this is true." (*HS*, 27C[A].22a)

Important features of this cult activity, as the historian Pan Ku (A.D. 3–92) and his colleagues report them in the *Book of Han*, are as follows. From the first month of the year until the autumn of 3 B.C., people became restive, and large numbers of peasants met on the roads. This would have interfered with planting and harvesting— the peasants' occupation in the traditional Chinese economic order—for a whole year. Questioned about their unlawful assembly, they claimed they were preparing for a royal advent and for worship of the Queen Mother of the West. Great movements of people and horses took place, disrupting normal activities. People rushed around chaotically, destroying crops in the field. Their processions even reached the capital city. Wherever they went, they raised a great uproar, carrying fire, beating drums, and shouting. Their appearance was bizarre: their hair was unkempt, their feet bare. They held services in village and field, dancing and singing to worship their goddess. They carried images of straw or hemp and exchanged tokens and emblems. They played games of chance, often associated with the cult of the transcendents. Cult followers, who called themselves envoys or servants of the Queen Mother, carried talismans to protect them from death. They believed that the Queen Mother of the West would grant immortality to the faithful. Nonbelievers, on the other hand, would find the white hairs of death on their doorstep.

Accounts in the *Book of Han* conjure up the ambivalent image of the Queen Mother so striking in the *Classic of Mountains and Seas* in Warring States times. There she was portrayed as both creator (weaver) and destroyer (tiger). Here she grants eternal life to believers and death to unbelievers; her actions depend on the individual's attitude. Her followers' behavior recalls the shamanistic aspects of her cult suggested by the *Classic of Mountains and Seas*. People moving in a collective trance, with disheveled hair and bare feet, dancing and playing games of chance, all suggest shamanistic behavior. Manikins, emblems, tokens, and talismans are paraphernalia of shamans. And the shaman's job is to transmit a message to the faithful such as the one preserved in the *Book of Han*.

The fervent and passionate religious activity of believers who did not fear disrupting civic or agricultural order foreshadows the Taoist-led peasant revolts in the late second century that contributed to the fall of the Latter (Eastern) Han dynasty (A.D. 25–220) and even resembles the millenarian peasant cults of the Ming and Ch'ing dynasties. The Queen Mother's cult has political implications: just as her approval and gifts can support the rule of an ancient sage-king, her worship by rebellious subjects can threaten the ruling dynasty's hold on the mandate of heaven.

In their classification and commentaries on the incident, the Han historians also identify the goddess with stars and with yin forces, two concerns of Shang ch'ing Taoism in later times. Activities such as group worship, processions, singing and dancing, playing games of chance, and exchanging talismans—all features of the Han dynasty cult of the transcendents—anticipate and form the basis of practices of the *chen jen* (realized persons) cult among Shang ch'ing Taoist believers in the Six Dynasties (222–589) period that follows. The most essential religious characteristics of the Queen Mother of the West that emerge from accounts in the *Book of Han* are her control of immortality and her gift of defeating death.[18]

Elite cult. The Queen Mother was also worshiped by Han elites: the imperial family, great clans, bureaucracy, and military. Their cult of the goddess, apparent from historical texts, archaeological remains, and poetry, contributes additional political and religious characteristics to her emerging image.

Reference to imperially sponsored construction of an altar to the goddess appears in the *Wu Yüeh ch'un ch'iu* (Springs and autumns of

Wu and Yüeh), an annalistic history compiled in the first century A.D. that purports to describe events of the Warring States but actually recounts beliefs of the Eastern Han dynasty. This chronological history describes the continuing struggles between the two rival states of Wu and Yüeh during the fifth century B.C. The first step in a nine-point plan for the conquest of Wu suggested to the king of Yüeh by his minister was to revere the spirits and seek their blessings. To put his reverence into practice, the king of Yüeh set up altars in the eastern and western suburbs of his capital. The altar in the west he dedicated to the worship of yin under the name of Hsi Wang Mu. The eastern altar was devoted to the worship of her counterpart, Tung Wang Kung, as the embodiment of yang. This done, the country avoided natural disasters for a year and accumulated the wealth necessary for carrying out the next phases of the conquest of Wu.[19] The final step in the plan involved sending the famous femme fatale Hsi Shih, as the ultimate embodiment of the destructive force of yin, to seduce the king of Wu and lead him to destruction. The often-told cautionary tale of one of the first state-toppling beauties of China thus begins with worship of the goddess. The ruler of a state worships the Queen Mother of the West as the essence of yin forces—her basic nature, according to later Taoists. In response to effective ritual, she grants him the benefits of both her protective and her destructive powers.

Han pictorial art. Numerous representations of the Queen Mother of the West in Han dynasty pictorial art provide evidence that her cult was widespread among Han elites. She appears in many media, including murals, lacquer paintings, stone reliefs, clay tiles, and bronze mirrors. She is depicted in most regions of China, indicating that her worship was widespread. Her image is associated with creation, cosmic harmony, immortality, and communication between divine and human realms. She appears in funerary art and ancestral shrines, works dedicated to the dead. The Queen Mother provides a model of transcendence and conducts souls of the dead to paradise.[20]

The Queen Mother's iconography first receives definitive form during the Han. Han artists depicted her image on tomb ceilings. The ceiling painting in the Western Han tomb of Po Ch'ien-ch'iu, dated 86–49 B.C., near Lo yang is one of the earliest depictions of the goddess (see Fig. 2). A figure wearing Chinese robes and a head-

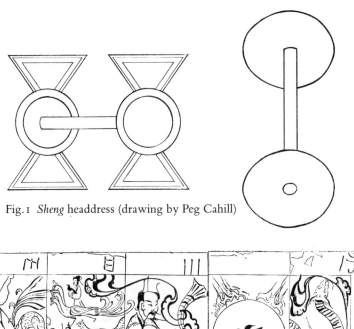

Fig. 1 *Sheng* headdress (drawing by Peg Cahill)

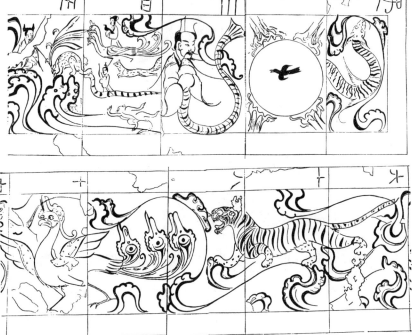

Fig. 2 Line drawing of ceiling painting from the tomb of Po Ch'ien-ch'iu at Lo yang, showing bricks 1–10, depicting the yellow serpent, sun with crow inside, Fu Xi, tomb occupant and his wife, Queen Mother of the West, white tiger, and vermilion bird (*Wenwu*, 1977.6)

Fig. 3 Painted lacquer bowl excavated at Lo lang, Korea, made in Szechwan in the first century A.D., showing the Queen Mother of the West and an attendant (*Wenwu*, 1977.6)

Fig. 4 Rubbing from stone relief of second century A.D. on western gable of Wu Liang shrine in Shantung, showing the paradise of the Queen Mother of the West (Edouard Chavannes, *Mission archéologique dans la Chine septentrionale* [Paris: Imprimerie National, 1913]: vol. 2, pl. 44)

Fig. 5 Rubbings from reliefs at I nan, Shantung, second–third century A.D., showing the Queen Mother of the West (Tseng, *I-nan ku hua hsiang*, pl. 25–26)

Fig. 6 (*Below*) Rubbing of pottery tile from Szechwan, first–second century A.D., showing the Queen Mother of the West and attendants (from the author's collection)

Fig. 7 Rubbing of section of a stone pillar from Shensi province, ca. first century A.D., showing the Queen Mother of the West (courtesy Shensi Provincial Museum)

Fig. 8 (*Below*) Eastern Han bronze mirror, second–third centuries A.D. Diameter 0.210 (8¼″). Surface—Back / dark olive green patina. Front / bluish gray with patches of light green. Decorations—figures and horse-drawn chariot in relief (courtesy Freer Gallery of Art, Smithsonian Institution, Washington, D.C., 37.14)

dress sits in three-quarter view at the far left of the painting. The painting also shows the celestial and directional symbols of yin and yang: moon and sun disks together with the dragon and tiger. Such cosmological symbols emphasize the goddess's role as creator and maintainer of cosmic balance. A nine-tailed fox and other mythical creatures appear, along with two mounted attendants and an exorcist. The Queen Mother welcomes the soul of the dead Po Ch'ien-ch'iu and enrolls him as a new transcendent, performing her function of bestowing immortality and sponsoring contact between human and divine worlds.[21]

The Queen Mother also appears on a painted lacquer bowl, dated A.D. 69, made in Szechwan province and found in a tomb in the Han dynasty colony of Lo lang in Korea (see Fig. 3). She wears a spotted cap as a headdress and sits facing outward on a spotted mat. The cap and mat are probably leopard skin, in view of descriptions in works like the *Classic of Mountains and Seas* that associate her with the leopard. Here, instead of being half-cat herself, as in the early texts, the Queen Mother is a beautiful woman dressed in the animal's fur. Her mat rests on top of a world mountain throne. One kneeling attendant waits on her.

When Han dynasty stone carvers of the second century A.D. depicted the Queen Mother in reliefs at the Wu Liang offering shrines in Shantung province, they showed her sitting facing outward, in the highest position on the western wall, presiding over the narrative and figural scenes below (see Fig. 4). Stone reliefs of the second to third century from the mausoleums at I nan represent the Queen Mother wearing her characteristic headdress, winged, and seated on a mountain throne with a tiger underneath. Two elixir-pounding hares flank her (see Fig. 5). Her consort wears the same headdress and robes; he is distinguished only by his mustache, the dragon beneath his throne, and his anthropomorphic attendants.[22]

A rubbing taken from a stamped clay brick excavated in a tomb in Szechwan province illustrates principal elements of the later Han dynasty image of the Queen Mother (see Fig. 6). A mature woman, fully human in form and wearing Chinese robes, the goddess sits facing the viewer, with legs crossed and arms folded in her lap. Important iconographic features include her *sheng* headdress, throne, animal companions, anthropomorphic attendants, and consort.

In the picture on the stamped clay brick, the Queen Mother wears her most significant and constant attribute, the *sheng* headdress or crown. The headdress, mentioned repeatedly in textual descriptions of the Queen Mother from the Warring States and Han periods, is here depicted in abbreviated form as two ornaments on either side of her topknot. Her special headdress associates the goddess with shamanism, weaving, and the stars.

The goddess's throne, another important iconographic marker, is a simple mat under a canopy with a dragon to the left and a tiger to the right, symbolizing yang and yin. The dragon, symbolizing east and yang, is the goddess's counterpart and a mount of her consort. The tiger, signifying west and yin, is her familiar and alter ego. The dragon represents life and energy; the tiger death and the spirit world. The dragon and tiger throne is a local feature of the Queen Mother's image in Szechwan province.

Stone reliefs from the northeast, in contrast, seat the Queen Mother on a mountain throne (see Fig. 7). Her throne rests atop a high, sheer-sided column, which may twist like a snake. Upward curving strips extending out from the platform on each side may represent clouds, and three tighter curls springing out from either side of the goddess's torso may be her wings. Column and platform represent the world mountain, K'un-lun. Mount K'un-lun, that perfect and complete microcosm, is the goddess's paradise and home. A heavenly horse grazes beneath the mountain. A celestial bird, perhaps a crane, the mount of transcendents, perches half way up. The mountain seat, like her dragon-tiger throne, associates the goddess with Han cosmogony, cosmic order, and the heavens.

In addition to the yin tiger and yang dragon on her throne, the goddess's animal companions on the clay brick include a nine-tailed fox, a hare holding numinous fungus (one ingredient of the elixir of immortality), a dancing toad, and a three-legged crow. Each of these appears elsewhere in connection with the Queen Mother, but it is rare to find them all together. The nine-tailed fox, a denizen of paradise, is a creature of auspicious omen. The hare inhabits the moon, where he prepares the elixir of immortality. The toad is another lunar resident. The three-legged crow, who represents the sun, serves as the goddess's messenger. Sometimes three blue birds replace him as her envoys. Her association with animals connected with both yang and yin, sun and moon, life and death, reveals the goddess's control over the universe. Her link to both yin and yang also suggests androgyny, completeness, and independence. The Queen Mother's usual anthropomorphic attendants are minor deities known as blue lads and jade girls, or followers seeking immortality. In the clay brick from Szechwan, two seated or kneeling female figures, perhaps goddesses, appear in the lower right corner, and two male figures, a deeply bowing attendant holding a jade tablet and a standing guard holding a halberd, fill the lower left corner. The Szechwan tile shows the goddess ruling alone above a hierarchy of spirits. In other contexts, such as the reliefs at the Wu Liang offering shrines and at I nan, she is accompanied by her divine consort, Tung Wang Kung (the King and Sire of the East), who is also called Tung Wang Fu (King Father of the East). She is yin to his yang; the pair embodies the divine marriage that creates the world and keeps it in balance.

The Queen Mother's pose on the clay brick, seated and facing straight out at the viewer, along with her clothing, which resembles a monk's robes, may reflect the influence of the seated Buddha image imported to China from Gandhara in northwestern India, to which it bears an uncanny resemblance. Buddhist texts and images were beginning to enter China along the Silk Route during this period. Han dynasty Chinese people may have perceived the Queen Mother and the Buddha as similar in function and meaning, since both were depicted in funerary contexts and associated with the dead and with hopes for an immortal afterlife in paradise. In addition, the Chinese may have noticed a similarity in form between the Gandharan Buddha and extant representations of their goddess. The goddess's image as it emerges in the Han may represent in art the beginning of the mutual influence between Taoism and Buddhism in China that we know from the scriptures of both religions to have been taking place on the doctrinal level at the same time. This reciprocal relationship between Taoism and Buddhism profoundly affected both faiths as they developed together in medieval China. The effects continue to make themselves manifest in the depiction of the Queen Mother in the centuries that follow the Han.[23]

The Queen Mother was also portrayed on objects buried with the dead, such as a "jade" screen with pierced carving dated after A.D.

174. This object, which shows the Queen Mother seated frontally in the upper register and her consort in the lower register, may have been intended to assist the soul of the tomb occupant in his journey to the next world by making present in his burial chamber the deities he would need to greet before registering as an immortal. Also intended to help the deceased with his adventures after death were the "money trees" buried with the dead in later Han times. Associated with worship of the earth god, prevalent in southwestern China at this time, the money trees may have been intended to provide funds for the soul's journey to immortality and for purchase of the burial plot from local gods of the soil. Seated images of the Queen Mother of the West sculpted in relief appear on the pottery bases of the bronze money trees. She faces forward, sitting sometimes on a dragon-tiger throne, and may be attended by immortals and by her consort.[24]

The Queen Mother also appears frequently on the non-reflective surface of bronze mirrors manufactured in large numbers toward the end of the Han dynasty and during the following centuries (see Fig. 8). The earliest extant image of the goddess on a mirror dates to A.D. 8. The mirror itself was considered a numinous object, reflecting only the truth and conferring on its possessor magic powers. At first a dynastic treasure and emblem of authority, the mirror became an important token of Taoist lineage and legitimacy and played a part in religious ceremonies and meditations. Bronze mirrors were buried with the dead to light the soul's way to the next world and provide it with blessings there. They bear images and messages expressing hopes of immortality. Inscriptions on the mirrors regularly mention the goddess. Mirrors are particularly important because they link visual image and text in a single object. Both depiction and word reveal, in condensed form, the story and functions of the goddess.[25]

Her image on the mirrors is standardized. She sits on a mat, facing outward, as in tomb reliefs and tiles. Her consort, Tung Wang Kung, may sit opposite her. Both goddess and her mate are occasionally identified by inscriptions. Male or female attendants frequently surround her. Other portions of the design may show the dragon and tiger, elixir-pounding rabbit, and horse-drawn carriages.

Accompanying inscriptions, often naming the Queen Mother and

King Father, request longevity, high position, material blessings, descendents, and protection from baleful forces. The earliest dated mirror inscription to mention the goddess, cast in A.D. 106, offers a wish for "longevity like that of the King Father of the East and the Queen Mother of the West."[26] This becomes a formula in later inscriptions. Some inscriptions describe the charmed life of the immortals. For example, a mirror showing the image of the goddess is inscribed: "On its surface are transcendent beings who do not know old age. When thirsty, they drink from the jade spring; when hungry, they eat jujubes. They go back and forth to the divine mountains, collecting mushrooms and grasses. Their longevity is superior to that of metal or stone. The Queen Mother of the West."[27] Still others identify the goddess as controller of seasons and directions, ruler of time and space who has attained the Tao. The inscriptions pray for the mirror's owner to possess the divine qualities of power, wisdom, and immortality they attribute to the Queen Mother. She has become an object of emulation as well as veneration.

The goddess's image on mirrors differs from that found in other contemporary media in that horse-drawn chariots, a favorite subject in Han dynasty art, frequently accompany her. These vehicles and steeds allow several interpretations. The horse itself is an emblem of both worldly power and transcendence in Han funerary art; one of the best-known pieces of early Chinese sculpture is the small bronze flying horse unearthed in a tomb in Kansu province.[28] Han people compared highly prized horses to dragons and believed they could fly. Whatever its specific reference, the horse on mirrors reinforces the goddess's connection with transcendence.

The horses and chariots juxtaposed with the Queen Mother on mirrors, in addition to general implications of worldly blessings for the tomb occupant and his descendents, suggest four related interpretations. They may represent the followers of the goddess, who, as Han historians related, raced across the countryside on horseback or in carriages to assemble in her honor. Alternatively, the scene may refer to her famous meetings with either of two early Chinese kings (discussed later): King Mu of the Chou dynasty or Emperor Wu of the Han. Finally, the vehicles and steeds may represent the Queen Mother descending to meet a worthy adept and conduct him to paradise. Each of these interpretations, and they are by no means mutually exclusive, expresses the goddess's role in assisting the tomb occupant on his journey to the heavens.

The goddess's image appears all over China during the Han. Regional variations in medium occur: stone reliefs prevail in the northeast, stamped tile bricks in Szechwan province, and mirrors in the central plain near the old capitals and in the south around the town of Shao hsing. Iconography varies as well: the exact form of her throne and headdress changes from one place to another. The cult to the goddess crosses class boundaries: her picture was created and used by members of Han elites and the peasantry alike.[29] And yet the images that survive are remarkably consistent. Pictorial evidence supports the textual record in suggesting that the Queen Mother's worship was widespread and beginning to become standardized in the Han dynasty.

Juxtaposing the goddess's image with symbols of yang and yin such as the dragon and tiger or sun and moon, Han art expresses her role as creator and maintainer of the cosmic order. Scenes pairing her with a divine mate suggest the hierogamy that produces and protects the world.

Han pictorial art represents the Queen Mother's control over transcendence and divine communion in several ways. First, her image appears in a funerary context, explicitly connecting her with death and the spirit realm. The image was intended to provide for the needs of the dead in the next life and to instruct their souls on how to proceed to transcendence, sometimes even illustrating the process of attaining immortality. Second, the narrative content of the image involves communication between the divine and human realms. Artists depict the Queen Mother in contact with humans: descending to visit believers or receiving followers in formal audience. She is depicted with symbols and instruments of transcendence such as the numinous fungus and the rabbit pounding the elixir of immortality. Third, the simple presence of the goddess's image in the tomb shows communion between the immortal and mortal realms; her image is often placed to the west, the direction of death and the spirit world, at the highest point of the wall or on the ceiling, allowing her to preside over the microcosm of the tomb. She frequently appears in paradise scenes. Finally, inscriptions directly link the goddess to the pursuit of immortality and suggest she was a model for seekers.

Han poetry. Han poems agree with other sources in depicting the Queen Mother as a goddess of longevity living on a magic mountain. Ssu-ma Hsiang-ju's (179–117 B.C.) *Ta jen fu* (Rhapsody on the great man), written between 130 and 120 B.C., portrays her as an old hag. (The *fu* was a literary form special to the Han that mixed elements of prose and poetry and is often translated as "rhapsody" or "prose-poem.") Apart from his humorous tone and clear delineation of age, Ssu-ma's description matches that found in the *Classic of Mountains and Seas*. The goddess wears a *sheng* headdress in her white hair and dwells in a remote mountain cave, where a three-legged crow brings her food. The poet comments: "If one were to live without dying, even for a myriad generations, what joy would one have?" (*SC*, 117.3060). Through satire and rhetoric, Ssu-ma Hsiang-ju criticizes the cult of immortality and warns the emperor, the "great man" of the title, against wasting his energy in vain pursuit of the worthless gifts offered by this old witch.

Yang Hsiung's (53 B.C.–A.D. 18) *Kan ch'uan fu* (Rhapsody on the Sweet Springs) commemorates an imperial sacrifice to the supreme heavenly deity known as T'ai I or Grand Unity. The long poem takes its title from the Sweet Springs Palace to the east of Ch'ang an, where the ritual was held. Yang Hsiung glorifies Emperor Ch'eng (r. 32–7 B.C.), whose sacrificial procession and ceremonial performance he compares to the shamanistic journeys of the "Elegies of Ch'u." He praises Emperor Ch'eng's palace, likening its buildings and grounds to the goddess's estate on Mount K'un-lun. Amid purple and turquoise palaces stand gardens planted with jade trees. There stands the Queen Mother of the West, attended by jade maidens and river goddesses. The narrator visualizes her during his ascent to transcendence. "Thinking of the Queen Mother of the West, in a state of joy he makes offerings to obtain longevity" (*WH*, 7.1a–14b). Yang emphasizes the adept's flight to immortality with the aid of the goddess. Han dynasty literati venerated the Queen Mother of the West as a major deity who dwelt in heaven, dominated other spirits, controlled access to immortality, and promised ecstatic flight through space.[30]

Han works in the Taoist canon. The history of the Taoist religion begins in the second century with the rise of two schools: the Celestial Masters or Five Pecks of Rice school in Szechwan and the Great Peace school around the capital city of Lo yang. They have left few surviving texts and fewer references to the Queen Mother. In fact, no contemporary record of either popular or elite cults to the Queen Mother during the Han dynasty survives in the Taoist canon. The earliest reference to her found in the patrology may be a line in the *T'ai-p'ing ching* (Classic of grand peace), a text originating in the Celestial Masters school. One line in a section of the classic entitled "Declarations of the Celestial Masters" reads: "Let a person have longevity like that of the Queen Mother of the West," a phrase almost identical to Han mirror inscriptions.[31] The Celestial Masters school connects her with long life but shows the goddess no special reverence.

Han texts in the canon neglect a cult other sources show to be widespread and continuous, centered on a goddess who was to become one of the highest deities. This may result from attempts on the part of early Taoist leaders to reform the native religions of China. Such tendencies may be seen in efforts by the Celestial Masters to eliminate ancestor worship, blood sacrifice, and monetary payments to the clergy. The Queen Mother's later readmission to the divine hierarchy of the official Taoist church would then represent one of the many victories of the native religion. But the goddess herself changes under the impact of the Taoist religion, as we shall see.

Shang Ch'ing Taoism, Paradise, Local Cults: The Six Dynasties

Shang ch'ing Taoism. The most important development concerning worship of the Queen Mother of the West during the Six Dynasties period was her incorporation into the religious system of Shang ch'ing Taoism. The school takes its name from the highest of three heavens where its gods dwell: the Realm of Supreme Clarity. This new lineage absorbed many archaic goddesses worshiped in earlier eras, such as local deities of the rivers and lakes. Alone among them the Queen Mother remained powerful and active rather than subservient. But her nature altered to suit new needs.

Shang ch'ing Taoism originated with revelations from the highest deities to a young visionary called Yang Hsi (330–ca. 386). Rising against the competition of the foreign faith of Buddhism, just then making great inroads with its missionary efforts all over China, Shang ch'ing Taoism quickly gained adherents among the Chinese elite in the south, many of whom had recently moved from the north under the pressure of conquest by non-Chinese peoples. The new school joined the Taoism of the northern capitals with the local shamanistic and elixir cults of the south in texts of the highest literary quality. Adherents to this school of Taoism concerned themselves with individual salvation through meditation, visualization, and other practices designed to extend the believer's life.[32] The ideal follower is the adept rather than the shaman of earlier times, and the goal is to become an immortal realized person. In works of the Shang ch'ing Taoists, the Queen Mother's image joins together old and new ideas to emerge as a coherent whole.

T'ao Hung-ching (456–536), the greatest Taoist writer of the period, edited the corpus of writings left by the great founders of his faith. He defined and systematized the doctrines of his school, incorporating many indigenous Chinese beliefs and practices and setting Taoism apart from its great rival, Buddhism. He attempted to organize and rationalize the host of deities venerated by his sect. He took the numerous gods and goddesses of different lineages, traditions, and localities and presented them in a unified, coherent, and hierarchical system in his *Chen ling yeh t'u* (Chart of ranks and functions of realized beings and numina; HY 167). The Queen Mother of the West ranks first among the female divinities in that work. As long as Shang ch'ing Taoism remained the school favored by the emperor and by the literate classes—that is, from the Six Dynasties period through the T'ang and well into the Sung dynasty (960–1279)—the Queen Mother of the West securely held the highest position occupied by a goddess in the Taoist and imperial registers, as well as in literature and art. T'ao Hung-ching ranks male and female divinities separately, and he does not make it exactly clear how the male and female lines correspond. Since the Queen Mother's teacher, Yüan shih t'ien tsun, the Celestial Worthy of the Primordial Commencement, stands supreme in the Shang ch'ing pantheon, the Queen Mother must rank just beneath him and above most other deities of the Realm of Supreme Clarity. T'ao Hung-ching refers to the goddess by what was thereafter her official Taoist title: The Ninefold Numinous Grand and Realized Primal Ruler of the Purple Tenuity from the White Jade Tortoise Terrace.[33] Contemporary and later Taoist writers favored this name and its abbreviations. Poets followed suit.

Another major work of the Shang ch'ing corpus, the *Chen kao* (Declarations of the realized ones; HY 1010), edited by T'ao Hungching from autograph manuscripts that constituted records of revelations to the patriarchs of the school, commands special authority. The *Declarations* contains a matrilineal system of clan and religious filiation traced through the female line with the Queen Mother of the West at its head. Her home on Mount K'un-lun is a celestial library, the source of definitive editions of the holy books of Taoism. She, her daughters, or her students become the teachers and divine brides of the patriarchs of the Shang ch'ing lineage. The Queen Mother of the West reveals essential scriptures to gods and humans, teaches Taoist masters, controls access to immortality, and acts as a divine matchmaker between humans and celestials.[34]

The Queen Mother of the West appears in other canonical works of the Shang ch'ing tradition from the Six Dynasties and later periods, works covering revelation, prayer, ritual, alchemy, and Taoist physical regimen. She functions as a focus of visions, recipient of prayer, power invoked in ritual, and bestower of practices intended to "nourish the vital essence." Such systems, devoted to nurturing the immortal embryo inside the adept so that he can eventually transcend the human condition, lie at the heart of the Taoist project.[35]

The Queen Mother is the leading female divinity in the oldest extant Taoist encyclopedia, the *Wu shang pi yao* (Compendium of unsurpassable essentials; HY 1130). This encyclopedia, compiled under the orders of Emperor Wu (r. 561–77) of the Northern Chou dynasty (557–81) and completed in 577, was intended to be an authoritative and exhaustive Taoist reference book. Various sections of the encyclopedia contain detailed descriptions of the goddess's appearance, palaces, and attendants.[36] The authors also describe her lineage as a teacher and note texts she has passed down to humans. Information on the Queen Mother found in the *Declarations of the Realized Ones* and the *Compendium of Unsurpassable Essentials* appears later in the writing of the T'ang dynasty Taoist master Tu Kuang-t'ing, translated in subsequent chapters of the present work.

An important category of texts in the Taoist canon concerns physiological microcosmology: the human body seen as a microcosm of the universe. Taoists believe that the body, like the greater world, is inhabited by a host of deities who correspond to gods in the greater world. If the adept learns to visualize, recognize, and properly address these deities, he may ask them for blessings. Texts in the canon help the adept establish correct relations with the body gods as an essential part of nourishing the vital essence. An important early member of this category is the *Shang ch'ing Lao-tzu chung ching* (Central classic of Lao-tzu from the Realm of Supreme Clarity), a text of perhaps the fifth century A.D. The classic instructs the adept on techniques for bringing down celestial divinities and lodging them in his own body and explains the benefits that will result. The Queen Mother appears as an object of inner visualization; she is the fourth deity considered.

She is the primal pneuma of grand yin. Her surname is So-of-itself; her cognomen Ruling Thought. Below she governs the Mountain of K'un-lun with its golden city walls in nine layers, its cloudy pneuma of the five colors, and its mountain passes tens of myriads of feet in height. On high, she governs the Northern Dipper and Floriate Canopy, beneath the Purple Chamber and Northern Chronograms.

Humans also have her. She resides in the center of a person's right eye, where her surname is Grand Yin, her name Mysterious Radiance, and her cognomen Supine Jade. A person must obtain the King Father [described in the previous entry as the primal pneuma of blue yang, the precedent one of the myriad divinities, who resides at the magic island of P'eng-lai in the Eastern Sea] and the Queen Mother and guard them in his two eyes. Only then will he be able to practice pacing the void, observing and looking up, and with acute hearing and eyesight distinguish and recognize good and evil. Then he can cause to flow down the various deities, just as a mother thinks of her child, and as a child also thinks of its mother. The germinal essence and pneuma will obtain each other, and for a myriad generations he will prolong his stay.

Now as for a person's two nipples, they are the germinal pneuma of the myriad divinities, where yin and yang pour down and bubble up. Below the left nipple is the sun; below the right nipple is the moon. These are the residences of the King Father and the Queen Mother. Above they rule in the

center of the eye and play on top of the head. They stop beneath the nipples
and lodge in the purple chambers of the Scarlet Palace. This is the pneuma of
yin and yang.[37]

Such Taoist practices were described in texts for the first time
during the Six Dynasties period, in response to the array of sophisticated techniques of meditation entering China as part of Buddhism.
During this era, Taoism and Buddhism influenced and competed
with each other. The Buddhist challenge forced Taoists to organize
and clarify their teachings and to define their deities. Shang ch'ing
texts from this time depict the Queen Mother as an assertively
native Chinese goddess. Her features and functions derive from
Chinese sources and owe little directly to Buddhism. Later, she
shares many traits such as compassion and activities such as individual salvation with Buddhist deities, in particular with the bodhisattva known as Kuan yin in Chinese and Avalokiteśvara in Sanskrit. This already begins in the T'ang, as we shall see. In millenarian
cults of the fifteenth and later centuries, both Buddhists and Taoists
worshiped her. Buddhists and Taoists in China today continue to
revere her.[38] But in the Six Dynasties, her image combines elements
from native deities of the Han dynasty and earlier, systematically
pulled together and defined by codifiers of the Shang ch'ing textual
corpus. As the Queen Mother's personality emerges as a coherent
whole during this period, her high stature as a Taoist divinity becomes clear. The goddess shaped by Shang ch'ing values and requirements is the one who permeates elite literature and art during
the Six Dynasties and T'ang periods.

Paradise. While Shang ch'ing systematizers were formulating
the definitive image of the goddess for medieval Taoism, texts of
mythic geography and folk ethnography such as the *Classic of Mountains and Seas* remained conservative. The goddess presented there
had been familiar since the Han dynasty. If her basic image remained
unchanged, it gathered embellishments. Han traditions continue of
Mount K'un-lun as an earthly paradise, a perfect and bounteous
microcosm of the macrocosm, and an *axis mundi*.[39]

The *Shih chou chi* (Record of ten isle-lands), attributed like many
works of fantastic geography to the Han dynasty hero of the cult of
immortality, Tung-fang Shuo (154–93 B.C.), records revelations

made to the author by the Queen Mother of the West. In answer to the Han emperor's request, Tung-fang Shuo reports on locales and inhabitants of the ten original geographical divisions of the world. The style follows that of the *Classic of Mountains and Seas*. The author describes Mount K'un-lun, giving details that match later canonical descriptions of the goddess's home, such as those found in Tu Kuang-t'ing's account. The section devoted to the Queen Mother's mountain reads:

Mount K'un-lun is located in Territory K of the Western Sea and Territory L of the Northern Sea [the letters translate longitudinal map markers], one hundred and thirty thousand *li* from their shores. There is in addition the Weak Waters River, which makes a circuit and returns, surrounding the mountain and spreading out. On the southeast, the mountain joins the Orchard of Piled-Up Stones. To its northwest are apartments of the North-Facing Doors. Its northeast presides over the Field of Great Satisfaction. To its southeast one reaches the Valley Receiving the Abyss. In these four corners are mountains that are branch supports of Mount K'un-lun.

At the southern head of the Orchard of Piled-up Stones is the place where the Queen Mother of the West told King Mu of the Chou: "Hsien yang [your capital city] is four hundred and sixty thousand *li* away from here." This mountain's height above level ground is thirty-six thousand *li*. At its summit are three corners. Its area is ten thousand *li*. Its shape is like an overturned basin. Below it is narrow; above, broad. Thus it is named K'un-lun.

As for the mountain's three corners, one of the corners is located in the true north, in the brilliance of the branches and chronograms (of the heavens). Its name is Lofty Whirlwind Pass. One of the corners is in the true west. Its name is Mysterious Orchard Audience Hall. One of the corners is in the true east. Its name is the Palace of K'un-lun.

In one of the corners is metal piled up to make the Heavenly Fortified Walled City. Its western aspect is a thousand *li* high. On top of the city walls are settled five metal platforms and twelve jade storied buildings. These are fresh like the broken glitter of flowing crystal. In their audience halls of cyan and jade, apartments of rose-gem efflorescence, and purple irridescent cinnabar chambers, phosphers are the lamps and the sun shines brilliantly. Vermilion auroral clouds emit a ninefold radiance.

This is where the Queen Mother of the West reigns, where the realized officials and transcendent numina are revered. Above it penetrates through to the Dark Mechanism [double star in the Big Dipper]. Primal pneuma flow and spread out. The Jade Crossbar of the Five Constants [handle of the

Big Dipper] governs the internal structure of the nine heavens and regulates yin and yang. As for categories and phenomena in their flocks being engendered, and rare and strange characteristics separately emerging: in all cases they depend on her.[40]

This account maps the heavens as though they were another Chinese province. The author emphasizes the satisfaction of the dwellers, the unscalable height of the mountain, its composition of precious and immortal gems, and the divine inhabitants. The Queen Mother's rule over stars and her role in creation are strikingly presented.

Divine marriage. Six Dynasties texts refer to the Queen Mother's periodic meeting with her consort; the meeting constitutes a hierogamy (divine marriage) required for creation and maintenance of cosmic harmony. The *Shen i ching* (Classic of deities and wonders), another work of fantastic ethnography falsely attributed to Tung-fang Shuo, has a commentary by Chang Hua (232–300) of the Chin dynasty (265–420), author of the encyclopedia called the *Po wu chih* (Monograph on broad phenomena). Chang Hua's commentary describes a bronze pillar as high as the sky on Mount K'un-lun and depicts the mountain as home for all transcendents.

Chang also emphasizes the theme of cosmic renewal. Above the mountain a huge bird covers the King Father of the East with its left wing and the Queen Mother of the West with its right wing. Every year the goddess visits her mate; she mounts the giant bird's wing and goes to meet him. Chang Hua concludes: "Yin and yang need each other; only when they meet are there abundant accomplishments."[41] The yearly meeting of goddess and god is required for mutual completion of yin and yang and for the periodic recreation of the universe. Shang ch'ing Taoists adapted the old Chinese notion of holy marriage in their belief that the adept must attain a perfect internal blend of yin and yang, preferably through union with a divine spouse, in order to achieve transcendence.

Cult of transcendents. Works of the Six Dynasties cult of transcendents, closely linked to Shang ch'ing Taoism, frequently mention the Queen Mother. One of the most entertaining and influential texts of this genre, existing in many recensions in medieval times and dating in its present form to the fifth century A.D., is the *Lieh hsien chuan* (Transmissions concerning the arrayed transcendents). The first immortal considered in that book of hagiographies of Taoist saints and wonderworkers is Ch'ih Sung-tzu (Master Red Pine). He visits the goddess in her stone chamber on Mount K'un-lun. He ascends and descends following the wind and rain. The ancient thearch Yen's youngest daughter follows him. The couple attains transcendence and then departs.[42]

The tale of Master Red Pine contains several features noteworthy for their reflection of Shang ch'ing Taoist beliefs and practices. The stone chamber on Mount K'un-lun is a type of paradise on earth called a grotto-heaven by the Shang ch'ing Taoists, a microcosm where the adept could consort with deities and learn special powers. The adept ascends and descends her mountain, a true cosmic pillar, like the angels on Jacob's ladder (Gen. 28.12). The master needs a mistress in order to achieve perfection; he selects a goddess of ancient lineage. The Queen Mother of the West possesses and bestows the secret knowledge that allows Master Red Pine to become a transcendent.

Peasant cult. Alongside the Shang ch'ing school and cult of the transcendents, both favored by literati, peasant cults of the goddess continued through the Six Dynasties period. A peculiar entry in the *Monograph on Broad Phenomena* confirms the gentry's continuing assumption that the Queen Mother was a deity of the people. The author declares that "Lao-tzu said that the myriad people in all cases rely on the Queen Mother of the West. It is only the fates of kings, paragons, vassals, realized ones, transcendents, and Taoist masters that depend on the Lords of the Nine Heavens" (*PWC*, 5).

Her popular cult was embodied in local shrines. The dynastic histories preserve information concerning popular temples to the goddess. In her concerns and actions, the deity they depict is a far cry from the aristocratic lady of Shang ch'ing Taoism. According to the *Chin shu* (Book of Chin), a northern ruler of the late fourth century on military campaign in the far west discovered a temple to the Queen Mother of the West near the Kokonor. He found inside the temple a mysterious divine chart, carved in stone. After ordering an official to compose a formal poem on the temple, the ruler himself wrote an account of a drought that was devastating the surrounding countryside and ruining the livelihood of the commoners. Soon afterward there fell a saving rain.[43]

Such incidents in the dynastic histories show official recognition of the goddess's popular cult, however grudging. The entries record religious contact between the local people and the government, showing the authorities intervening with a deity on behalf of the common people. Perhaps the officials are trying to co-opt the potentially disruptive goddess and make her part of the pantheon of deities answerable to the imperium. Their interactions with her suggest later officials' relations with the city gods. Although the historians tell nothing about the content of popular beliefs, they indicate a northwestern center for the cult and suggest some circumstances under which people turned to the goddess: in times of drought and fire, they prayed for life-giving rain. Association with welfare of the crops and control of the weather may go back to the Shang dynasty directional deity.

The *Book of Chin* mentions another shrine, in an entry interweaving imperial and popular concerns. A western commandant submitted a memorial requesting construction of a shrine dedicated to the goddess at South Mountain. The purpose of the new shrine would be to obtain blessings for the emperor and to secure the mandate of heaven for the dynasty forever. The location of the shrine at South Mountain had special significance. South Mountain, near Wine Springs Township on the Silk Route, was considered the earthly embodiment of Mount K'un-lun. The present emperor could only increase his prestige by building on such a numinous site, already the location of numerous religious structures. Here we have an example of cooperation between the Taoist church and the Chinese state: the state financed and cared for the shrine, and the shrine gave evidence of the support of local religious leaders and the faithful for the ruling dynasty. Permission to construct was granted.[44]

The scarcity of information regarding popular cults of the goddess may reflect an official decision to suppress it. If the goddess was already the focus of such heterodox and outlawed sects as we know her to have been during later periods, the imperium may have expressly forbidden references to her popular worship, in hopes that what historians did not transmit would pass out of existence. Most mentions of shrines of the goddess occur in accounts of disaster, war, and popular unrest, falling squarely into the category of events of ill omen for the reigning dynasty. Historians mention them to build up a picture of mounting crises. It was in the interests of both the government and the dominant Taoist orthodoxy of the time to ignore local cults to the goddess. Shang ch'ing Taoists suspected heterodoxy; members of the imperium feared revolution. Such cults formed dangerous and disruptive elements in both the church and the social fabric. The result was that peasant practices were suppressed and ignored while elite worship was fostered and patronized by both Taoist church and Chinese state.

Six Dynasties pictorial art. Archaeologists have excavated few pictorial images of the Queen Mother from the Six Dynasties, but abundant iconographic materials in the Taoist canon dating to this time make it certain that many existed. Her familiar Han image continued to be produced, and new variations were introduced. Icons of the goddess were now needed for meditation, visualization, and worship by adherents of Shang ch'ing Taoism, as well as for funerary purposes. Bronze mirrors of the Six Dynasties period feature the goddess in designs that originated in the Han, along with new combinations and arrangements of deities. New patterns include one showing deities arranged in tiers, reflecting the tendency in contemporary Shang ch'ing Taoism to organize the heavens in hierarchical order.

The Queen Mother of the West continues to figure in funerary art, her iconography somewhat modified under the influence of Buddhism. A lacquer painting on the cover of a wooden coffin dating to the Northern (Toba) Wei dynasty (386–534) shows the Queen Mother seated inside a small square pavilion similar to those in which the Buddha preaches the *Lotus Sutra* in stone carvings of the same period. The Queen Mother sits in profile, under a canopy. Opposite sits her consort, the King Father of the East. Both wear Chinese robes, leading archaeologists to date the painting after 475–94 when the Toba Wei dynasty ruler Wen ti (r. 471–99) decreed that his people, who were of Turkic stock, should adopt Chinese clothes. A long serpentine pillar represents the world mountain, K'un-lun. The sun and moon appear above the deities, symbolizing celestial rule and harmony. The appearance of the Queen Mother on the coffin confirms the transfer of Chinese beliefs to a foreign ruling class, and the form taken by the goddess reveals influence from images of the Buddhist religion to which the Toba Wei rulers adhered. Her presence proves a continuing belief, spreading even to areas not under Chinese rule, in the Queen Mother's power to link heaven and earth, death and eternal life, and human beings and gods.[45]

A new image of the Queen Mother appears in Buddhist art during the Six Dynasties period. Depictions of the goddess flying across the heavens to worship the Buddha, found in two ceiling paintings from the Northern Wei dynasty and two from the Sui dynasty (581–618) in the Buddhist cave temples at Tun huang on the Silk Route in Chinese Central Asia, provide evidence of the Buddhist conquest of China. In form, the image derives from depictions of the goddess flying down to receive the occupant in Han dynasty tomb paintings. She wears her characteristic *sheng* headdress. This image constitutes an example of the foreign faith absorbing elements of the native religion and transforming these elements to suit its missionary aim. Buddhist proselytizers could hardly put forth a more convincing visual argument on behalf of their deity; the Buddha must surely be supreme if the highest deities of Taoism worship him.[46]

Shang ch'ing sensibilities shape the image of the goddess in texts and arts of the Six Dynasties. Fragments of older images combine to form that of a single high goddess. Canonical works describe her nature, lineage, appearance, residence, and companions, defining her relations with human and supernatural beings. Sacred texts spell out her functions as a cosmic force and Shang ch'ing Taoist divinity. In common with other high deities of Taoism, she shares in the cyclic creation of the world and its transient inhabitants. Once the phenomenal world is created, the Queen Mother, as the highest Taoist goddess, helps sustain it. Her special duties are legion. As essence of the ultimate yin, she maintains cosmic harmony by adjusting the balance of yin and yang. She legitimizes divine and worldly power. She transmits texts, talismans, and practices associated with the Shang ch'ing school and the cult of transcendents. She bestows the word of the sacred scriptures; the word is the intermediary between gods and humans. She sanctions ascents to transcendence by men and women, registering the new immortals. She serves as matchmaker in Taoist divine marriages. In short, she controls access to immortality and relations between humans and deities.

The ambivalence between creator and destroyer, expressed in earlier times by the dual images of weaver and tiger, persists. As goddess who presides over communication and continuity, the Queen Mother also governs separation and death. As stories of her meetings with human emperors will show, she is goddess of termination as well as of renewal and return. She can help or harm her human followers. She can connect or sever the sacred and profane realms.

By the end of the Six Dynasties period, the visual and textual image of the Queen Mother of the West, in the form it was to take for the next four hundred years, was substantially complete. Her transformation from archaic goddess to central divinity of a popular cult to high goddess of aristocratic Shang ch'ing Taoism has been accomplished. Fragments of different images combine to create a single high goddess who is more than the sum of her parts. From this time on, her image calls up two themes: the human pursuit of transcendence and the longing of men and gods to communicate. Ruler of love and separation, immortality and death, knowledge and ignorance, she offers hagiographers and poets a vocabulary of images of extreme flexibility and strength.

Meetings

Medieval Chinese people told stories about the Queen Mother and her encounters with humans, especially Chinese emperors. These tales are not separate from her worship; in fact, they are the literary context in which her actions as a deity become apparent. But they are so important a feature of both canonical literature and T'ang poetry that they will be separately treated here. Following Tu Kuang-t'ing's practice in his biography of the goddess, we will examine in putative chronological order the tales of her meetings with Chinese emperors, rather than in order of the dates of the respective traditions. A T'ang reader would have imagined the encounters taking place in a historical progression going back to the Yellow Thearch and continuing up to Ming Huang (the Brilliant

Thearch) of the T'ang. A Taoist adept might even hope to meet her personally. To understand the meanings of stories about meeting the goddess, we must return again to Chou and Han dynasty texts.

Yellow Thearch

The tradition of a meeting between the Queen Mother and the Yellow Thearch was well known in medieval China. The story links the ancient goddess with the legendary first ruler of all China and the first man to become immortal. Yet the tale is no earlier than the Han dynasty. It probably resulted from a joining of the Han cult of the Queen Mother with the Huang-Lao cult of the same era.

The cult of the Yellow Thearch and Lao-tzu in the Han had military and political overtones; medieval stories of the Yellow Thearch and the Queen Mother involve war and the mandate of heaven. During the Han dynasty, the *Huai nan-tzu* already links the two. A passage tells how the great gods react when the Tao is lost: "The Old Lady of the West breaks her *sheng*; the Yellow Thearch whistles and intones" (*HNT*, 6.13a). The *sheng* headdress, as we have seen, identifies the old lady as the Queen Mother as weaver of the world. Wild animals and birds respond to the gods' actions, and a series of calamities takes place in the natural and supernatural worlds. When she smashes her headdress, which represents her loom, the structure of the cosmos she created and maintains by weaving falls to pieces.

In the Six Dynasties, Shang ch'ing Taoism absorbed both earlier cults and redefined the deities to suit its own needs, making the Queen Mother the Yellow Thearch's teacher. Shang ch'ing writers did this by placing the Queen Mother at the top of a hierarchy of goddesses that included Hsüan nü, the Mysterious Woman, and Su nü, the Natural Woman, instructors of the Yellow Thearch in war and sexuality since the Han.[47]

Shun

Warring States and later sources associate the Queen Mother of the West with the legendary emperor Shun, predecessor of Yü the Great. The *Chu shu chi nien* (Bamboo annals), a historical text discovered in a tomb late in the third century A.D. that purports to have been transcribed during the third century B.C., preserves some surprisingly accurate information about events in the Chou dynasty. That annals-style history records that in the ninth year of Shun's reign "the Queen Mother of the West came to his court."[48] Reports of encounters between the Queen Mother of the West and Shun continue. The *Ta Tai li chi* (Record of the rites according to the Elder Tai), a Han dynasty edition of the Warring States period classic known as the *Li chi* (Record of the rites), notes that:

Formerly Yü Shun succeeded Emperor Yao because of the charisma of heaven. He broadcast achievements and spread charisma; he made a rule of the rites. . . . In Shao fang, the Yu tu tribes came and submitted as vassals; in the south he soothed the Crossed Toes; wherever the sun and moon came out and went in, none did not follow and abase themselves to him. The Queen Mother of the West came and submitted as tribute a certain white tube.[49]

The white tube, a ceremonial object used exclusively by the emperor to regulate the seasons, signifies both the goddess's power over time and the legitimacy of Shun's rule. In tales of the Queen Mother and Shun, his virtue attracts her to his court to present tribute—a dynastic treasure in the form of a symbolic ritual object. In response to a ruler's virtue, then, the Queen Mother appears and grants tokens of political power and legitimacy; these features prefigure later accounts of her visits to emperors and Taoist adepts.

Writers of the Six Dynasties continued the tradition of the goddess's visit to Shun. The *Ti wang shih chi* (Records of generations of thearchs and kings) combines the story with material from the *Classic of Mountains and Seas*:

To the north of K'un-lun is the divinity of Jade Mountain. She has a human body, a tiger's head, and a leopard's tail. She wears a *sheng* headdress and flourishes a loom mechanism and staff. Shining brightly: the white rock city walls and apartments where she dwells. To the south is a blue bird, which regularly seizes food for her. Her name is Queen Mother of the West. In the time of Shun, she came and submitted a white jade circlet and half-circle. She also contributed charts of the earth to [his minister] Yi.[50]

Yü the Great

The Warring States rhetorician Hsün-tzu states, as we have seen, that Shun's successor, Yü the Great, studied with the Queen Mother of the West.[51] The statement appears in a list of masters of the great sage-emperors of antiquity, including teachers of the Yellow Thearch and Shun, as well as Yü the Great. Warring States political theorists referred to these emperors as their highest models of virtuous, effective rule. Depicting the Queen Mother as Yü the Great's teacher grants her enormous power, since the teacher surpasses the pupil in generation and wisdom. The sacred, superior, and legitimizing role of the teacher remains an important part of the goddess's image in Han and Six Dynasties texts and is emphasized in the Shang ch'ing tradition. That Taoist school also places great importance on teaching lineages as an organizing principle for both divine and human society.

During the Six Dynasties and the T'ang, most writers lost interest in the Queen Mother's visits to the model rulers of high antiquity favored by Warring States rhetoricians and concentrated instead on narrative cycles concerning two later emperors. The first of these was King Mu of the Chou dynasty.

King Mu of the Chou

Bamboo Annals. The *Bamboo Annals* record an encounter between the Queen Mother and King Mu (r. 1001–946 B.C.) of the Chou dynasty. An entry for the thirteenth year (989 B.C.) of King Mu's reign reads: "He went on a punitive expedition to the west and reached the spot where blue birds rest." That is, he reached the place where the sun sets. Later, in his seventeenth year (985 B.C.), "he went on a punitive expedition to the west and reached the K'un-lun hill. He had an audience with the Queen Mother of the West. The Queen Mother of the West detained him. . . . That year the Queen Mother of the West came to his court, where she was received as a guest in the Brilliant Palace."[52]

The laconic account in the *Bamboo Annals* gives the first outline of the story that later develops into a major narrative cycle involving the goddess. The essential elements are few. King Mu sets off on a military expedition to the far west, reaching lands with fanciful names beyond the borders of Chinese civilization. The female ruler of a western country receives him in court audience, as his superior, at a hill called K'un-lun. Later the same year the goddess comes as a guest to the court of the king. Her return visit does not appear in later stories about King Mu: later traditions transfer the notion of a visit from the goddess to other kings. Otherwise, the bare outline of the tale set forth in this annalistic account forms the core around which generations of Chinese authors expanded, creating narrative structures filled with startling and moving detail.

Elegies of Ch'u. The Queen Mother's connection with a western mountain paradise and with longevity are early associations of the King Mu narrative cycle. These associations appear in a long and enigmatic poem collected in the southern anthology known as the *Elegies of Ch'u.* This collection of poems contains shamanistic hymns and other material on early myth and religious practice. The poem called "Heavenly Questions," which has, among other speculations, been interpreted as an explanation of the iconographic program of a set of wall paintings depicting religious subjects in a royal palace or as a Warring States catechism, features a narrator who inquires about various figures and places of ancient myth and religion. The answers are either lost or never existed. The narrator poses three pairs of questions alluding to King Mu and the Queen Mother. The first presents K'un-lun as a pillar joining heaven and earth, whose depth cannot be fathomed and whose top cannot be scaled. The second places longevity in the goddess's control. The third set asks:

> King Mu was crafty and greedy—why did he drift about in a circuit?
> Making his circular tour and penetrating the inner structure of the world—what was he seeking?[53]

The reply must be that King Mu sought the Queen Mother of the West and, through her, immortality. The "Heavenly Questions" link the goddess with a western mountain paradise, immortality, and the personality and adventures of King Mu—associations that continue through the T'ang dynasty.

The Lieh-tzu. The meeting between the Queen Mother of the West and King Mu of the Chou received its first extended prose treatment in Chapter 3 of the *Lieh-tzu*, "King Mu of the Chou." This text, which probably dates from the third century A.D., draws on a body of tales concerning King Mu already in circulation for some time. In an account reminiscent in tone and plot of the encounters of the Han emperor Wu with technicians and proto-Taoist "recipe masters" that appears in the "Monograph on the *feng* and *shan* Sacrifices" in Ssu-ma Ch'ien's (ca. 145–ca. 85 B.C.) *Shih chi* (Records of the historian), the author of the *Lieh-tzu* writes:

> In the time of King Mu of the Chou dynasty, there was a magician from a country in the far west who came. . . . His thousand changes and myriad transformations could not be exhausted or finished. . . . King Mu revered him as if he were a deity and served him as if he were a sovereign. [King Mu accompanied the magician on an ascent to the latter's celestial realm, and returned dissatisfied with life and work in the Middle Kingdom.] . . .
> Projecting his intentions into far wandering, he ordered his vehicles drawn by eight steeds to be harnessed. The inside pair of horses consisted of Flowery Bay on the right and Green Ears on the left. The outside horses were Red Thoroughbred on the right and White Sacrifice on the left. As for the main chariot, Father Ts'ao held the reins. Shang was to the right. In the team of the next vehicle, the inside horses were Big Yellow on the right and Faster-than-Wheels on the left, while the outside horses were Robber Black on the left and Son of the Mountain on the right. Pao Yao was in charge of the chariot; Ts'an Pi acted as rein-holder. P'ai Wu was to the right.
> They galloped quickly for a thousand *li*, then reached the Chu-sou country. The Chu-sou people offered as tribute white snow-goose blood for the king to drink, and provided cow's and mare's milk to wash the king's feet. They did the same as well for the men of the two vehicles.
> After they drank, they went on, then spent the night in a cleft of Mount K'un-lun, on the sunny side of the Red Waters River. On another day, they ascended K'un-lun Hill, in order to see the Yellow Thearch's palace. They placed a lump of dirt there as a memorial for later generations. Then King Mu was a guest of the Queen Mother of the West, and they toasted each other on the banks of the Turquoise Pond. The Queen Mother of the West composed a song for the king; he composed one for her in return. Their words were sad. Then he looked toward where the sun entered. In a single day, it went a myriad *li*. The king then sighed and said, "Alas, I, the one man, am not overflowing with virtue; moreover, I am given over to pleasure. Later generations will look back and number my transgressions."
> How was King Mu a divine person?! He was able to exhaust the pleasures of this body, but still after a hundred years he went off. The world then thought that he had climbed up into the sky.[54]

The *Lieh-tzu* author may have opposed the cult of the transcendents: he criticizes King Mu's extravagance, sensuality, and credulity, scoffing at the notion that such a one could have achieved immortality. Editorial comments aside, the *Lieh-tzu* account includes basic features of the story of King Mu and the Queen Mother of the West as it appears in works of poets thereafter. The story begins with a journey to the far west, in chariots drawn by fine chargers, and has its climax in the meeting between king and goddess. The meeting, a feast and exchange of poems, takes place beside the Turquoise Pond. The king leaves reluctantly, relinquishing his chance for immortality. The Queen Mother seems human: she treats the king with ceremonial behavior appropriate for a medieval Chinese noble woman, and exhibits emotions.

Transmissions Concerning Mu, Son of Heaven. The most extended treatment of the tale occurs in the *Mu T'ien-tzu chuan* (Transmissions concerning Mu, son of heaven). This controversial text, supposedly discovered in A.D. 284 at a site called Chi chung in modern Honan province, in the same grave with the *Bamboo Annals*, bears a preface by the Chin dynasty scholar Hsün Hsü dated A.D. 289. In recent years, scholars have assigned the text dates ranging from the fifth century B.C. to the late third century A.D. The final decision must await careful philological study. Meanwhile, on the basis of language, style, and content, I tentatively consider it a late third century A.D. text that incorporates earlier materials.[55]

The *Transmissions Concerning Mu, Son of Heaven* takes the shape of a commentary to an annalistic history; it is related to the *Bamboo Annals* as the *Tso chuan* is to *Ch'un ch'iu* (Spring and autumn annals). The commentary explains the laconic entries in the annals with quoted speeches, narrative accounts, and fanciful topography. The information it contains also appears in the *Lieh-tzu*, and in Kuo P'u's (276–324) commentary on the *Classic of Mountains and Seas*, which it may follow. Whatever its date, the *Transmissions Concerning Mu* became an authoritative text for Six Dynasties believers in the cult of transcendents and one of their early canonical works. It provided a source from which T'ang dynasty poets drew their picture of King Mu and his fabulous journeys. King Mu's encounter, dated 985 B.C., forms only part of the whole story.

The account elaborates on the entry in the *Bamboo Annals*. With eight fine horses and his excellent driver Father Ts'ao, King Mu makes his circuit of the known world, a combined quest of the goddess and kingship-asserting tour of his realm. As he proceeds, local tribes submit or pay tribute. King Mu pays a ceremonial visit to the Queen Mother at the Turquoise Pond. He carries symbols of his rank and gifts of tribute. She bows in response. Their exchange resembles ceremonies surrounding Sino-foreign treaties, as well as later Taoist rites in which a master bestows texts on a disciple. They toast each other with wine, listen to music, and exchange melancholy poems. These poems celebrate the brief meeting of opposites: the mortal "son of the people of this world" and the immortal daughter of the Lord on High. Although tempted to stay, the king returns to his earthly duties without attaining immortality. He never comes back. The author, sympathetic to King Mu, presents his biography in a favorable light.

On the auspicious day, A-Rat [*chia tzu*], the son of heaven paid a formal visit to the Queen Mother of the West. Grasping a white jade tablet and a dark jade circle, he had an audience with the Queen Mother of the West. He submitted one hundred lengths of multi-colored damask and three hundred lengths of [X].[56] The Queen Mother of the West repeatedly bowed and accepted them.

On the B-ox [*i chou*] day, the son of heaven toasted the Queen Mother of the West beside the Turquoise Pond. The Queen Mother composed a ballad for the son of heaven:

> White clouds are in the heavens;
> Mountains and mounds emerge of their own accord.
> Our ways and byways are distant and far-off;
> Mountains and rivers separate them.
> If I take you and make you deathless,
> Perhaps you'll be able to come again.

The son of heaven replied to her:

> I will return home to the eastern earth,
> To harmonize and set in order the various Chinese tribes.
> When the myriad people are peaceful and equitable,
> I will turn my head back to see you.
> Three years from now,
> I will return to this wild place.

The Queen Mother of the West chanted again for the son of heaven:

> I'm going off to that western land,
> Where I reside in its wild places.

With tigers and leopards I form a pride;
Together with crows and magpies I share the same dwelling
      place.
Fortune and destiny cannot be transcended.
I am the Thearch's daughter.
Who are these people of the world,
Who can take you up and make you depart?
Blow the pipes and sound the reeds!
My heart is soaring and wheeling!
Oh, son of the people of the world—
You are what is looked at from afar in heaven!

The son of heaven subsequently galloped to ascend Cover Mountain.
Then he inscribed his name and traces on a rock on Cover Mountain,
planted a saphora tree, and named the place the Mountain of the Queen
Mother of the West. (*MTTC*, 3.15–16)

This story is condensed, some parts copied verbatim, into Tu
Kuang-t'ing's hagiography of the Queen Mother, as we shall see in
Chapter 3. The authors of both the *Transmissions Concerning Mu* and
the *Lieh-tzu* humanize the Queen Mother. Combining two earlier
notions of the goddess as a powerful figure possessing the arts of
immortality and a female ruler who meets a Chinese king, these Six
Dynasties writers depict her as a regal teacher with human emotions. She drinks, falls in love, composes poetry, and promises to
share her secrets. Presenting the goddess in the guise of a human
woman makes her more accessible and less frightening than she
seemed in her earlier feline form. Humanization of the great goddess, once started, became an irreversible process that continues up
to the present day.[57]

T'ao Ch'ien. The story of the Queen Mother of the West and King
Mu appears occasionally in Six Dynasties poetry, prefiguring the
outburst of poetic references in the T'ang. One of the best-known
and most loved poets of the Chin dynasty, T'ao Ch'ien (365–427),
mentions the tale repeatedly in a cycle of poems entitled "On Reading the *Classic of Mountains and Seas*." The poems refer more to Kuo
P'u's commentary on the *Classic of Mountains and Seas* than to the text
itself. In his commentary, Kuo retells the story of King Mu much as
we have it in the *Transmissions Concerning Mu, Son of Heaven* (see

SHC, 2.19b). As in the works of T'ang poets yet to come, the meeting of the goddess with a mortal king, here King Mu, dominates T'ao Ch'ien's poems. The first one sets the tone for the series:

> In early summer when the grasses and woods grow,
> The trees surrounding my chamber spread and provide shade.
> Flocks of birds delight to have a refuge there,
> And I too cherish my thatched hut.
> I have already plowed the fields and planted seed as well,
> And the time for reading books returns.
> This poor lane has no deep-worn ruts,
> And tends to send back my friends' carts.
> Joyfully I ladle out spring wine,
> And pick some greens from my garden.
> Scattered showers come from the east,
> Accompanied by a good wind.
> I take a fleeting glance at the *Transmissions Concerning the Chou King*,
> And look through the *Classic of Mountains and Seas*.
> Looking up and looking down, I reach the ends of the universe—
> If this is not pleasure, then what can be?[58]

The *Transmissions Concerning the Chou King* that the poet reads at leisure in his peaceful country home is the text referred to above as *Transmissions Concerning Mu, Son of Heaven*. T'ao Ch'ien, like his contemporary Kuo P'u, drew on some version of the familiar tale of King Mu and the goddess.

The second poem in the cycle mentions a jade tower where the narrator sees the Queen Mother:

> Where the jade audience hall skims the auroral clouds' profusion—
> The Queen Mother's delighted and wondrous face.
> She was born together with heaven and earth,
> I don't know how many years ago.
> Her numinous transformations are inexhaustible,
> Her lodging and shelter no single mountain.
> High and intoxicated, she puts forth a new ballad;
> How could one liken it to the words of this world?

According to T'ao Ch'ien, she was born when the cosmos was created, an immeasurably long time ago. The poet recalls the goddess of the *Chuang-tzu*, another text he favored. Mistress of ceaseless transformations, the Queen Mother travels between divine mountains. High on wine and the Way, she sings songs not of this world. T'ao refers to the poems she exchanges with King Mu beside the Turquoise Pond. Her image in T'ao Ch'ien's poetry reflects the beautiful goddess described in the Shang ch'ing corpus more than the therianthropic deity described in the *Classic of Mountains and Seas*.

The third poem mentions Mount K'un-lun and its Mysterious Orchard Hill. There one finds elixir minerals growing beside the Queen Mother's Turquoise Pond. The narrator concludes: "I regret that I cannot reach Mu of the Chou, / And ask him to take me on just one trip."

The fourth poem names elixir plants ingested by the Yellow Thearch that prolong the life of the one who takes them. The Queen Mother transmits drugs of immortality growing on Mount K'un-lun to the Yellow Thearch.

Poem number five celebrates three blue birds who serve as the Queen Mother's messengers. He wants to accompany them and deliver his own request for longevity to the goddess:

> Wheeling and soaring: the three blue birds,
> The color of their plumage is outstandingly moving.
> Mornings they act as the Queen Mother's messengers;
> Evenings they return to the Triple Precipices Mountain.
> I wish I could follow along with these birds.
> In this world all I need
> Is wine and prolonged years.

T'ao Ch'ien decorates the seventh poem with bejeweled trees and other treasures and splendid oddities of the goddess's paradise. More auspicious divine birds dance and sing, winning over the Queen Mother:

> Gleaming and glittering, the triple-beaded tree
> Lodges and grows on the shady side of the Crimson Water.
> Standing erect, the cinnamon trees that skim the wind:

Eight trunks together make a forest.
The numinous phoenix dances, rubbing the clouds.
The holy simurgh resonates, harmonizing with the jade
     sounding stones.
Although these are not treasured in the world,
Still they caught the heart of the Queen Mother.

T'ao Ch'ien's series of poems on the *Classic of Mountains and Seas* captures the spirit of the earlier *Elegies of Ch'u* and follows the same theme of a quest for the goddess. Now the poet names King Mu as the seeker, the Queen Mother as the object of his quest, and Shang ch'ing Taoist practices as the method.

Han Wu-Ti

The next ruler to encounter the Queen Mother of the West was the Martial Thearch of the Han (Han Wu-ti; r. 141–87 B.C.). His is the best-known story of all, even today. Their meeting in 110 B.C. becomes the model for meetings between the Shang ch'ing Taoist adept and his transcendent female teacher.

Monograph on Broad Phenomena. The third-century *Monograph on Broad Phenomena* gives our earliest account of the meeting of the Han emperor and the goddess. It tells how Han Wu-ti loved the Way of the divine transcendents and sacrificed to numinous mountains and watercourses in order to seek the Way. In response:

One time the Queen Mother of the West sent her messenger on a white deer to inform the emperor that she would certainly come. In preparation he furnished the Ninefold Floriate Basilica with curtains and waited for her. Then on the seventh day of the seventh month, at the seventh notch of the clepsydra, the Queen Mother, riding a purple cloud chariot, arrived west of the basilica, and sat on the south facing eastwards. On her head she wore seven layers of blue pneuma, dense like clouds. There were three blue birds as big as crows. Messengers and attendants flanked her. Then they set up the Ninefold Tenuity Lamp. The thearch sat on the east facing westwards. The Queen Mother asked her attendants for seven peaches. They were as big as crossbow pellets. Giving five to the thearch, the Mother ate two. The thearch ate the peaches, then immediately took their pits and put them in front of his knees. The Mother said, "Why are you taking these pits?" The thearch replied, "These peaches are so sweet and lovely. I want to plant them." The Mother laughed and said, "These peaches bear fruit once in three thousand years." The Mother and the thearch were sitting by themselves, opposite one another. None of their followers got to approach. Then Tung-fang Shuo stealthily spied on the Mother from the southern side room of the basilica, through the Vermilion Bird window lattice. The Mother saw him. She said to the thearch, "This small boy is spying through the window lattice. Formerly he came three times to steal my peaches." The thearch then greatly marveled at him. On account of this, people of the world say that Tung-fang Shuo is a divine transcendent.   (*PWC*, 3.17)

The *Monograph of Broad Phenomena* exhibits plot elements, characters, and details present in later, fully developed versions of our story. The emperor's zeal and ritual correctness attract the goddess's attention. After her message arrives by divine envoy, he prepares for her visit. She comes by celestial transport, accompanied by divine attendants on the transcendents' special meeting night—the festival of Double Seven. A heavenly lantern lights the peach feast. The emperor receives and eats the transcendent peaches, but cannot gain immortality from them: he cannot plant their seeds. The immortal prankster Tung-fang Shuo watches the proceedings. The Queen Mother explains that he has already stolen her peaches three times; he must have lived nine thousand years or three peach cycles to do so. He, rather than Han Wu-ti, is the divine transcendent in the tale.

The *Monograph on Broad Phenomena* provides the earliest clear association of the Queen Mother of the West with the peaches of immortality, which remain her major emblem today. Earlier texts including bronze mirror inscriptions of the Han dynasty associate her with other foods such as dates and jujubes. Han dynasty pictorial art links her with such symbols of immortality as the magic mushroom and the hare pounding the elixir of immortality. Pre-Han texts already credit peach wood with apotropaic powers. Han dynasty materia medica refer to curative properties of peach soup.[59] The peach, an independent auspicious and protective symbol during the Han, became associated with the Queen Mother as her special elixir shortly thereafter. During the following centuries, further treatments add information and standardize the story of the Han emperor and the goddess. Later versions tend to reconcile the tale with

Shang ch'ing Taoism, incorporating that school's emphasis on ritual, textual transmission, and exact description of deities.[60]

Esoteric Transmissions Concerning the Martial Thearch of the Han. The fullest version of the story appears in the classic *Han Wu-ti nei chuan* (Esoteric transmissions concerning the Martial Thearch of the Han).[61] This beautifully written narrative, ancestor of the Ming and Ch'ing novel, has traditionally been attributed to the Han historian Pan Ku. It takes the structure of an official biography from the dynastic histories, borrowing the credibility and authority of this sober form and loading it with the most incredible contents. The text probably dates to the sixth century A.D. The action, setting, and characters are the same as in the *Monograph on Broad Phenomena.*

The epiphany of the goddess in the *Esoteric Transmissions* is dated 110 B.C., an eventful year in Han dynasty religious history. This year Han Wu-ti performed the greatest and rarest of all imperial rituals: the *feng* and *shan*, thanksgiving sacrifices to heaven carried out when the empire prospered and found itself in harmony with the cosmos. The thearch performs the rites with devotion and displays contempt for the world and for his power and position. These qualities, rather than charisma like that of the legendary emperor Shun, attract the Queen Mother. A beautiful serving girl precedes and announces the goddess. She arrives with a full entourage. The text contains a detailed description of the goddess who appears to be about thirty years old. Her physical appearance as well as her costume accords with her iconography in Shang ch'ing Taoist texts. Han Wu-ti provides a feast for the goddess that includes jujubes, mentioned in Han dynasty mirror inscriptions as food of transcendents, and grape wine, associated with the west. The emperor pleads for instruction as a humble Taoist acolyte. The Queen Mother then summons another high goddess and, after some debate, gives the emperor sacred texts. After lecturing him on Taoist self-cultivation, the goddess reads off a long list of transcendent elixirs, ranked in classes according to efficacy. Religious rituals, ceremonies, and songs punctuate the action. Although the goddess bestows several potent esoteric texts on the emperor, in the end he cannot benefit from the teachings they contain and the manuscripts literally go up in smoke when his palace library burns. This text is condensed into Tu Kuang-t'ing's biography of the Queen Mother, as we shall see later.

Here is the description of the Queen Mother of the West from the *Esoteric Transmissions*:

The Queen Mother ascended the basilica and sat facing east. She was wearing a long unpadded robe of multi-colored damask with a yellow background; its patterns and colors were fresh and bright. Her radiant propriety was clear and serene. Belted with the great cord of the numinous flying beings, at her waist was a sword for dividing heads. On top of her head was a great floriate topknot. She wore the cap of the Grand Realized Infants of the Dawn. She stepped forth on shoes studded with primal rose-gem, with phoenix-patterned soles. To look at her, she might have been about thirty years old. Her stature was about average. Her heavenly appearance eclipsed and put in the shade all others. Her face and countenance were incomparable. Truly, she was a numinous person.   (*HWTNC*, 2)

Shang ch'ing Taoism permeates and structures this text. The major revelations, rituals, ceremonies, and songs, as well as parts of the plot, derive from a lost biography of the Mao brothers, divine founders of the Shang ch'ing school.[62] Language and contents depend equally on the Shang ch'ing textual legacy. The *Esoteric Transmissions* provided the basis of the T'ang dynasty version of the meeting of goddess and emperor set down by Tu Kuang-t'ing and celebrated in T'ang poetry. From direct references in their works, we know that T'ang dynasty poets read the *Esoteric Transmissions*; the picture they draw of the Queen Mother agrees substantially with that text.

Mao Ying

Another meeting between the Queen Mother and human pupils changed the world and—according to legend—resulted in the founding of Shang ch'ing Taoism: her encounter with Lord Mao and his two younger brothers on Mount Mao near Nanjing. Numerous Six Dynasties accounts of this meeting must have existed. Parts of one early version survive in the Yüan dynasty *Mao shan chih* (Monograph on Mount Mao). There the Queen Mother, accompanied by other great goddesses, visits Lord Mao, grants him many revelations along with supernatural powers and titles, and departs after introducing him to his divine spouse and teacher: Lady Wei Hua-ts'un. His younger brothers are also entitled and espoused.

The three Mao brothers, in contrast to the emperors, make a success of their efforts to attain transcendence. From the Six Dynasties
on, Lord Mao and his younger brothers provide Shang ch'ing Taoist
adherents with a positive model of the project of transcendence.[63]

Worshiping at Her Shrine: The T'ang Dynasty

Worship and meetings, themes of the first two sections of this
chapter, are never really separate. During the T'ang dynasty, we can
examine how they join in the example of the shrine to the goddess.
The Queen Mother of the West remained the highest female deity in
the Taoist pantheon throughout the T'ang dynasty. Unlike other
archaic goddesses whose cults declined in medieval times, she was
actively worshiped. Whereas deities like the Nymph of the Lo River
Fu Fei and the moon goddess Ch'ang Oh became just pretty faces,
the Queen Mother remained important in the imagination and religious practices of the people and the elite. She continued to govern
immortality and communication between gods and humans. A central symbol of her T'ang cult is the shrine, celebrated by poets,
where she was worshiped. Our main sources of information about
worship of the goddess during this era include archaeology, Taoist
canonical literature, and poetry.

Archaeological discoveries include inscribed stelae and traces of
shrines. Compared to the abundance of funerary art portraying the
Queen Mother from earlier periods, no pictorial images from the
T'ang survive. This puzzling lack of images may result from a
change in the context of her worship from the cult of the dead
during the Han dynasty to individual practices favored by Shang
ch'ing Taoism, such as meditation and nourishing the vital essence,
during the Six Dynasties and T'ang. Although she no longer seems
to appear in tombs or tomb furnishings, she is abundantly mentioned and described in writing.

Accounts of the goddess's life and acts found in texts collected in
the *Tao tsang* shed light on her worship. Canonical works on sacred
geography, hagiography, ritual, meditation, and practices for nourishing the vital essence mention the Queen Mother. A gazetteer on
the sacred mountain of the west, the *Hua shan chih* (Monograph on
Mount Hua),[64] provides information about the goddess's shrine.

The hagiographical account of the Queen Mother found at the beginning of the *Records of the Assembled Transcendents of the Fortified Walled City* by Tu Kuang-t'ing tells her life story and testifies to the importance of her cult among T'ang literati. Works of the medieval poets preserved in the *Complete T'ang Poetry* anthology show best how T'ang literati perceived the Queen Mother. There she receives her fullest literary definition. Poetic references also provide information about the cult of the goddess. She appears in poems that themselves fall into distinct groups, with characteristic plots, language, and religious contents. We will encounter many such groups in later chapters. One series of poems on the goddess's shrine concerns worship of the Queen Mother of the West and her meetings with humans.

The Shrine of the Goddess

State cult. During the T'ang dynasty, stone inscriptions provide evidence about the imperial cult to the goddess. Limestone stelae dated 661–798 that stand to this day on Mount T'ai, the sacred mountain of the east located in modern Shantung province, bear inscribed texts describing performances of the rite of "tossing the dragons and tallies," a Taoist ritual connected with the Queen Mother. Performed by Taoist monks, this rite consists of throwing cast metal dragons into a body of sacred water, accompanied by tablets inscribed with accounts of the ceremony itself including texts of prayers recited. Such prayers requested longevity and blessings for emperor and dynasty.[65]

The ceremony was performed at the most sacred places in the empire. A large temple compound stood on Mount T'ai during the T'ang. Inside this compound, at the mountain's foot, in front of a small audience hall dedicated to Lao-tzu, was the Turquoise Pond, informally known as the Queen Mother's Pond. Even today, pilgrims climbing the holy mountain drink water from the pond as they set out. In 1909, when French archaeologist Edouard Chavannes visited Mount T'ai, locals called this pool the Queen Mother's Pond. It still goes by that name, now official enough to appear on maps issued by the Chinese government for tourists. The Queen Mother's Turquoise Pond on Mount T'ai and her Turquoise Pond on Mount K'un-lun are equivalents in mythical geography. A T'ang inscription on two stelae still standing next to the pool records that the ceremony of tossing the dragons and tallies was performed on this spot.[66]

The poem by Li Po that opens the Introduction attests to both the presence of a shrine to the Queen Mother at the foot of Mount T'ai and her veneration by one of the greatest poets of the era. Preceding his ascent in 742 of the holy mountain of the east with a "drink from the Queen Mother's pond," Li was the most famous of an endless stream of pilgrims passing through that shrine from then until now.

The same ceremony of tossing dragons and tallies that monks performed at the foot of Mount T'ai also took place at a nearby site associated with the Queen Mother on Mount Wang wu in modern Honan province. According to inscriptions there, Taoist monks performed the ritual under imperial sponsorship on behalf of the ruling dynasty. This site, known as Lesser Existence Grotto, was the first of 36 grotto-heavens holy to Shang ch'ing Taoists mentioned by Tu Kuang-t'ing in his sacred cartography of the known world.[67] The same grotto-heaven appears, explicitly connected with the goddess, in T'ang poems.[68] Tu's inclusion of the Wang wu grotto and its association with the Queen Mother in poetry make it likely that Taoists performed the ceremony there during the T'ang, even though the earliest inscriptions on the mountain date from 1311.

The single most important place of worship dedicated to the Queen Mother in the T'ang dynasty was her shrine on Mount Hua, one of the *wu yüeh*, five marchmounts, or holy mountains of the four directions plus the center worshiped in ancient China. Mount Hua, the sacred mountain of the west, was located in modern Shensi province between the two capital cities of Ch'ang an and Lo yang. Medieval Chinese people would naturally connect the Queen Mother with the western sacred mountain: both were associated with the west, death, spirits, metal, autumn, the tiger, and paradise. Mount Hua was prominent in imperial ritual during the T'ang dynasty, when Shang ch'ing Taoism was the official state religion. A major Taoist monastic establishment, including a shrine to the Queen Mother, stood on Mount Hua. According to the *Monograph on Mount Hua*, a religious history of the mountain compiled during the thirteenth century, an old belvedere dedicated to the Queen Mother was part of the Mount Hua temple complex.[69]

Poems on her shrine. During the T'ang, several authors wrote poems about a shrine or a temple dedicated to the Queen Mother on Mount Hua. The *Complete T'ang Poetry* preserves six poems on this subject. These poems reveal something about T'ang worship of the goddess at the same time as they draw on earlier stories of her meetings with mortals.

The shrine poems belong to a general category of works commemorating visits to cult centers of archaic goddesses, such as Nü Wa, the Nymph of the Lo River, and the Hsiang River Consorts (Hsiang chün and Hsiang fu jen).[70] Such verses follow an identifiable scenario that has its own literary history. The typical poem opens with a night visit by a solitary narrator to the goddess's deserted shrine, followed by descriptions of the shrine, setting, and gloomy atmosphere. The work continues with allusions to legends concerning the goddess and mortal Chinese rulers, an epiphany of the goddess (in the form of rain, mist, clouds, or incense smoke), and some communication between divine and human realms. Such poems conclude with the goddess's departure and reflections by the narrator.[71]

Although individual works may omit parts of this scenario, it accounts for the major structural elements of each poem. The same scenario is present in poems about visits to shrines of other ancient goddesses. What sets poems about the Queen Mother's shrine apart is the specific detail of her legend and appearance. The detail in turn derives from canonical texts and from prose narratives of the Six Dynasties period concerning meetings of the goddess with King Mu of the Chou dynasty and Han Wu-ti (see above). T'ang poems on stories contained in these narratives will appear in Chapters 3 and 4. Medieval poets certainly knew and referred to these popular and often-quoted texts. The author Li Shang-yin (813?–58) even mentions the *Esoteric Transmissions Concerning the Martial Thearch of the Han* in his poem "The Cyan Walled City," no. 3 (*CTS*, 3246).

The shrine poems share themes as well as details with the prose narratives celebrating King Mu of the Chou and Han Wu-ti. Allusions to tales of these two rulers distinguish poems on visits to the Queen Mother's shrine from those commemorating pilgrimages to the holy places of other ancient goddesses. The poems are meditations on ideas evoked by the actual shrine. The narrator identifies with the ancient ruler: he too meets the goddess, falls under her spell, and finally parts from her. The shrine where all this happens is transformed into the Turquoise Pond on Mount K'un-lun and the Han palace in the capital city of Ch'ang an. The poetic present contains moments that occurred in ancient times. When narrator and goddess meet at the shrine, human and divine realms make brief contact; when they separate, discontinuity between the two is re-confirmed. The Queen Mother promises extended life to her followers, but in the end she withholds immortality. Shrine poems express awareness of distinctions between gods and mortals and doubts about the possibility of transcendence.

The great eccentric Li Shang-yin wrote two poems on his visits to the shrine of the Queen Mother on Marchmount Hua. Referring to King Mu, they contain a strong memento mori theme. One of these, entitled "At Mount Hua: On the Shrine of the Queen Mother," reads:

> Beneath Lotus Flower Peak—locked-up carved pillars;
> From here to the Turquoise Pond—lands together extending.
> I might as well go to the Eastern Sea for Ma Ku's sake,
> And urge her to plant yellow bamboo, not to plant mulberry.
>
> (CTS, 3236)

The poet describes the shrine and its setting on Mount Hua. "Carved pillars" represent, through synecdoche, the closed and locked shrine. Her Turquoise Pond, on Mount K'un-lun, where the goddess met King Mu, is far to the west of this place. Ma Ku (Ms. Hemp), another powerful Taoist goddess, is associated with the east and with passage of enormous spans of time measured by alternation of the Eastern Sea with mulberry fields. The Queen Mother has already departed west; reaching her would be as difficult as persuading Ma Ku to give up her mulberries. "Yellow bamboo" alludes again to King Mu's journey; after he left the Queen Mother to return to his subjects in the Middle Kingdom, he passed Yellow Bamboo Hill, where he sang his "Yellow Bamboo Song," a mournful lament for flawed and mortal humanity.

Li Shang-yin's quatrain, a sophisticated literary manipulation of the shrine scenario and legendary materials, provides our only extant written record of the exact location of a shrine beneath Lotus Flower

Peak on Mount Hua—a piece of medieval religious geography that would otherwise remain unknown. Li not only refers to sources in earlier literature but also records his visit to an actual place. He calls a second short poem on the same subject "Beneath Marchmount Hua: On the Temple of the Queen Mother of the West":

> Divine transcendents are distinct from mere mortals: how can we connect feelings?
> Eight horses vainly followed the setting sun's progress.
> Don't regret the famed noblewoman's disappearing in the middle of the night,
> While you still can't extend your own life.
>
> (CTS, 3262)

The eight horses are King Mu's famous chargers; the questing journey following the sun's path recalls King Mu's western travels. Li refers in the same poem to the meeting a thousand years later of Han Wu-ti and the Queen Mother. The noblewoman who disappears from the imperial palace before daybreak is the goddess; the person addressed in the last line is the Han emperor. Regret over failure to attain longevity is useless, the narrator implies. Humans and deities are separate; goddesses leave, and men die.

One rainy night late in spring, sometime in the late ninth century, Liu Ts'ang visited an unspecified shrine of the goddess; references to Han Wu-ti suggest a site near the capital city of Ch'ang an. Liu's eight-line poem "On the Queen Mother's Temple" describes an elegantly decorated but deserted shrine. He compares the fading incense smoke of long-concluded Taoist ceremonies to the perfume of the vanishing goddess and conjures a vision of her palace in the dawn clouds. The narrator remembers a story of her visit to the Han capital and identifies with the emperor's mental state after the Queen Mother has departed. In a final couplet, Liu finds consolation for his intimations of mortality in the beauty of the setting and incidentally mentions a fine altar that furnished the shrine:

> Quiet and empty: its pearls and kingfisher remind me of sounds she left behind,
> Gates closed, incense smoke faint—the Water Basilica clears.
> At first sweep of daybreak, purple auroral clouds give rise to ancient walls;

> What year was the scarlet token sent down from her
>   multistoried city?
> Cranes return to Liao Sea; spring's radiance wanes.
> Flowers fall on fence and stairs; evening's rain has cleared.
> The Martial Thearch may not have his name on transcendent
>   registers,
> But at the jade altar, stars and moon shine forth in an empty
>   night sky.
>   (CTS, 3552)

The poet Wu Jung (d. ca. 903), in "The Queen Mother's Temple," evokes an even more despondent mood. Wu probably refers to the same shrine near the capital—he mentions the emperor's tomb and calls upon the ghost of Han Wu-ti. Wu imagines the building a relic of the goddess's visit to that Han emperor and fancies it has stood there for a thousand years, its distant view of the imperial burial mound reminding the visitor that someday he too must die.

> Dragon and simurgh descended one night from K'un-lun Hill;
> The temple they left behind has pillowed a thousand years on
>   the cyan flow.
> But all she obtained was for the Martial Thearch's heart to wear
>   out,
> And now I must endure seeing autumn's grasses on the Fertile
>   Tumulus.
>   (CTS, 4103)

Yü Fu (fl. 840) concentrates on the faraway scenery visible from a southern shrine dedicated to the goddess in his "Describing the Distant View in Front of the Queen Mother's Shrine." The narrator's spiritual experience in this deserted but still numinous spot, as much as the vista, forms the subject of the poem. The goddess is long gone as the poet sits in a building surrounded by willows, watching the sun set over the darkening Yangtze.

> Clouds and auroral haze of a thousand old tales,
> Peach and plum—familiar flowery faces.
> The fragrant letter is lost with the blue bird;
> Her empty shrine conceals evening mountains.
> Incense transmitted, the whole building darkens;
> Willows surrounding them, the myriad households locked.
> How much more does it wound spiritual places?
> The river darkens between here and the setting sun.
>   (CTS, 3298)

Private shrines were dedicated to the Queen Mother, as to other important deities, by the T'ang royal family. One stood inside the Floriate Clear Palace on Black Horse Mountain outside the T'ang capital city of Ch'ang an. The Floriate Clear Palace was a royal hotsprings resort, the favorite winter retreat of the T'ang dynasty Taoist emperor Li Lung-chi (r. 712–56), posthumously known as Hsüan tsung, and his beloved consort Yang Kuei-fei. This imperial shrine to the goddess appears only once in literature, in a long descriptive poem by Cheng Yü (*CTS*, 3438–40).

T'ang poems on the Queen Mother's shrine preserve the memory of her cult, the sacred places where she was worshiped, and the stories medieval people told each other about her. The poems also join the ancient Chinese tradition of songs about ancient goddesses with another old tradition of tales about men's encounters with such goddesses. The interlocked themes of worship and legend unite in the T'ang; the shrine poems are just one example.

Religious and literary images of the Queen Mother from the past create the warp and weft threads that come together in the T'ang to weave a rich and complex tapestry that is the substance and pattern of the goddess herself. The medieval picture of the Queen Mother of the West survives in two repositories of elite culture: her official Taoist biography by Tu Kuang-t'ing, and the works of numerous poets. The main body of this book interweaves information from these two complementary but distinct sources to reveal the life and acts of the goddess familiar to literati of the T'ang.

✥ The Primordial Ruler, Metal Mother

Biography of the Goddess by Tu Kuang-t'ing

The Queen Mother of the West, as people of the T'ang dynasty knew her, appears in a hagiographical account written around 910–20 by the Shang ch'ing Taoist master Tu Kuang-t'ing. Tu includes a lengthy chapter on the goddess in his *Records of the Assembled Transcendents of the Fortified Walled City*, a collection of lives of female deities and saints revered by his school. The author was unquestionably the most important Taoist writer and editor of his time.[1] Tu Kuang-t'ing worked at the end of the creative period of Shang ch'ing Taoism, at a time when he could survey and sum up the great teachings of his school. He had survived the fall of the T'ang dynasty, with its attendant chaos and heavy loss of texts and writers. One of his purposes in compiling the *Records* was to save, organize, and edit as much of the Shang ch'ing scriptural heritage as possible, establishing orthodox versions of the texts he preserved. He also wanted to recommend Taoism to his royal patrons and testify to the efficacy of his faith in times of turmoil. He created his account of the Queen Mother of the West by selecting, rewriting, and combining parts of older texts. He used Taoist, classical, historical, Buddhist, and popular sources, always giving precedence to works of his own tradition. His writing is condensed and allusive. Tu places the Queen Mother's biography first in his *Records*, expressing her primacy in both power and lineage. His account is our single most complete source of information about T'ang perceptions of the goddess.

Tu Kuang-t'ing's hagiographical account of the Queen Mother of
the West takes the form of a traditional biography of an important
ruler or government official from the dynastic histories. He gives it
the same name: *chuan* (transmissions). Like any Chinese biography
of royalty, it begins with her names and titles, followed by information about her lineage and birthplace. Like any Chinese account of a
notable woman, it records her marriage next. Tu then describes her
appearance and special characteristics, names her teachers and associates, and narrates her deeds. The author expresses himself in old-
fashioned formal language fitting for the most serious utterances.
Using the structure and diction of a dynastic biography, Tu avails
himself of its familiarity, legitimacy, and credibility. Yet he explodes
the form. His text is quite long—many times the length of his
models. Tu fills his borrowed structure with information that might
startle the dynastic biographer: many of the actors (including the
principal character) are not human, much of the action does not take
place on earth, and the subject does not die at the end.

In this chapter and those to come, I follow the order of Tu Kuang-
t'ing's biography. Here we will examine the goddess's name, lineage,
home, appearance, and associates; later chapters address her actions
in the world of men and women. In each chapter, I present first Tu's
words on each subject, then examine the works of T'ang poets, and
finally compare the two. Concordances and contrasts between the
sacred and secular image of the goddess in literature will emerge.
Viewing the goddess from various perspectives, we may construct a
total image that will be more than the sum of its parts.

Names of the Goddess

Personal names are important in Chinese biography to establish the
lineage and individual identity of the subject. In addition to defining
kinship and personal identity, names of Taoist high gods have a
special significance: Taoists believe you must know the correct name
of a deity in order to address that deity properly, establish communication, and obtain benefits. Deities' names possessed great power
throughout the ancient world. The proper name of the deity of the
ancient Israelites, shrouded in secrecy and reverence, is an issue of
great concern in the early books of the Hebrew Bible, as seen in the
story of God's call to Moses in Exodus 3: 13–15. With medieval

Taoists as with the people of ancient Israel, the name itself is holy, for it is or embodies the deity's identity.

In the heading of his account, Tu calls the goddess *Chin mu yüan chün* (The Primordial Ruler, Metal Mother; *CMYC*, 24158). I translate *chin mu* as "Metal Mother," despite its harsh and cold sound, because it seems both accurate and appropriate. Earlier the metal in question would have been bronze (*t'ung*); today it would be gold. But in the T'ang *chin* still referred to metals in general and had not yet assumed its modern significance of gold (called *huang chin* or "yellow metal" at that time). As a deity who rules the west, she is associated with metal, the element of that direction. To the modern ear, "Metal Mother" sounds distant and chilly, far from maternal. But perhaps this name is meant to be formal and forbidding, reminding us that she is not only a nurturing and compassionate mother goddess but also a governor of death, another primary association of the west. High Taoist goddesses are entitled primordial rulers. Tu Kuang-t'ing's opening statements list her names and their alternatives: "The Primordial Ruler, Metal Mother, is the same as Metal Mother of Tortoise Mountain, She of the Nine Numina and the Grand Marvel. One source calls her Metal Mother of Tortoise Terrace, She of the Grand Numina and the Nine Radiances. Another source calls her Queen Mother of the West. She is, in fact, the Perfected Marvel of the Western Florescence and the Ultimate Worthy of the Grotto Yin" (*CMYC*, 24158).

The goddess's names and titles express her lineage, essence, and individual identity. Once the Taoist adept knows her correct names, he may call on her or address her if she appears in a vision. Without the proper name, he can do nothing and may even summon a demon. Tu does not divulge her esoteric names, which would be learned at initiation and known only to a few advanced masters. The titles he cites first are public, formal, and official. They place her at the top of the hierarchy of Shang ch'ing Taoist deities, as the greatest of the spirits and their ruler. Naming the goddess, Tu connects her with motherhood, with the element metal, with cosmic mountains, and with the nine original cosmic powers known as the Nine Numina. As mother, she precedes and brings to birth the universe. Metal is the element of the west—the twilight world of yin, death, and the afterlife. Nine is the perfect yang number, balancing her essential yin to make her complete and androgynous. In charge of the "marvel" of Shang ch'ing teachings, she herself is a source of radiant light. She is the perfected essence of yin, the dark female force. Along with her official titles, Tu gives her most common and popular name, the one by which she was known to the general public: Queen Mother of the West.

The goddess appears in T'ang poetry under a slightly different constellation of names. As we might expect, T'ang poets most often refer to her as the Queen Mother of the West or simple abbreviations of that popular name: Queen Mother or Western Mother. Some writers call her the Divine Mother, a general title applied to the highest goddesses, one that does not occur in her biography. Many poets refer to her by the intimate expression Amah (wetnurse or nanny). This familiar usage occurs especially in contexts in which the goddess is portrayed as a mother figure or a teacher. In the works of Taoist poets, she may be called Metal Mother or the Queen Mother of the Nine Heavens. Her full titles specifically associated with Shang ch'ing Taoism do not appear in poetry.[2]

The special requirements of poetry explain some of the differences between canonical and poetic texts in naming the goddess. The limited space in a poetic line makes the use of most long titles impractical. In addition, not all authors and audiences of T'ang poetry even knew her official Taoist names. Poets did not share the concern of the hagiographer with order, hierarchy, and classification. Finally, poets and hagiographers have different attitudes toward their subject: the poets name her with affection and delight; hagiographers such as Tu with distance and authority. The intimate tone of many poems encourages the use of informal nicknames over imposing epithets.

Genesis of the Goddess and Her Consort

In Chinese society, kinship structures provide one major form of order and definition. The Chinese biographer emphasizes lineage, since it establishes the group and individual identity of the subject. Deities are no exception. Like important Chinese clans, they have complicated and hierarchical family relationships. These relations, which determine the gods' power and functions, are carefully traced by their followers. All over the ancient and medieval world, ties between deities were depicted as family relationships. Taoists follow a general tendency to organize deities according to a family model, strengthened by the intense emphasis on kinship in Chinese culture.

Tu Kuang-t'ing shares the genealogical concerns of the historians. After naming her names, Tu describes the genesis, birthplace, and inherent characteristics of the goddess and her mate: Mu Kung, the Wood Sire. He is also known as Tung Wang Kung, the King and Sire of the East, or Tung Wang Fu, King Father of the East.[3] Wood is the element associated with the east, as metal is with the west. Following a general introduction, Tu turns to the Queen Mother's mate:

At the time of the former Way, the breaths were congealed and quiescent, deeply imbued with and embodying non-action. About to disclose and lead to the mysterious accomplishment of creation, and to produce by transformation the myriad phenomena, first the Way produced Wood Sire by transformation from the breath of the perfected realization of the eastern florescence. Wood Sire was born beside the Cyan Sea, in the Barrens of the Gray-Green Numen, where he governs the breaths of yang harmonies, and arranges the internal structure of the eastern quadrant. He is also called King Sire.

Then the Way produced Metal Mother by transformation from the breath of the perfected marvel of the western florescence. The Queen Mother was then born at the I River in Divine Island. Chüeh is her surname and K'ou her clan. As soon as she was born, she soared up in flight. She governs the breaths of yin numina and arranges the internal structure of the western quadrant. She is also called the Queen Mother.

In all respects, she derives her substance from the great non-existent; she nurtures her spirit with the mysterious enigma. In the midst of the impenetrable clouds of the western quadrant, the unmixed seminal breaths of the great Way were divided, and the breaths were bound together to make her shape. Together with the Eastern King, Wood Common-lord, through structuring of the two primal breaths, she nourishes and raises heaven and earth, firing and casting the myriad phenomena. She embodies the basis of the pliant and yielding, functioning as origin of the ultimate yin. Her position corresponds to the western quadrant. She mothers and nourishes the classes and categories of beings. In heaven, beneath heaven, in the three worlds, and in the ten directions, all women who ascend to transcendence and attain the Way are her dependents. (CMYC, 24158)

Tu Kuang-t'ing sets the stage for the goddess's activities with an account of her origin and essence that uses the standard language of

Taoist creation and divine lineage stories. Her birth takes place before the creation of the universe and just after that of the two primal breaths of yin and yang. First her consort is born beside the Eastern Sea, in the territory of the Blue Thearch, Lord of the East, who is called the Gray-green Numen in the text.

Next the Queen Mother arises beside the I River (a tributary of the Lo River in modern Honan province), westernmost of the four original rivers divided from the primordial flood. Giving her both surname and clan, Tu preserves a usage observed in antiquity of distinguishing names derived from the land from those originating in the clan. Both of the goddess's names are unusual and do not reappear in Tu Kuang-t'ing's works or in T'ang poetry. Her putative descendents are more likely to have the surname Wang.

Together with her consort, she creates and maintains the universe and all its phenomena. Located in the west, she herself is the ultimate yin. Tu describes her using the analogies of mother, potter, and metallurgist, images of the creator important in earlier texts considered sacred by the Taoists such as the *Chuang-tzu* and the *Tao te ching* (Way and its power).[4] Attributing creation to the Queen Mother establishes her pedigree and power among Taoist deities. Otherwise Tu Kuang-t'ing shows little interest in the Queen Mother's role in cosmogony. He is more concerned, as we shall see, with what the goddess does after creation, with her relations with humans, and with salvation. She nurtures all creatures but maintains a special protective relationship with women in Taoism.

Although the Queen Mother's consort was a Shang ch'ing deity in his own right, T'ang dynasty writers mostly ignore him in poems concerning the goddess. He does appear briefly in "Twenty-three Poems on Horses," no. 7, a quatrain by Li Ho (791–817) that refers to the yearly feast of the god and goddess, a repetition of the hierogamy or divine marriage that created the world:

> The Western Mother's wine is about finished;
> The Eastern King's cooked rice is already dried up.
> Had you, Lord-King, wanted to go to the feast,
> Who would have pulled your chariot shaft for you?
> (*CTS*, 2328)

The poem is the complaint of a neglected servant, addressed to his ruler. The divine marriage feast is over, and the emperor has missed the celebration. He had no means of reaching it in any case. None of the officials in the royal stable is worthy to serve, and the ruler is incapable of recognizing true virtue. The narrator compares himself to a noble steed capable of conveying his ruler to the holy table if only his talents were recognized.

Other poets refer to the goddess's consort in works describing the Taoist adept's flight through the heavens. As part of the ceremony preliminary to ascending to transcendence, the adept performed a ritual salutation to the Queen Mother and her mate. The late eighth-century adept Wei Ch'ü-mo depicts this clearly in the fifteenth of his nineteen "Cantos on Pacing the Void." The song portrays travel even beyond the nine traditional layers of the celestial vault:

> At the Western Sea, I take leave of Metal Mother;
> At the eastern quadrant, I salute Wood Sire.
> Clouds progress—I suspect they contain rain;
> In my star pacing, I'm about to skim the wind.
> My feathered sleeves wave on the cinnabar phoenix;
> My auroral cloud turban drags a variegated rainbow.
> Whirling upward, I go outside the nine empyreans;
> Looking down, I gaze from afar on the palaces of the
> transcendents.
>
> (CTS, 1865–66)

In a description of wondrous sights seen by the Taoist adept during ecstatic flight, "Lyrics on the Realm of Supreme Clarity," Li Chiu-ling, who passed the imperial examination to become a *chin shih* ("advanced scholar") at the end of the T'ang, includes the goddess's mate. Li refers to him as the Eastern Illustrious One, a lofty title that testifies to his power as essence of the supreme yang:

> Storied buildings locked in by red-lacquered auroral clouds—the
> ground absolutely without dust.
> Cyan peach blossoms issue forth—spring in the nine heavens.
> The Eastern Illustrious One, as day approaches, indolently
> wanders to the feast.
> Leisurely in the extreme—five-colored *ch'i-lin* by the Turquoise
> Pond.
>
> (CTS, 4342)

In the spotless gardens of paradise, peach trees flower; pink blossoms set against their dark blue-green foliage signify spring. Taking his time, the god joins the yearly feast while his divine vehicles relax by the Queen Mother's pond. The *ch'i-lin* is a composite creature made of feline, raptor, and deer. Often called the Chinese unicorn, it has both auspicious and apotropaic functions. The label of Kirin Beer (*kirin* is the Japanese pronunciation of the graphs pronounced *ch'i lin* in Chinese) sports a handsome picture of the beast. Favored mount and draft animal of the high Taoist gods, legend has it that a *ch'i-lin* appeared just before the death of Confucius.

T'ang poets add little to what Tu tells us about the genesis of the goddess or her relation with her consort. They ignore the Queen Mother's role in creating and maintaining the universe, except for the story of her divine marriage and yearly meeting with her heavenly mate, Tung Wang Kung. The annual feast means ritual to the Taoist and romance to the poet. Like the hagiographer, poets emphasize another aspect of the deity: her actions in the lives of people.

Local Habitation of the Goddess

The home of the gods has inspired curiosity and awe in most ancient and medieval religions. Often visualized as a paradise full of every desirable and perfect thing, the gods' dwellings might be palaces modeled on the splendors of earthly rulers, such as Mount Olympus of the Greeks, the Brahma Heavens of the Hindus, or the Western Paradise of the Buddha Amitabha. Or it might be a state of innocence and natural harmony with the divinity, such as the Garden of Eden in the Hebrew scriptures (Gen 2–3). The scriptures of all major religions contain descriptions of the gods' abode. A few adepts can go there during this life by shamanistic flight or mystical transport; the faithful can go at death after a life of virtue and correct practice. Taoists have several traditions concerning heaven. Shang ch'ing Taoists believe in the three realms of clarity (Jade Clarity, Supreme Clarity, and Grand Clarity) far above the earth's atmosphere as well as several grotto-heavens and holy mountains here on earth. The Queen Mother's sacred microcosm is a perfect and complete paradise. In addition to being an afterlife destination for human beings, like the paradises of Pure Land Buddhism and of Christianity, her home is a meeting place for the gods and a cosmic pillar where communication between gods and humans is possible.

Tu Kuang-t'ing provides a clear and very specific description of the goddess's home, a cold and hard realm of pure minerals, a complete microcosm made of precious substances that will last forever:

The palaces and watchtowers where she lives are located in the capital city of the Western No at Pestle Mountain in the Tortoise Mountain Range, and in the hunting parks of Mysterious Orchard and Vacant Wind Peaks at Mount K'un-lun. There are metal city walls of a thousand layers, surrounding twelve jade storied buildings, with watchtowers of rose-gem florescence, halls of radiant cyan, nine-storied mysterious terraces, and purple kingfisher cinnabar chambers. On the left the palace compound is girded by the Turquoise Pond; on the right it is ringed by Kingfisher River. Beneath the mountain, Weak River, in nine layers of swells and rolling waves, rushes along for one hundred thousand feet. Unless one has a whirlwind cart with feathered wheels, he cannot reach this place. The jade watchtowers mentioned above stick up into the heavens; green terraces receive the empyrean. Under azure blue-gem eaves, inside vermilion purple chambers, joined blue-gems make variegated curtains, and the bright moon shines distinctly on all four sides.

. . . Precious canopies screen reflections. Feathered banners shade the courtyard. Beneath the balustrade and steps of the shaded courtyard, the grounds are planted with white bracelet trees and a cinnabar diamond forest. There are a myriad stalks of "hollow blue" mineral, a thousand lengths of turquoise tree trunks. Even when there is no wind, divine reeds spontaneously harmonize sounds, clinking like jade belt pendants. In all cases they perform the timbres of the eight unions. (*CMYC*, 24158–59)

The stones composing this paradise all have meaning. Jade, buried with the dead in China since neolithic times, suggests immortality and incorruptibility. Lapis lazuli with its flecks of golden pyrite crystals stands for the night sky. Cinnabar (mercuric sulfide) was the elixir of eternal life. All the minerals Tu names were ingredients used in elixir alchemy. They were also used in powdered form as pigments for painting. Together they build a colorful image of a permanent, static world, perfect and unchangeable, that stands in poignant contrast to the transient and imperfect world of humans. T'ang poets exploit this contrast to great effect.

Tu harmonizes several canonical accounts of the goddess's realm here, preserving as much detail as possible.[5] The specific details are important so that iconographers in their depictions and the faithful in their visualizations can be certain of conjuring up the true form of the goddess in her proper setting and not some demonic double. T'ang poets also showed the greatest interest in the Queen Mother's dwelling place. Thanks to the general popularity among T'ang literati of such texts as the *Esoteric Transmissions Concerning the Martial Thearch of the Han*, which contains a detailed description of the goddess's paradise derived from Shang ch'ing Taoist sources, we can assume a high degree of familiarity on the part of poets with her home. They associate her first with a mountain paradise. She also wanders freely through the nine heavens, the celestial regions of old, as well as the three paradises of Shang ch'ing Taoism. The writers have mapped out her habitation for us bit by bit, especially in works describing the Taoist adept's flights through space.[6]

Hsü Neng (fl. 806–821) locates the goddess's Turquoise Pond in the highest heaven, the Realm of Jade Clarity. He writes a humorous quatrain in answer to one by a Taoist monk from a famous T'ang temple known as the Belvedere on the Sunny Side of Mount Sung for its location on the eastern slopes of that holy mountain. Mount Sung, sacred mountain of the center, was traditionally given thirty-six peaks. In "Harmonizing with 'Recollecting People of the Realm of Supreme Clarity on a Moonlit Night,' by a Stranger from the Sunny Side of Mount Sung," Hsü imagines a lonely vigil during his stay at the mountain temple:

> Alone at night on the sunny side of Mount Sung, I recollect the
>   supreme transcendents,
> As the moon shines forth brilliantly before the thirty-six peaks.
> The moon at the Turquoise Pond is even brighter than the moon
>   on the sunny side of Mount Sung,
> So do people in the Realm of Jade Clarity sleep or not?
>   (CTS, 2853)

Unlike the human world of the poet and the temple, the Queen Mother's is jade-like, eternal, fixed. Sleep is a marker of human time in a changing world. Hsü's question means: with all that bright light, can the transcendents sleep? Are the immortals like us? A chilling thought beneath the humor—the reader knows they are not.

Located in the heavens, the Queen Mother's realm is difficult of access. Constellations separate us from her. She lives beyond the Heavenly Barrier Pass, across the Mysterious Barrier Pass, and past the Silver Han (our Milky Way). To reach her from earth, one must set out to the west, go beyond even the four wildernesses and the eight extremities, up into uncharted space. After crossing the Boundless Abyss and the Realm of Utter Silence, one finally arrives at her mountain.[7]

The idea of the Queen Mother's paradise on a mountain in the far west, strong in literature and art since the Han dynasty, remains popular in T'ang poetry. Following older authors, T'ang poets occasionally link the goddess to a vague Western Mountain, to Jade Mountain, and to Tortoise or Sea Turtle Mountain. But by far the most frequent association is with the cosmic Mount K'un-lun, sometimes called Highgate or the Triple Mountain. The name Triple Mountain derives from the three main peaks of K'un-lun, which the poets also mention by name: Lofty Hunting Park, Mysterious Orchard, and Lofty Whirlwind Palace.[8]

The Taoist poet Ts'ao T'ang (fl. 860–874), in the forty-third of ninety-eight pieces entitled "Lesser Wanderings in Transcendence," describes a visit to the mountain orchard of the goddess:[9]

> Wind from the eight phosphors turns back my five-phoenix
>   chariot;
> On top of Mount K'un-lun, I see peach flowers.
> If we instruct an envoy to purchase spring wine,
> He'll have to search the Amah's household in Yü hang.
>
> (CTS, 3833–34)

The eight phosphors are brilliant luminaries of the eight directions in the sky; wind emanating from these bright lights provides the source of energy to turn back the narrator's chariot. If he wants to bring an offering to the goddess's feast, he'll have to send back for fresh wine to Yü hang (the main urban administrative district of Hang chou). Hang chou, like the Queen Mother's paradise, was known for its lush scenery, beautiful women, and fine wine. Perhaps, in granting the goddess an earthly home, the poet expresses the same thought as the traditional saying still heard today "Heaven above; Suchou and Hangchou below."

Wu Yün (d. 788), in the twentieth of twenty-four poems called "Wandering in Transcendence," mentions a visit to the goddess's palace on Lofty Whirlwind:

> Flourishing parasols, we reach the chronograms' extremity;
> Riding on the mist, I wander to Lofty Whirlwind Peak.
> The Lady of the Supreme Primordial descends through jade
>   interior doors;
> The Queen Mother opens her Blue-gem Palace.
> Celestial people—what a crowd!
> A lofty meeting inside the Cyan Audience Hall.
> Arrayed attendants perform Cloud Songs;
> Realized intonations fill the Grand Empty Space.
> Every thousand years, her purple crabapple ripens;
> Every four kalpas, her numinous melon produces abundantly.
> This music differs from that at the feast in the wilderness—
> So convivial, and certainly infinite.
>   (*CTS*, 4942)

The adept participates in a transcendent meeting in the Queen Mother's palace beyond the North Pole (the chronograms' extremity), attended by divine musicians. The participants eat divine foods, ripened over world ages. This feast, unlike that of the goddess and King Mu in the Western Wilderness, will go on forever. Its music is correspondingly cheerful.

Although the goddess's home is on K'un-lun, she may also be found on far distant mountains. Sometimes she can be enticed to visit P'eng-lai, the Island of the Blest in the eastern sea. Ts'ao T'ang, in the first of his "Lesser Wanderings in Transcendence," shows us an immortal hermit preparing for her:

> Jade syrinx and metal zither produce the autumnal tuning.
> Mulberry leaves wither and dry; waters of the sea clear.
> He cleans and sweeps the lower road to Mount P'eng-lai,
> Planning to invite the Queen Mother to discuss long life.
>   (*CTS*, 3832)

The melancholy *shang* tuning of musical instruments signifies autumn. White jade and metal point to the Queen Mother, whose season is at hand. The eastern sea, which alternates in different eons between a mulberry field and a body of water, is in its oceanic phase.

Ts'ao's transcendent cleans the water path to his residence in anticipation of the goddess's visit.

The goddess also travels to the holy mountains of the earth, to grace her shrines on Mount Hua, Mount T'ai, and Mount Wang wu or to honor worthy followers at Mount Sung or Mount Mao. Sometimes she may be found in the grotto-heavens beneath the sacred mountains.[10]

But the poets lavish their descriptive powers most of all on Mount K'un-lun, furnishing the goddess's home with all manner of divine buildings and gardens. Her palace compound has tiered walls, twelve layers thick and twelve stories high. Their color is dark blue-green or cyan. Nine watchtowers of turquoise protect the compound. Inside are various buildings: a nine-storied terrace known as the Turquoise Platform where she receives guests and holds ceremonies, the Metal Basilica where she holds formal court audiences, and a jade storied building named the Blue-gem Palace where she gives transcendent feasts.[11]

Shen Pin, a poet who took the "advanced scholar" examination at the end of the T'ang dynasty, reminisces about a trip to the goddess's palace in his "Rhymes Recollecting Transcendence":

> Wind blew among the white elms, whirling the nine heavens
> into autumn;
> The Queen Mother, returning from court, gave a feast at the
> jade storied building.
> As days and months gradually lengthened, paired phoenixes
> slept;
> When mulberry fields were about to be transformed, six giant
> sea turtles became despondent.
> Then cloud-soaring syrinxes and woodwinds departed
> following one another;
> Star-soaring flags and standards each floated spontaneously.
> Now wine and poetry may bring me close—I go mad with not
> attaining it, then
> Straddling a dragon, I drop into my recollections of wandering
> in the Realm of Supreme Clarity.   (CTS, 4388)

The narrator is a banished immortal remembering the good old days. White elms are the stars. The feast goes on so long that the eastern sea changes into mulberry fields, a periodic event occurring at the end of eons of time. The huge sea turtles who normally hold up the Isles of the Blessed become depressed at the thought of losing their oceanic home. When the party is over, divine musicians ascend in procession even higher in the heavens. The deserted narrator grieves and fears for his sanity as he recalls, with the help of wine and poetry, his transcendent flight to the goddess's realm.

Surrounding the Queen Mother's buildings is a celestial park, designed in the style of Chinese royal compounds as a microcosm. It includes a scarlet courtyard and a rose-gem orchard. The most famous elements of the landscape are the Turquoise Pond and the peach garden, locations of meetings between humans and immortals. These two places where men had a chance to love a goddess and transcend death inspired the T'ang dynasty poets most of all. Hu Tseng (fl. 806) tells the story of the meeting of the Queen Mother and King Mu of the Chou dynasty in his "Turquoise Pond":

> The Amah feasted King Mu at the Turquoise Pond;
> To the accompaniment of music by transcendents from the nine
> heavens, they passed around rose-gem broth.
> How moving! When the eight chargers, proceeding like
> lightning,
> Returned home and arrived among humans, his state had
> already perished.   (CTS, 3873)

Chang Pi (fl. 804) recalls the meeting of the goddess and Han Wuti in "Remembering the Flowers," no. 2:

> The old crow beats its wings, hurrying across the basin of space,
> Making me suspect that this floating life resembles a wink and a
> breath.
> The Amah's twisted peach trees' fragrance has never been
> equaled,
> But the Han Illustrious One's bones are entombed in autumn
> mountains turning cyan.   (CTS, 2833)

The old crow is the sun whose flight across the heavens reminds us of the transience of our lives in contrast to the eternal existence of the Queen Mother. The peach orchard was as famous for its fruit of immortality as for its beauty. Those insurpassably fragrant fruits did not preserve the Han emperor's life. T'ang poets associated the Turquoise Pond with King Mu and the peach trees with Emperor Wu; they reappear in Chapters 3 and 4.

Like Tu Kuang-t'ing, T'ang poets pay close attention to the Queen Mother's home, reveling in descriptive detail. The poet depicts divine realms he visits while transported by wine or meditation. Like Tu's hagiography, poems reveal the frozen immutability and flawless beauty of paradise. Their visions correspond remarkably well with the canonical account. They use the same language and images. But the poets show a more varied, complicated, and ambivalent attitude toward paradise. They place the goddess's eternal and perfect realm in explicit and poignant contrast to the transient, imperfect world inhabited by humans. Where Tu praises the splendors of heaven and seems to promise eternal life there to the believer, the poets grieve over the limited but warm beauty special to our short lives. They do not always seem convinced that heaven as depicted in the scriptures is preferable.

The Appearance of the Goddess

Appearance is a concern of the religious writer, not the dynastic biographer. Historians rarely describe their subjects' physical characteristics. The biographer of deities, on the other hand, takes pains to describe his subject in detail so that an adept can tell whether the deity he sees is genuine and benevolent or false and evil. Visualization is a precise and exacting practice. Near the beginning of his account, Tu Kuang-t'ing sets forth the briefest description of the goddess's appearance: "She wears a flowered *sheng* headdress and carries at her belt numinous emblems" (*CMYC*, 24159).

Next Tu turns to early canonical descriptions of the goddess, taking pains to rationalize the ferocious and animistic features of her ancient image. Han dynasty commentaries, explains Tu, err when they portray her as half human, half wild beast: "[The commentaries] also say, 'The Queen Mother has disheveled hair and wears a *sheng* headdress. She has tiger's teeth and is good at whistling.' Now this is actually the Queen Mother's envoy, the spirit of the white tiger from the metal quadrant; it is not the Queen Mother's veritable shape" (*CMYC*, 24159).

Tu cannot utterly ignore older descriptions of the goddess as part human and part feline, since they were well known and appear in the *Tao tsang*. No matter how full of contradictions, sacred scriptures must be respected. They can be reinterpreted but not changed. For example, the description of the Queen Mother that Tu quotes in this passage occurs in a fourth-century A.D. commentary on the *Classic of Mountains and Seas*.[12] What he cannot deny, Tu explains and reshapes to suit his view of the goddess.

The image of the goddess has changed greatly since Warring States times. No longer animalistic and thirsty for blood sacrifices, she has been reformed, refined, and humanized under the influence of Shang ch'ing Taoism. Like the gods in the texts of that school, the Queen Mother has become a Chinese aristocrat, and Tu is eager to strengthen this image. She is, in his book, no cult figure of a peasant or folk religion, but a figure worthy of worship by the highest classes of society.

In fact, Tu's fullest description of the goddess is lifted almost verbatim from a Six Dynasties text with close connections to the Shang ch'ing lineage, the *Esoteric Transmissions Concerning the Martial Thearch of the Han*. That narrative presents a dignified, mature woman:[13]

The Queen Mother rides an imperial carriage of purple clouds, harnessing nine-colored dappled *ch'i-lin*. Tied around her waist, she wears the whip of the Celestial Realized Ones; as a belt pendant, she has a diamond numinous seal. In her clothing of multi-colored damask with a yellow background, the patterns and variegated colors are bright and fresh. The radiance of metal makes a shimmering gleam. At her waist is a double-bladed sword for dividing phosphors. Knotted flying clouds make a great cord. On top of her head is a great floriate topknot. She wears the crown of the Grand Realized Ones with hanging beaded strings of daybreak. She steps forth on shoes with squared, phoenix-patterned soles of rose-gem. Her age might be about twenty. Her celestial appearance eclipses and puts in the shade all others. She is a realized numinous being. (*CMYC*, 24161)

We might compare her stately and elegant figure to the ladies in waiting in the murals found in the early eighth-century tomb of the princess Yung-t'ai near modern Xian. But this is not just any upper-class female: the Queen Mother's numinous radiance and power are unmistakable. Tu's description expresses the standard medieval iconography of the goddess.

Some changes have taken place in her description since the early texts, changes that reflect the concerns of Shang ch'ing Taoists. Believers visualized deities in order to communicate with them. For visualization to be effective, the divinity must appear in the adept's mind in a form that was correct down to the last detail. Correctness was defined as absolute congruence with a standard image set forth in canonical texts. In response to the adept's need for reliable guides to visualization, descriptions in texts become quite specific and detailed. Tu's depiction of the Queen Mother thus attempts to provide the adept with a correct image of the goddess for use in religious practices. He harmonizes various older pictures of her, sometimes leaving out a piece of information that does not fit, or selecting one description over another.

Tu Kuang-t'ing's hagiography sets forth the standard image adhered to by writers and artists of the T'ang. Although a poet might occasionally revert to a more ancient image, borrow attributes of other high deities to give to the Queen Mother, or show deviation in some detail, most T'ang poets present the same picture as Tu. The poets pay close attention to her person, attire, and attributes. Her figure is white and frost-like. She moves with dignity and grace. Her makeup, with brows reshaped to look like moths, matches that of the great beauties of the T'ang. No poet mentions the *sheng* headdress, her single most important identifying mark during earlier times. In its place she now wears the nine-starred crown characteristic of the highest Taoist goddesses. Clothed in a rainbow chemise and moon-colored jacket, she is adorned with jade bracelets, belt pendants, and rings. At her belt hangs a double-edged sword for dividing heavenly lights. In various poems, she carries gifts for human adepts. She brings territorial charts, letters of appointment, bags, tallies, and texts. She also carries elixirs and magical fruits such as peaches and pears from her own garden to bestow on the fortunate. Her appearance in T'ang poetry, as in Tu's account, is a compromise between medieval ideals of female beauty and the requirements of Taoist iconography.[14]

Poets, although describing the goddess in canonically correct form down to her smallest piece of jewelry, take more drastic steps toward humanizing her than a hagiographer would deem appropriate. The poet may presume a more intimate relationship with the goddess than the hagiographer, even when both are Taoist masters.

Ts'ao T'ang, in the ninety-third of his "Lesser Wanderings in Transcendence," depicts the goddess as a mournful beauty, missing an absent husband. Taking the forlorn pose of an abandoned mistress, she leans on the cinnamon tree that grows on the moon. She wishes she had offered to share her lover with other wives in the hope of keeping him by her side. This poem reflects the dilemma and emotions of the senior wife in a polygamous household.

> The Queen Mother of the nine heavens wrinkles her moth
>   brows;
> Depressed and despondent, she leans on a cinnamon tree branch
>   without speaking a word.
> She regrets that she could not detain Mu, the Son of Heaven,
>   and even
> Let him bring his wives and concubines, to stop at the
>   Turquoise Pond.
>   (*CTS*, 3836)

Liu Pi, a *fang shih* ("recipe master" or magician) at the court of Hsien tsung (r. 805–20), presents a more imposing image of the Queen Mother, one closer to Tu's stately ruler of spirits. Liu calls her a realized illustrious one, an honorific title granted high gods by Shang ch'ing Taoists, and describes her regal dress and comportment. Liu's "Lines on the Realm of Jade Clarity" recounts his participation in immortal ceremonies in her Stamen Palace atop Mount K'un-lun. The narrator, like a shaman in flight to celestial realms, travels across the void of space above the world and solar system.

> Far, far away, in the bitter cold winter season,
> Wind soughing and sighing, I tread the Grand Nothing.
> Looking upward, in the distance I see basilicas of the Stamen
>   Palace;
> Crossing the heavens, I look down upon the non-empty realm.
> Below, I see the white sun flowing;
> Above, I see the Realized Illustrious One's dwelling.
> At her western window panel, the sun gate opens;
> At the southern crossroads, stars and lunar lodgings spread out.
> The Queen Mother comes to the Turquoise Pond;
> Felicitous clouds press on her rose-gem chariot box.
> High and steep, her cinnabar phoenix crown;
> Swinging as it drags, her purple auroral cloud skirt.

Illuminating and penetrating, her sagely comportment is strict;
Drapery whirling and lashing in the wind, her divine steps are
    grave and stately.
Transcendent squires grasp jade tallies,
While attendant women offer up metal writs.
Numinous incense scatters its variegated smoke;
At the Northern Watchtower Road, palanquins rumble.
Their dragon horses progress without leaving a trace;
The sound of their songs and bells bubbles up to heaven.
Driving the winds, she ascends her precious throne;
In dense phosphors, we hold a feast upon floriate mats.
Marvelously performed—the "Three Springs" tune;
In the Lofty Brahma Heavens—transcendents of the myriad ages.
Seven treasures fly to fill all the seats;
Nine fluids are ladled out as if from a spring.
Numinous belt pendants hang down from the balcony railing;
Standards and banners are arrayed in front of the curtains.
The awesomeness of lion and *ch'i-lin* strikes fear all around;
Simurgh and phoenix shadows lift their wings, fluttering and
    flapping.
I turn my head back and gaze for just an instant,
And already it's been several thousand years.

(CTS, 3039)

Mortal though he is, the poet has attended a transcendent banquet at the Turquoise Pond, presided over by the goddess. She arrives in splendor, with her entourage of divine boys and girls. In language closely related to such well-known descriptions of the Buddha's lectures as the one in Chapter 11 of the Lotus Sutra, with their showers of gems and audiences numbering in the myriads, Liu describes the Queen Mother's role at her feast. Instead of Indian divinities, however, Chinese star gods attend the ceremonies, and instead of Buddhist teachings, the Queen Mother bestows elixirs of immortality and protective talismans. The poet returns home to human space and time, finding several thousand years have passed in a single instant of epiphany.

The poems by Liu Pi and Ts'ao T'ang illustrate the tremendous variety in the goddess's appearance as captured by the T'ang poets. They show her different moods and activities and describe her bearing, costume, and attributes. They set forth individual resolutions of the conflict between medieval Chinese notions of feminine beauty and canonical descriptions of the great goddess. Unlike other goddesses of the past such as the Nymph of the Lo River, who were reduced in T'ang literature to frail and submissive beauties, the Queen Mother is sexual but never simply a sex object. She remains powerful whether lovelorn or aloof. The T'ang poets reveal different solutions to the problems inherent in representing a goddess who was at once the embodiment of all that was admired and all that was feared in women.

The Goddess's Companions

The Queen Mother makes her trips to the earth in the company of other high gods and transcendents, whom Tu Kuang-t'ing lists faithfully in his account. Her most important companion, Shang yüan fu jen, the Lady of the Supreme Primordial, deserves consideration in her own right.

The Lady of the Supreme Primordial figures in the texts of Shang ch'ing Taoism, where she appears in tales of Han Wu-ti and of the three Mao brothers, serving holy food and revealing sacred texts, talismans, and chants. Her origins are shrouded in mystery. The *Compendium of Unsurpassable Essentials* mentions that she was banished from heaven for transmitting Taoist esoterica to those unworthy of receiving them (*WSPY*, 9.1a). She may originally be the same deity as the Lady of the Three Primordials, with whom she is frequently confused. Tu Kuang-t'ing, however, keeps the two separate in his account of the Queen Mother and grants them distinct biographies in his *Records of the Assembled Transcendents of the Fortified Walled City* (*YCCHL*, 24164–70, 24171–72).

In Tu Kuang-t'ing's *Records*, the Queen Mother summons the Lady of the Supreme Primordial to the ceremonies in the Han palace at the conclusion of the peach feast, almost as an afterthought. Upon her arrival, a second sacred meal begins. At its conclusion, the Queen Mother orders the Lady to bestow holy texts on the Martial Thearch. It looks as though two old stories of investiture of the emperor by two different goddesses have been conflated. Tu shows the Lady's rank among the goddesses as high but inferior to that of the Queen Mother through her obedience to politely but firmly stated summons and commands.[15]

The Queen Mother, having commanded that her vehicles be harnessed, was on the point of departing, when the thearch got down from his mat, kowtowed, and requested that she stay. The Queen Mother then commanded her serving girl to summon the Lady of the Supreme Primordial to descend and join them at the thearch's palace. After a good long while, the Lady of the Supreme Primordial arrived. Again they sat. She provided a celestial feast. After a long time, the Queen Mother ordered the Lady to bring out the Writ of the Eight Unions, the Veritable Shape of the Five Marchmounts, the Talismans of the Six Cyclicals of the Five Thearchs, and the Numinous Flying Beings: altogether twelve items. She said, "These texts may be transmitted from above the heavens only once in four myriad kalpas. Once they are among humans, every forty years they may be bestowed on a gentleman who possesses the Way."   (CMYC, 24162)

The Lady of the Supreme Primordial makes another short and sudden appearance at ceremonies conferring honors on the three Mao brothers. The Lady bestows the Taoist canon on Lord Mao Ying's younger brothers. Again, the Queen Mother's superiority is emphasized: "The Queen Mother commanded the Lady of the Supreme Primordial to bestow on Mao Ku and Mao Chung the Hidden Writs of the Supreme Empyrean, the Seminal Essence of the Way of Cinnabar Elixirs and Phosphors, and the like, all the precious scriptures of the canon in four sections" (CMYC, 24163).

The Lady of the Supreme Primordial, a powerful goddess in her own right, is reduced in Tu Kuang-t'ing's biography to a transcendent serving-girl whose function is to assist the Queen Mother in handing over sacred texts. One suspects she is being offered as an unwilling divine bride to the Chinese emperor and perhaps to the younger Mao brothers as well. The books the Lady reveals are all works of Shang ch'ing Taoism, some corresponding to titles preserved in the canon today.[16] Tu reveals here the hagiographer's concern with glorifying his subject, the Shang ch'ing master's concern with clear order and hierarchy, and the religious editor's concern with proper transmission of texts.

Although recognizing that she held a lower rank than the Queen

Mother, medieval poets seem to have appreciated the Lady's mysterious loveliness and power. In "The Lady of the Supreme Primordial," Li Po writes in wonder about a vision of her:

> The Supreme Primordial: what sort of lady is she?
> She's obtained more than her fair share of the Queen Mother's
> seductive beauty.
> Jagged and serrated: her three-cornered topknot.
> The rest of her hair, spread out, hangs down to her waist.
> Cloaked in blue-furred, multi-colored damask,
> She wears a red frost gown next to her body.
> She takes Ying Nü-erh by the hand;
> Casually accompanying them, phoenixes blow syrinxes.
> With eyebrows and conversation, the two spontaneously laugh,
> And suddenly whirl upward following the wind.
>
> (*CTS*, 1014)

Li Po's poem resembles an aid to visualization, such as those found in the Taoist canon. The Lady wears a three-pointed hairdo, her iconographic mark on Han dynasty mirrors. Her damask cloak, with blue-glinting black down woven into it as decoration, covers a thin dress made of the crust that forms in an alchemist's crucible. She is accompanied by Lung Yü (also called Ying Nü-erh, Daughter Ying), a legendary maiden of noble birth whom a syrinx player of divine talent wooed and wed, leading them both to ascend to transcendence astride phoenixes. The goddess and the transcendent girl disappear gracefully to the accompaniment of divine music after granting the poet a glimpse of them.

The Lady of the Supreme Primordial also appears in a peculiar set of poems from the late T'ang dynasty of which she is the purported author. These poems remind us of the crime for which she was banished from heaven: revealing sacred mysteries to the wrong people. In contrast to the aloof goddess of Tu Kuang-t'ing's biography who barely deigns to bestow texts on the Han emperor, or the independent creature who allows the eager narrator a brief view of herself in Li Po's poem, this Lady comes to earth in search of a worthy mortal to wed. She mentions famous transcendents, including Lung Yü and her husband Lord Hsiao (Hsiao Shih), in her impassioned argument to her intended. Let the preface and the three poems tell the story:

In the middle of the Treasure Calendar reign period (A.D. 826), there was a certain Feng Pu. Filial and modest, he dwelt at the Minor Apartment Peak of Mount Sung. His aims resided in the classics and mounds [traditional divisions of ancient literature]; his inner nature was quite upright and subtle. The Lady of the Supreme Primordial suddenly descended from the void seeking a mate. Pu did not recognize her as a transcendent. Preserving a correct appearance, he did not follow her. She left a poem making an appointment to return in seven days. Later, on the seventh day, when she arrived again, Pu once more did not follow her. She left a poem once again, making an appointment for seven days hence. Seven days later she arrived again and said: "If you follow me, you can increase your longevity, Milord." Pu railed at her as a sorceress, drove her away, and did not follow her, just as in the beginning. She wrote a poem, and leaving it, parted from him.

After three years, Pu suddenly passed away. Sent by the Stygean Bureau, he went to Mount T'ai. To the left of the road, he encountered the beautiful transcendent woman of former times. She said: "Since I could not stop my passionate feelings for this person, I ordered the Stygean Bureau to decree that you must return." That was when he first realized that she was the Lady of the Supreme Primordial. Pu grieved noisily, crying and blaming himself.

Given to Feng Pu

Dwelling in exile from the isle of P'eng-lai, separated from the Turquoise Pond,
Amid spring beauties and misty flowers, there is something I brood about.
Through love your heart could be purified and whitened;
I'm willing to grasp the broom and dustpan, to hold in my hands the bedscreens and curtains.

Given Again

Lung Yü had a husband; both attained the Way;
Liu Kang and his wife both climbed to transcendence.
If you are careful and attentive to detail, you too can look upon the morning dew,
Then in an instant follow cloud chariots to salute at the grotto-heavens.

Left Behind at Parting

Lord Hsiao did not turn back his head toward the people in the Phoenix Storied Building;
But at the cloud obstruction, I turn my chariot around, tears on my cheeks renewed.
With despondent thoughts of the islands of P'eng-lai and Ying, I depart on the road back home;

It will be hard to view the cyan peach spring in our former
hunting preserve.   (*CTS*, 5000)

This remarkable document argues the importance of hierogamy
for the divine partner as well as for the mortal one.[17] Even the Lady
of the Supreme Primordial seeks a human bridegroom to teach the
ways of transcendence. She chooses him on the basis of filial piety
and scholarly discipline. As we see from the virtuous Feng Pu's
startled and terrified reaction to the manifestation of the Lady, it was
a well-known fact of life in T'ang times that ghosts, tigers, and
foxes—those negative manifestations of yin force—might appear in
the guise of beautiful goddesses. The Lady's poems resemble those
attributed to the great Taoist goddesses courting human soul mates
for purposes of instruction and mutual progress, as recorded in the
Declarations of the Realized Ones and other works of the Shang ch'ing
school. Perhaps its author is to be found among T'ang members of
that school. The Queen Mother of the West stands off to the side
here, as the patron and ruler of the home of the goddess and the
governor of divine marriages.

The Queen Mother appears as a role model as well as a ruler in
another set of poems attributed to someone identified only as a
Woman of Mount Sung, whom I also take to be the Lady of the
Supreme Primordial. The story of these two poems, told in a prose
preface, also involves a virtuous but fearful young man who chases
off a goddess thinking she is a witch and thereby loses his chance for
immortality.

Jen Sheng dwelt in seclusion at Mount Sung, reading texts. One night there
was a woman, perhaps twenty or thereabouts, with a seductively fascinat-
ing face and delicate beauty. Two blue-clad attendants preceding her, she
opened his beaded curtain and entered. She herself said: "The numerology
of the dark stygean realm has joined us to make a marriage contract." She
composed a poem on his table top, seeking to become his mate. Sheng,
suspecting bewitchery or weirdness, warded her off. The woman repeated
the gist of the poem, then parted from him, flying gradually into the void
and away. After a number of months, Jen fell ill and dreamed of the woman,
who spoke to him: "Mount Sung has a thin life allotment, young man. Your
number is exhausted. You will be given three more years and then your life
will be over." In the end it was so. The poems that had been written became
thunder and lightning; she took them and departed.

Text Written on Jen Sheng's Table
I was originally registered at the Realm of Supreme Clarity;
Dwelling in exile, I wandered the Five Marchmounts.
Taking you, Milord, as not bound by the common,
I come to urge you to divine transcendents' studies.
Even Ko Hung had a wife!
The Queen Mother also had a husband!
Divine transcendents all have numinous mates;
What would you think of getting together, Milord?
(*CTS*, 5001)

Ko Hung, mentioned in the final poem, was a Six Dynasties period champion of the cult of transcendence, author of a famous treatise called *Pao p'u-tzu* (Master of the uncarved block).[18] His grand-uncle Ko Hsüan was an important transmitter of Shang ch'ing texts, whom Tu Kuang-t'ing mentions in his account of the Queen Mother. Both sets of poems from the Lady glorify divine marriage and suggest the importance of marriage as a religious vocation for Taoist human couples.

The voice of the Lady of the Supreme Primordial speaks in one final poem preserved in the *Complete T'ang Poetry* anthology. This anonymous work derives from theatricals performed at the court of Shu, the same court that honored and employed Tu Kuang-t'ing late in his life. One set of performance pieces consists of dramatic short poems spoken by goddesses and transcendents. The actress playing the Lady delivers these mournful lines:

Thinking over and calculating bygone affairs: my single
    despondent face.
Once in her wanderings the Amah reached the Han palace.
Its city walls and watchtowers no longer exist—not a person
    remains;
The Fertile Tumulus has turned to grass and my resentment
    become inexhaustible.
(*CTS*, 5001)

Here the Lady remembers sadly a visit to her royal but mortal lover, Han Wu-ti, long entombed in the Fertile Tumulus beneath the hills outside the capital city of Ch'ang an.

In contrast to Tu Kuang-t'ing, who presents the Lady of the Supreme Primordial as a dignified and gracious attendant of the more powerful Queen Mother, and to Li Po, who finds the Lady alluring but aloof, poems attributed to the goddess herself show her as familiar, heartbroken, and dangerous. Far from divine equanimity and indifference, she seems moved by human feelings of despondency and resentment. The poets preserve an image of the goddess as an ambivalent force in human life, potentially hostile or even fatal. Like the deities worshiped by ancient shamans, she may enter people's lives and create havoc. T'ang verses of the Lady's courtship and reminiscences assume Shang ch'ing Taoist beliefs in the saving grace of divine marriage and in the danger of angering a potent deity. They also display the poets' love of a good ghost story, their penetrating investigation of psychology and emotions, and their consciousness of the pathos of the human condition.

The Goddess's Messenger

Tu Kuang-t'ing's biography ignores one popular figure associated for centuries with the Queen Mother of the West: the blue bird. Birds, with their ability to fly from earth to heaven, provide a natural symbol of communication between gods and men and figure in many early religious traditions. In the ancient Israelite story of the world flood recorded in Genesis 8.11, for example, a dove brings Noah a branch to signify the end of the inundation and of God's punishment. The blue bird has appeared in Chinese art and literature since the Han dynasty as the Queen Mother's special harbinger and messenger. In its most famous act, the bird descends to Han Wu-ti, preparing him for the goddess's visit. That function is served by a jade girl in Tu's account. The year is 110 B.C.

In the fourth month, on E-Dragon day, the Queen Mother sent the jade girl from the Fortified Walled City, Wang Tzu-teng, to come speak to the Thearch. She said: "I have heard that you are willing to slight the emoluments of the four seas and put away the noble rank of a myriad vehicles in order to seek the veritable Way of extended life. How diligent! On the seventh day of the seventh month, I will certainly come for a little while." (*CMYC*, 24160)

Despite Tu's attempt to substitute a goddess, popular imagination continued to evoke the avian messenger and to connect it with the

Queen Mother. The blue bird, sometimes shown as three birds or as a three-legged bird, is associated with the crow that the Chinese believed to inhabit the sun, another yang creature. The bird—so light, swift, beautiful, and free, and possessed of the ability to fly—was a primary Chinese symbol of the soul and of transcendence. As such, it figures in funerary art and in literature as well. A person who had ascended to transcendence was termed a "feathered person," in recognition of a bird-like capacity for flight not possessed by ordinary, unenlightened mortals. At the end of mortal life, the transcendent was believed to "ascend to heaven in broad daylight."[19]

T'ang poets did not forget the goddess's messenger. Poems on the blue bird or birds play variations on the theme of communication and separation between the human and divine realms. These lively servants of the goddess acted as message bearers, linking heaven and this world. But the need for a link also signifies distance between the two realms, and poets exploit this meaning.

Two poems by Li Po employ blue birds to mediate between the human and divine worlds. One is called "Lodged in Words," a reference to the ancient notion that poetry puts feelings into words.

> A pair of variegated phoenixes from the distant hem of the world;
> Sensuously beautiful—three wild blue birds.
> They wander back within reach of the Turquoise Platform,
> Crying out as they dance by the isolated peaks of Jade Mountain.
> This way they welcome the Ch'in beauty's aims,
> And also fulfill the Queen Mother's intentions.
> So small—the essence-guarding birds,
> Holding wood in their beaks, chant grievously in empty space.
>
> (CTS, 1024)

Li Po populates his poem with numinous birds: phoenixes from beyond the borders, three blue birds who fly past one of the Queen Mother's official buildings on Mount K'un-lun and then past her Jade Mountain, and the essence-guarding birds from Dove Mountain who fly back and forth from east to west, carrying bits of wood and stone to carry out the impossible task of damming the eastern sea.[20] All these creatures flock together to welcome the soul of an unidentified dead woman to transcendence. Li Po compares her to the transcendent Lung Yü, the Duke of Ch'in's beautiful daughter, who ascended with her husband astride a phoenix. The decedent answers the Queen Mother's summons and fulfills that goddess's intentions by registering as a new immortal. The narrator's grief is expressed by the piteous and hopeless crying of the tiny birds in the final couplet.

The second poem by Li Po is called "Entrusted to the Far Distance."

> Three birds separate from the Queen Mother;
> Bearing texts in their beaks, they come and pass me.
> This severs my guts like a string snipped with scissors;
> Why am I having such despondent thoughts?
> In the distance I recognize someone inside a jade window,
> Her slender hand manipulating a Cloud Harmony zither.
> The tunes she performs have deep intent:
> Blue pines intertwined with female lichen.
> She delineates a landscape in the middle of a well:
> From the same source—what different waves!
> Ambitions of Ch'in together with the grief of Ch'u:
> Her white-shining, dazzling fairness—whom does it benefit?
>
> (CTS, 1031; no. 1)

This poem concerns a premonition of death. The narrator sees the Queen Mother's messengers on their way to call someone, maybe himself; then he is granted the vision of a transcendent maiden. The woman in the window has been a powerful image of unfulfilled longing since the Nineteen Old Songs of the Han.[21] She performs two very different songs for him on her zither. First she plays an alluring tune of love between a man and a woman in the guise of a pine and the lichen that drapes it; her next piece suggests the insignificance of this world viewed from the perspective of paradise by comparing it to a landscape reflected in a well. The miniature garden in turn recalls the perfect microcosm of the Queen Mother's home on Mount K'un-lun. The music calls to mind two different sorts of goal: the ambition of Ch'in shih huang ti, first emperor of all of China, to conquer the world, and the unrequited love of the King of Ch'u for the goddess. Death, the great equalizer, puts a permanent end to all such vain desires. The last line asks the rhetorical question Who benefits from all this shining beauty and talent? The reader knows nobody does.

Three birds appear again in a poem entitled "Sacrifice at Sire Chang's Grotto," no. 2, by Huang-fu Jan, who obtained his advanced scholar degree in 756. The poem commemorates a ritual in honor of Chang Tao-ling (trad. 34–156), the father of the Taoist religion. Here her messengers deliver the sacrifice to the recipient, one of the Queen Mother's flock:

> Clouds open at the Lesser Existence Grotto;
> The sun comes out in the Great Brahma Heavens.
> Three birds follow the Queen Mother,
> While paired lads aid Tzu-hsien.
> At what seasons have you planted peach seeds?
> How many times have you seen the mulberry fields?
> In a twinkling, mist and auroral clouds scatter
> Making cliffs in space as the mounted envoy returns.
>
> (*CTS*, 1499)

Sire Chang was Chang Tao-ling, the religious and political leader of the Celestial Masters or Five Pecks of Rice school of Taoism centered in Szechwan near the end of the Han dynasty. Sire Chang's cult was important on Blue Walled-city Mountain, where Tu wrote his *Records of the Assembled Transcendents of the Fortified Walled City*, for it was there that the deified Lao-tzu made a series of appearances to Chang, beginning in 142 A.D. The origins of Taoism as a religion go back to these revelations. Shang ch'ing Taoism owes much of its organization, doctrine, and practice to the Celestial Masters. Tu Kuang-t'ing in his writings honors the older school as part of the tradition leading to the final and perfect Shang ch'ing teachings. Although Tu does not mention Chang in connection with the Queen Mother, he does describe Sire Chang's grotto in another work on sacred geography, classifying the cave as "sacred ground."[22] That grotto, which during the T'ang featured a shrine to Chang Tao-ling, is located in modern Kiangsu province.

In his first couplet, Huang-fu compares the shrine to other holy places. The Lesser Existence Grotto-heaven was located on Mount Wang wu, a mountain sacred to the Queen Mother where ceremonies were performed in her name. Tu classifies it as a "grotto-heaven." Its name and location were first transmitted by Lord Mao himself.[23]

The Great Brahma Heavens are the heavens presided over by the god Brahma, Hindu creator of the world. Indian Buddhists inherited Brahma's paradise as part of a celestial cartography they adopted from the Hindus; Chinese Buddhists imported the idea of this paradise from India. Finally, Chinese writers of the T'ang, including both Buddhists and Taoists, used the name as an elegant term for the sky.

On this holy ground, the narrator is granted a vision of the Queen Mother's envoys and of an ascending immortal. Tzu-hsien was a legendary transcendent and hero of the cult of the perfected. After reaching the age of over a hundred, Tzu-hsien mounted a dragon and ascended to heaven in broad daylight from Floriate Yin Mountain. Mention of the birds and Tzu-hsien point to the narrator's success in communicating with the spirit of Chang Tao-ling.

The Queen Mother's peaches and Ma Ku's mulberry fields, both images of long eras, show the great age of the spirit of Chang Tao-ling. After all these images of immortality, the author returns to a specific day. The weather clears; the narrator finishes his ritual and rides away.

The Queen Mother's messenger sets a standard of beauty and holiness for birds. Comparing the bird to the goddess's envoy, Wei Ying-wu (737–ca. 792) devotes the "Song of the White Mynah Who Presides over the Precious Belvedere" to a splendid bird that lived in a Taoist temple compound in Ch'ang an.

> Mynah bird, mynah bird—
> All the flock looks like black lacquer;
> You alone look like jade.
> Oh, mynah bird!
> While all the flock descends from P'eng-lai and Mount Sung,
> You alone come from Triple Mountain.
> Resident squire of Triple Mountain, you've descended among
>   humans,
> Modest and plain, without adornment, with your countenance
>   of ice and snow.
> Transcendent bird, you obediently fly over and alight on my
>   palm,
> You alight on my palm—at times you push and strike.
> With human heart and bird thoughts, naturally without
>   suspicion,
> Your jade claws and frosty down basically the same color.

At times you depart alone to skim the watchet sea.
Mornings you wander the infinite flow; evenings you spend at
    the Jade Audience Hall.
In the rain at Shamanka Gorge, your flight is temporarily rained
    out;
Inside the Apricot Flower Forest, your passage brings fragrance.
Day and evening you depend on human kindness, despite your
    completely feathered wings;
If you should cross the void with a jade ring in your mouth,
    isn't that a response to virtue?
Why not act like the blue bird from the Amah's household,
And transmit news of comings and goings in the Han palace?

(CTS, 1091)

Rare or odd creatures such as the albino mynah Wei Ying-wu describes were considered omens pertaining to the rule of the current emperor. The poet clearly takes this bird as a most auspicious sign. He claims it hails from K'un-lun. Like a shaman, the bird is the goddess's messenger. He spends his leisure time flying to palaces of Taoist gods and to earthly spots sacred to the cult of transcendence, such as the gorges near Shamanka Mountain where a powerful goddess resided and the Apricot Forest Transcendent Tung had planted. The mynah's presence in court was a sign of divine approval. He might bring a jade ring from the Queen Mother to the T'ang emperor in token of her grace; she had sent such gifts to other exemplary rulers of the past. Or, the narrator hopes in his final couplet, the bird might divulge the secrets of the meeting between the Queen Mother and Han Wu-ti when they met in his palace on the night of Double Seven.

Tu Fu (712–70) uses the image of the blue bird in his "Lines on the Beautiful People," describing a lavish court procession on the Taoist festival held on the third day of the third month. The presence of the goddess's envoy suggests intimacy between the T'ang royal family and the Taoist high gods; their communications kept messengers busy, especially on important holidays. During the festivities, "the blue bird flies away, carrying a red cloth in its beak" (TSYT, 25/4). Tu's allusion to the messenger of the gods also implies that the Li clan is so far above ordinary mortals that they celebrate Double Three with the deities.

In the same vein as Tu Fu, Li Hsien-yang (fl. 873) uses a glimpse of the blue bird rushing away to suggest an active love life. His "Regrets of the Light and Thin," voiced by an old lady remembering her youth at court, recalls a passionate affair that kept the envoy on the wing:

> The Western Mother's blue bird lightly whirled and twirled
>   upward;
> We divided a jade ring and smashed a jade disk—our comings
>   and goings were exhausting.
>   (CTS, 3849–50)

The couple split a jade band and the ritual token of feudal loyalty as signs that each was one half of a whole—traditional gestures of love used to pledge faithfulness during times of separation.

Sending and receiving messages implies separation as much as contact. When Yü Fu wants to express the utter desolation of the goddess's shrine, he writes: "Her fragrant letters are lost along with the blue bird" (CTS, 3298). The departure of the bird signifies permanent absence, without even a trace left behind. The Queen Mother is long gone and far away.

The blue bird symbolizes separation for earthly lovers as well as for worshipers of a goddess. She is addressed in a melancholy poem by Li Shang-yin describing the plight of a pair who cannot meet:

> Seeing each other is difficult; parting is also difficult.
> The east wind has no strength; a hundred flowers fade away.
> Spring silkworms at the point of death—their thread just now
>   all reeled out:
> As the wax candle turns to ashes, my tears just begin to dry.
> The dawn mirror only depresses her; her cloud-shaped temple-
>   locks are changing.
> At night I chant poetry in response to my feelings; the moon's
>   radiance is bitter cold.
> There aren't many roads going from here to Mount P'eng-lai;
> Oh, blue bird—please try to see her for me!
>   (CTS, 3246)

The last couplet is reminiscent of lines from an American folk-song: "If I had wings like Noah's dove, I'd fly away to the one I love." The blue bird provided medieval poets with a sign of communication across a significant barrier. It could be the boundary between the human and divine worlds, between life and death, between nobility and the rest of humanity, or between parted lovers. Although Tu Kuang-t'ing substituted bird-like goddesses for the Queen Mother's messenger, T'ang poets continued to invoke the blue bird as long as barriers remained a major theme of Chinese literature.

The Queen Mother's Attendants

Important deities in many traditions appear to the faithful in the company of huge crowds of lesser spirits, all giving glory and praise to their god. God as seen by the prophet Isaiah is surrounded by a heavenly host (Isa 6); when the Buddha begins to preach in the opening chapter of the Lotus Sutra, a great company including divine musicians and lesser deities attends. The Queen Mother is no exception.

Early in his record of the Queen Mother, Tu Kuang-t'ing mentions that "her attendants on the left are transcendent girls; her attendants on the right are feathered lads" (*CMYC*, 24159). A fuller description of her companions and vehicles appears in the story of the goddess's midnight descent to the Han palace. Tu's account relies substantially on that found in the *Esoteric Transmissions Concerning the Martial Thearch of the Han.*

On the night of Double Seven, after the second watch [9–11 P.M.], a white cloud arose in the southwest. Dense and thick, it arrived and crossed over the courtyard of the palace. It gradually drew near; then came clouds and evening mists of nine colors. Pipes and drums shook empty space. There were semblances of dragons, phoenixes, men, and horses, with a guard mounted on *ch'i-lin* and harnessing deer. There were ranks of chariots and heavenly horses. With rainbow banners and feathered streamers, the radiance from the thousand vehicles and myriad outriders illuminated the palace watchtowers. Celestial transcendents, both followers and officials, arranged in ranks, numbered one hundred thousand multitudes. All were ten or more feet tall. Once they arrived, the followers and officials disappeared. The Queen Mother was riding an imperial carriage of purple clouds, harnessed with nine-colored, dappled *ch'i-lin.* . . . Descending from her chariot, she was supported under the arms by two female attendants. (*CMYC,* 24160)

Another serving-girl brings a jade basin of peaches, of which the emperor eats four. Then the goddess orders more divine maidens to perform ritual music, forming a finale to the feast and a prelude to her instruction. The musicians are minor goddesses of the Taoist pantheon who serve the Queen Mother, glorifying her with their worship and talent. They appear in the occasional poem or story. The care with which Tu recounts each detail attests to the importance of music in Taoist ceremony.

Thereupon the Queen Mother commanded the serving-girl Wang Tzu-teng to play the eight-orbed chimes, Tung Shuang-ch'eng to blow the Cloud Harmony Mouth Organ, Shih Kung-tzu to strike the jade sounding stones from the courtyard of K'un-lun, Hsü Fei-ch'iung to sound the Thunder Numen Flute, Wan Ling-hua to hit the musical stone of Wu-ling, Fan Ch'eng-chün to strike the lithophone of the grotto yin, Tuan An-hsiang to make the "Harmony of the Nine Heavens," and An Fa-ying to sing the "Tune of the Mysterious Numen." The whole ensemble of sounds was exciting and distinct: the numinous timbres startled empty space.   (*CMYC*, 24161)

Later in his biography, when Tu recounts the visit of the goddess to the adept Mao Ying, attributive founder of the Shang ch'ing lineage of Taoism, the Queen Mother is attended by males rather than females. Realized transcendents, blue lads, representatives of the highest gods, and the Thearchs of the Five Directions all follow her to earth (*CMYC*, 24163–64).

In her travels, the goddess rides a divine vehicle, capable of heavenly flight. Following Tu Fu, poets often refer to it as an "eight-phosphor carriage." The eight phosphors, celestial sources of light and energy from the eight directions, symbolize her rule over the cosmos. In poetry, her chariot may be pulled by *ch'i-lin* or by dragons, the sun serving as charioteer. Sometimes she drives a five-colored cloud-chariot, clouds being a traditional sign of the presence of a great goddess. She may even mount a five-colored dragon herself.[24]

As in Tu Kuang-t'ing's account, T'ang poets populate the goddess's entourage with divine servitors. Simurghs and phoenixes follow her. Jade lads, feathered people, and divine transcendents regularly form part of her retinue. The majority of her servants are nubile goddesses: the jade girls.

Wei Ying-wu describes these minor goddesses and contrasts their immortal lives to those of ordinary people in "The Jade Girls' Song," a poem he puts in the Queen Mother's voice.[25]

> Flocks of transcendents wing up to the Divine Mother;
> With feathered canopies they arise, following the clouds.
> Above, they wander the mysterious extremes, inside obscure
>   stygean realms;
> Below, they view the Eastern Sea as a single cup of water.
> By the banks of the sea, how many times have I planted peach
>   trees?
> Every thousand years they open their flowers; every thousand
>   years they form seeds.
> Jade complexions, so subtle and otherworldly—where can their
>   like be sought?
> While in the human world, without limit, people just
>   automatically die.   (CTS, 1090)

Attendants of the Queen Mother, portrayed as lovely nymphet musicians, figure in many a T'ang dynasty poem. The eccentric Buddhist monk Kuan Hsiu (832–912), a figure painter and poet who was Tu Kuang-t'ing's friend, sketches the leisurely life of these jade maidens in "Dreaming of Wandering in Transcendence," no. 2. Kuan's words conjure up strong physical images, impressionistic versions of more detailed descriptions of deities found in iconographic texts:

> Three or four transcendent girls,
> Their bodies clothed in lapis lazuli garments,
> Take up bright moon beads in their hands,
> To knock down gold-colored pears.
>   (CTS, 4790)

Do they seem a little bored in their perfect mineral kingdom? Even their vehicles are unearthly, allowing them to travel freely in the heavens. Kuan reports in another quatrain called "Dreaming of Wandering in Transcendence," no. 3:

> There is no dust in their chariot ruts
> As they go and come at the banks of the Turquoise Pond.
> Beneath the tall, dense cedrela trees,
> A white dragon comes to snort at people.
>   (CTS, 4790)

The cedrela, a fragrant Chinese cedar, was a fit inhabitant of paradise because of its great height and starry spring blossoms. In "Wandering in Transcendence," no. 1, Ssu-k'ung T'u (837–908) captures some adolescent transcendents: already women but still girls. After making a contest of giving bouquets to the Queen Mother and taking their music lessons, they play indolent games of chance on her palace staircase:

> Moth eyebrows newly painted, they sense their own beauty and grace,
> As they compete to take flowers to the Amah's side.
> Lessons in transcendent tunes completed, they seem sluggish and disorganized;
> Jostling each other on the jade staircase, they pitch gold coins.
>
> (CTS, 3795)

Ts'ao T'ang, in the twenty-fifth poem in his long series "Lesser Wanderings in Transcendence," describes an encounter on Mount K'un-lun with a more mature and contemplative transcendent who bears the Shang ch'ing honorific title of *chen fei* "realized consort." She plays music in the melancholy tuning traditionally associated with autumn, the goddess's season:

> A jade-colored female dragon with a golden bridle:
> The Realized Consort goes out astride her, in free and easy wandering.
> On top of the K'un-lun Mountains, beneath peach blossoms,
> With a single melody of song in *shang* tuning, heaven and earth become autumnal.
>
> (CTS, 3833)

Some transcendents the T'ang poets recognize in the Queen Mother's entourage are famous heroines of the old cult of the immortals. Tu Kuang-t'ing's biography does not mention Lung Yü, but T'ang poets could not resist putting them together. Lung Yü appears in a poem attributed to her that was written for the court theatricals of Shu, where Tu Kuang-t'ing lived in his old age. Here the transcendent newlywed shyly recalls her husband giving her a push as they took off from her father's palace on their heavenly flight:

> A multi-colored phoenix came flying up to the forbidden enclosure;
> Then followed the Queen Mother to stop at the Turquoise Pond.

> I just remembered that on top of the Ch'in storied building,
> Someone stealthily spied Squire Hsiao nudging his
>   handmaiden.
>
>   (CTS, 5001)

In the sixtieth poem in the series "Lesser Wanderings in Transcendence," Ts'ao T'ang encounters a heartbroken Lung Yü whose drunken husband has deserted her for the pleasures of the Turquoise Pond.

> The Queen Mother detains him and won't let him return;
> Inadvertently sunk in drink, he beds down on the Turquoise
>   Platform.
> "Please, Milady, tell Squire Hsiao—
> Instruct him to ride his blue dragon and come get your
>   handmaiden."
>
>   (CTS, 3834)

The melancholy and poignant picture of love among the minor goddesses presented by T'ang poets is clearly meant to be compared to the human situation. On occasion, their conniving and earthy Queen Mother contrasts strongly with the serenely benevolent goddess Tu Kuang-t'ing describes. Poets, free of the constraints of orthodox hagiography, can explore links between emotion and religious devotion that Tu dares not acknowledge.

Some members of the Queen Mother's entourage were divine men. T'ang poets' fantasies about male transcendents differ from those about female transcendents. The males are objects of identity rather than desire. Fascinated with their freedom and pleasure, and perhaps wishing to lead such lives themselves, the poets imagine what immortals do. In "The Transcendent Person," Li Ho gives us a look at one:

> Plucking his zither on top of a stone wall,
> Flapping his wings—a transcendent person!
> His hand holding a white simurgh's tail,
> At night he sweeps the Southern Mountain's clouds.
> As deer drink beneath the bitter-cold mountain ravine,
> And fish return to the Clear Sea's shores,
> So, just at the time of the Martial Thearch of the Han,
> He wrote, reporting of a peach blossom spring.
>
>   (CTS, 2334)

Male transcendents enjoy travel, music, feasts, and communication with the Queen Mother. This one must be very ancient: he was present last time the goddess's peach trees flowered, a thousand years earlier.

In "Tune of the Divine Transcendents," Li Ho spies on a group of transcendent boys and girls, gilded youth playing in the surf around the Isles of the Blessed in the eastern sea, and shows how they enjoy themselves in their free time. They send the Queen Mother an invitation written in magic graphs to a feast in their scarlet palaces on the Isles of the Blessed. They choose the blue dragon of the east to transmit their celestial mail, since he is faster than the crane, that symbol of longevity and vehicle of the gods. Finally, two transcendent maidens, Hanging Dew and Beautiful Hair-coils, personally carry the word.

> At Cyan Peaks, where the sea's surface hides numinous texts,
> The Supreme Thearch selected and made divine transcendents'
>   dwellings.
> Pure and bright, their laughter and talk is heard in empty space;
> They race, riding huge waves or mounting whales.
> On spring netted gauze they write graphs inviting the Queen
>   Mother
> To feast together with them in the most remote spot of their red
>   storied buildings.
> Crane feathers pick up the wind, but are slow for crossing the
>   sea,
> So they'd rather send off the blue dragon instead.
> Still afraid the Queen Mother might not promise to come to
>   them,
> Hanging Dew and Beautiful Hair-coils transmit the word again.
>   (*CTS*, 2346)

The male and female attendants composing the Queen Mother's retinue fascinated T'ang poets as well as the hagiographer. They served as models for Taoist adepts, and fantasies about their activities provided an outlet for hopeful speculation about the world to come. Poets, not constrained by the serious task of religious biography, seem more flexible, playful, and imaginative than Tu Kuang-t'ing in describing the lives and appearances of the goddess's immortal attendants.

The Goddess's Master

Since Chinese society tends to order the world and human relations in terms of kinship, lineage is always a primary concern of the historian. Groups outside the family, such as religious communities and schools of thought, are also organized in kinship terms. Biographers take special care to note the teaching line of a great thinker or religious figure. Deities receive the same treatment. Tu Kuang-t'ing pays careful attention to the Queen Mother's lineage, naming her master, his charge to her, and the texts she received from him. We could argue that teacher-student relationships are the most important ones for the Queen Mother.

Her line begins with Yüan shih t'ien wang, the Celestial King of the Primordial Commencement, first among the deities of the Realm of Jade Clarity and highest god of the Shang ch'ing pantheon. Indestructible and eternal, extant before the dawn of creation, he is claimed as master by both the Shang ch'ing and Ling pao schools of Taoism. His relationship to the Queen Mother illustrates the rule in Shang ch'ing Taoism that transmission of sacred texts must take place between members of opposite sex. The Celestial King of the Primordial Commencement is also known as Celestial Worthy of the Primordial Commencement; the titles are interchangeable. (Both "celestial king" and "celestial worthy" came into Taoist terminology under the influence of Buddhism.)

The Celestial King of the Primordial Commencement bestowed upon her the Register of the Ninefold Radiance from Tortoise Mountain, from the Primordial Unification of the Myriad Heavens, commissioning her to control and summon the myriad numina, to unify and gather the realized ones and the paragons, to oversee oaths, and to verify faith. At all formal observances of feathered beings of the various heavens, at meetings during court appearances or feasts of celestial worthies and supreme paragons, at the places for examining and editing texts, the Queen Mother in all cases presides, reflecting divine light on the proceedings. Precious Scriptures of the Realm of Supreme Clarity, Jade Writs of the Three Grottos, and in general whatever is bestowed at ordination: all these are either obstructed or given by her. (*CMYC*, 24159)

T'ang poets mention not only the Celestial King of the Primordial Commencement but most of the highest gods of Taoism as masters, patrons, and supervisors in their poems about the Queen Mother. Prominent among them are the Illustrious Ones, rulers of the three Realms of Clarity and of the five directions. The Queen Mother's master, the Celestial King of the Primordial Commencement, appears under the shorter name of Celestial Thearch in "Canto on Pacing the Void," no. 1, by Liu Yü-hsi (772–842):

> The Amah planted her peach trees at a juncture of clouds and
> sea;
> Their flowers fall and seeds mature once every three thousand
> years.
> When a sea wind blows, breaking off the most heavy-laden
> branch,
> I kneel and lift it in a rose-gem basin to offer as tribute to the
> Celestial Thearch.
>   (CTS, 2170)

Yang Chiung (650–ca. 694) evokes the Celestial King of the Primordial Commencement in "Harmonizing with Elder Fu's 'Entering the Stellar Observatory of the Vast Heaven Belvedere,'" a poem celebrating his visit to an astronomical observatory. He compares the "stellar observatory," located within the precincts of the Vast Heaven Belvedere, a Taoist monastery in the capital city of Ch'ang an, to the Queen Mother's home.

> Celestial calculations are done in the Illustrious Hamlet,
> Stellar observations performed in the Grand Unity Palace.
> The Heavenly Gates open—glittering and glinting;
> Beautiful vapors are dense and abundant.
> The cyan drop-off stands outside the three luminaries;
> Yellow charts map all within the four seas.
> City dwellings are surrounded by the Semblance River;
> Watchtowers in the city walls look down on New Abundance
> Township.
> Jade balustrades by K'un-lun's side,
> The metal pivot points east of the earth's axis.
> The highest realized ones go to court at the Northern Dipper,
> While the Celestial King of the Primordial Commencement
> sings eulogies to the southern wind.
> The ruler of Han sacrificed and prayed to the Five Thearchs;
> The Prince of Huai performed rituals to the eight worthies.
> Bamboo tallies of Taoist texts and chapters,
> Numinous infusions poured into paulownia-wood vessels.

> Grasses in profusion turn rose-gem steps green;
> Flowers weighing them down, gem trees turn pink.
> The stone loft buildings are variegated, resembling a painting;
> The earth mirror seems a vast flood, like empty space.
> At the Mulberry Sea, years must be accumulating;
> The peach spring road is not yet exhausted.
> As for Yellow Hsüan, if you ask after him,
> He went in the third month to the K'ung-t'ung Mountains.

(CTS, 372)

The goddess's unseen presence hovers around the stellar observatory. Yang Chiung, author of other poems on stars, praises the building, calling the activities that take place there divine and comparing it to a star palace. The honorific "Illustrious Hamlet" in the first line refers to the capital as residence of the emperor; what follows glorifies the T'ang rulers as well as the Taoist church and the establishment he visits.

The narrator performs cosmic calculations to determine auspicious and inauspicious days according to a technique known as "concealing the *chia* [cyclicals]" transmitted by the Queen Mother's master and revealed by her to humans. He observes signs in the sky. Astronomical interpretations take place, the poet asserts, in the Grand Unity Palace, itself part of the Palace of Purple Tenuity found among the northern circumpolar constellations and home of the highest Taoist gods, including the Celestial King of the Primordial Commencement. The portals of heaven open in response to Taoist ceremonies; numinous vapors flow down. The narrator stands in the observatory and looks to the edge of the sky, beyond the celestial luminaries (sun, moon, and stars). He sees the whole world mapped by the divine charts. He who possesses maps of heaven and earth—gifts of the Queen Mother—controls the entire universe.

The observatory looks down on the suburbs of Ch'ang an. At the same time the stellar platform is a world pillar that governs all four directions: it straddles Mount K'un-lun to the west and serves as a compass pointing east. From this spot deities, including the Queen Mother's master, look to the north and south. Stepping off from Mount K'un-lun, the narrator accompanies the realized ones as they pace the void and receive instruction from Celestial King of the Primordial Commencement. That great god sings for joy.

The poet hints that textual transmission and alchemical transformation take place at the observatory as in days of old. The Martial Thearch and the Prince of Huai-nan, famous mortal alchemists, performed their rites and received their revelations from the Queen Mother just here. The effects can still be felt. The place itself is magical: grasses grow spontaneously from gemstone staircases and trees of precious stone bear flowers. The stellar observatory becomes a paradise on earth, visited by the highest transcendents. All time and space spread out before the poet as the observatory becomes a true microcosm. According to Yang Chiung, the building has lasted from the beginnings of time and will continue eternally. The Yellow Thearch, another disciple of the Queen Mother from whom we might ask the secrets of immortality, has only just departed westward.

Because of the Chinese concern with lineage and affiliation, Tu Kuang-t'ing takes great care with the Queen Mother's teacher. T'ang poets are not so interested in the aloof and distant Celestial King of the Primordial Commencement, mentioning him more as a hoary authority figure than as a compelling character in his own right. One of Tu's principal intentions as a hagiographer is to transmit information about the orthodox teaching of Shang ch'ing Taoism in specific and correct detail. The poets, not sharing this intent, show less interest in enumerating the texts bestowed on the Queen Mother or giving the reader their full, standard, or even correct titles. There is no reason to assume that all T'ang poets knew such information in detail. Despite variation among poets, the case of the Queen Mother's divine master reveals a consistent contrast in aims between the poet and the hagiographer: the poet's primary task is to write good literature; the hagiographer's to impart orthodox information clearly.

3

❖ *Singing of White Clouds Beside the*
Turquoise Pond: Encounters with
Legendary Rulers and Sages

After introducing the Queen Mother of the West, Tu Kuang-t'ing
narrates her encounters with legendary heroes of antiquity. To medieval Chinese people as to the people of ancient Israel, the most
noteworthy feature of a deity was that deity's intervention in human
history. According to Chinese belief, the Queen Mother acted repeatedly in the lives of men. Among the roles open to a female deity
in relation to mortals, she plays lover, teacher, and kingmaker. The
pursuit of divine communication, dynastic legitimacy, and immortality dominate stories of her meetings. The meetings take place in
sacred and separate time and space: in primordial chaos, paradise, or
special states of mind such as dreams or drunkenness. These stories
are parables of the human condition, tales of love and death that
contrast hope with limitations. They reveal the power of religion in
medieval life, the importance of the relationship between the Taoist
church and the Chinese state, and the way early Chinese people
viewed men and women and their relationships.

   This chapter concerns early meetings of the Queen Mother with
men: those that took place during what T'ang people would have
considered ancient times. The greatest of these was with King Mu of
the Chou dynasty. But first she visits the Yellow Thearch, mythical
first emperor of all China and progenitor of the Chinese people. The
Yellow Thearch is important to Taoists: he restored cosmic order
through military victory over the dark forces of chaos and became
the first human to achieve immortality. His cult during the Han
dynasty and later provides an excellent example of the power of

religion to support or disrupt the state. His followers generally lent legitimacy to the current rulers, upholding their possession of the mandate of heaven. Legend has it that the Yellow Thearch ruled at the beginning of the third millennium B.C.[1]

The Yellow Thearch

Tu Kuang-t'ing's biography of the goddess places the story of the Yellow Thearch at the head of all her human encounters, granting him her power and protection. She instructs and aids him in saving and civilizing the world:

Formerly the Yellow Thearch punished Ch'ih Yu's violence and aggression. Before he was checked, Ch'ih Yu performed illusionistic transformations using many methods. He raised the wind and summoned the rain; he blew smoke and spat mist. The leaders and masses of the Yellow Thearch's army became greatly confused. The Thearch returned home to rest in a fold of Mount T'ai. Bewildered, he went to bed depressed. The Queen Mother sent an envoy wearing a dark fox cloak to bestow on the Thearch a talisman that said: "Grand Unity is located on the front; Heavenly Unity is located on the back. He who obtains them will excel; when he attacks, he will overcome." The talisman was three inches wide and a foot long, with a blue luster like that of jade. Cinnabar-colored drops of blood formed a pattern on it. The Yellow Thearch hung it at his waist.

Then, once he had done with this, the Queen Mother commanded a woman with a human head and the body of a bird to come. She addressed the Thearch: "I am the Mysterious Woman of the Nine Heavens." She bestowed on the Thearch the Plan of Yin and Yang of Five Intentions from the Three Palaces, along with Arts of the Grand Unity for Concealing *Chia* Cyclicals, Calculating the Six *Jen* Cyclicals, and Pacing the Dipper, as well as the Mechanism of the Yin Talisman, the Five Talismans of the Numinous Treasure, and the Pattern of Fivefold Victory. Consequently he subdued Ch'ih Yu at Chung chi. After he had exterminated this descendent of Shen Nung and executed [the rebel] Yü Wang at Pan ch'üan, the empire was greatly settled. Then he built his capital at Cho lu on the Upper Valley.

Again after a number of years, the Queen Mother sent her envoy, the white tiger spirit. Then, riding a white tiger, she perched in the Thearch's courtyard and bestowed on him some territorial maps.

In later years she further bestowed on the Thearch the Rectified and Realized Way of Pure Quietude and Non-action. The words to it went: "If drinking and pecking [eating grains] do not cease, your body will not become light. If thinking and worrying do not cease, your spirits will not become pure. If sounds and forms do not cease, your heart will not become tranquil. If your heart is not tranquil, then your spirits will not become numinous. If the spirits are not numinous, then the Way cannot accomplish its requisite marvels. It does not depend on paying homage to the stars and treating the Dipper with ceremony, causing yourself bitter suffering and exhausting your frame and wealth. It depends on not "building" anything and yet building the Way of the divine transcendents deep within your heart. Then you can extend your life." (*CMYC*, 24159)

Here Tu Kuang-t'ing takes an old Chinese myth of the battle at the beginning of the world, similar to those found in many ancient cultures, and recasts it in orthodox Shang ch'ing Taoist form. The place-names Tu mentions are all located in the great plain of the Yellow River, the cradle of Chinese civilization. Ch'ih Yu, who became a Chinese god of war during the Han dynasty, struggles with the Yellow Thearch for dominion of the universe. High gods of Taoism help the Thearch, contributing arts and talismans.

The Mysterious Woman of the Nine Heavens, an old goddess of sexuality and warfare, is brought into the Shang ch'ing pantheon, serving as the Yellow Thearch's teacher.[2] This absorption of an indigenous cult is typical of the relation of Shang ch'ing Taoism to earlier local traditions. The disciple-master relationship of the Yellow Thearch and the Mysterious Woman follows the Shang ch'ing pattern of transmission of teachings between adepts of opposite sex. The Queen Mother herself has an indirect and formal relationship with the emperor as the founder of his religious lineage and source of his instructions. She dispatches the Mysterious Woman and later her tiger avatar to bring him numinous writings. The overwhelming Shang ch'ing concern with texts and transmission shows in Tu's insertion into the tale of names and teachings of several works of his school. He claims great age for these scriptures by associating them with the first emperor.

The Yellow Thearch himself was an old culture hero whom Taoists had worshiped since at least the Han dynasty as a protector of world order and one of the first humans to attain immortality. Through his account, Tu Kuang-t'ing incorporates the earlier cult figures of the Yellow Thearch and the Mysterious Woman of the Nine Heavens into the orthodox fold of his school. This process of absorption of older deities by newer schools is prevalent in Taoism and especially characteristic of the writings of the great systematizing editors of the Shang ch'ing school such as Tu Kuang-t'ing. One of Tu's goals is to harmonize and organize the teachings of the various schools he valued, and he shows this nowhere so clearly as when he tells stories of relations among the gods. Earlier references show people already believed the Queen Mother and the Yellow Thearch had met; Tu simply supplies the details of their meeting. Strangely enough, Tu leaves the question of the Thearch's transcendence vague.

T'ang dynasty poets were much more certain about the Yellow Thearch's immortality. In their eyes, he was the first adept who ascended to heaven in broad daylight, becoming a model for later aspirants. Poets played down his primal battle for world dominion and his contributions to Chinese civilization, emphasizing instead the practices that led him to immortality. They created a standard plot structure for the story of the Yellow Thearch: he prepares himself and visits the goddess, she confers legitimacy and immortality on him, and he ascends to transcendence. The theme of these poems, which have as their literary ancestors shamanistic hymns such as those found in the *Elegies of Ch'u*, is a quest for the goddess. Unlike its precursors, however, this quest meets with success.

Two poems entitled "Flying Dragon Conductus," by Li Po, describe the Yellow Thearch's ascent to paradise on a dragon. (A "conductus" [*yin*] was a poem set to zither music. Its lines might vary in length.) The first chronicles the Yellow Thearch's preparations:

> The Yellow Thearch cast tripods at Mount Ching,
> To refine powdered cinnabar.
> With powdered cinnabar he made yellow gold,
> Then, riding astride a dragon, he ascended in flight to
>   households of the Realm of Grand Clarity.
> Clouds grew despondent, seas thoughtful, making people sigh
> Over the Selected Women inside the palace, their faces like
>   flowers.
> Suddenly whirling, they waved their hands and skimmed purple
>   auroral clouds,
> Stretched up their bodies to follow the wind and climbed into
>   simurgh-belled chariots.

> They climbed into simurgh-belled chariots,
> To wait upon Hsüan-yüan.
> Rambling and roaming within the blue heavens,
> Their delight cannot be put into words.
>
> (*CTS*, 924)

The second poem starts with his departure:

> In the flowing waters of Tripod Lake, so pure and protected,
> When Hsüan-yüan departed, were a bow and double-edged
>   sword.
> People of old told how these things had been left among them,
> And how his bewitching charmers from the rear palace—so
>   many flowery countenances,
> Flew, riding simurghs on the mist: they too did not return.
> Astride dragons, they climbed up to heaven and advanced to the
>   Heavenly Barrier Pass.
> They advanced to the Heavenly Barrier Pass,
> Where they heard heavenly conversation.
> Assembled cloud river chariots carried the jade maidens;
> They carried the jade maidens,
> Past the Purple Illustrious One.
> The Purple Illustrious One then gave them prescriptions for
>   drugs pounded by the white hare,
> So they would not age until heaven did; they would make even
>   the three luminaries seem faded.
> Looking down at the Turquoise Pond, they viewed the Queen
>   Mother,
> Her moth eyebrows bleak and chilly, resembling an autumn
>   frost.
>
> (*CTS*, 924)

The Yellow Thearch, whose personal name is Hsüan-yüan, casts bronze tripods at Mount Ching in present-day Honan province. The *ting* tripod was a bronze ceremonial vessel used for offering food in the ancestral sacrifices. The set of vessels the Thearch cast at Mount Ching becomes a symbol of dynastic legitimacy sought by subsequent rulers such as Ch'in shih huang ti. Compounding the elixir of immortality in those tripods, the Thearch ascends to heaven in broad daylight. He passes upward through Taoist heavens, starting with the Realm of Grand Clarity. His concubines, beauties holding the office of Selected Women, follow him in chariots decorated with bells in the shape of mythical birds (in the second poem they ride the birds themselves), to continue waiting upon their lord and enjoy the delights of heaven. The second poem opens as the Thearch leaves his weapons behind at a lake near Mount Ching named for the famous tripods. The palace women ascend to the Heavenly Barrier Pass, a constellation of five stars also known as the Gate of Heaven, through which the sun and moon were believed to depart on their daily cycles. Hearing divine instruction, they become minor goddesses themselves. The Purple Illustrious Thearch sends them elixir drugs from the mortar and pestle of the moon rabbit (the Queen Mother's creature). The Purple Illustrious Thearch, one of a divine triumvirate, governs the Realm of Supreme Clarity, the highest heaven. Flying over the Turquoise Pond they salute the Queen Mother, an elegantly made-up but cold and ancient matriarch—the final ritual required before ascending into transcendence.

Ch'en T'ao, a late T'ang poet who became a recluse after the fall of that dynasty, also wrote a poem entitled "Flying Dragon Conductus." Here the Yellow Thearch (whom he calls Lord of Yu Hsiang) and his consorts share a feast with the Queen Mother at her Turquoise Pond.

> The Lord of Yu Hsiang loved divine transcendents;
> Making his meals of auroral clouds, he smelted stone for three
>   thousand years.
> One morning a yellow dragon descended from the Nine Heavens;
> Mounting the dragon, he slowly ascended to the purple mists.
> The multitudes seized its beard; whiskers fell to the ground.
> With a shriek and a whoosh—his bow and double-edged sword
>   whirled into the bitter cold waters.
> Eight or nine purple simurghs dropped jade mouth organs;
> His metal mirror, retained in vain, reflected only local demons.
> Feathered standards in full plumage, he experiences the Silver
>   Han in autumn;
> While in the six palaces, with distant gazes severed, his lotus-
>   faced beauties grew despondent.
> Responsive-winged dragons descend, shake themselves off in
>   the central enclosed garden, and laugh,
> Causing vast, engulfing water to surround the Green Moss Isle-
>   land.

An auspicious wind whips up and returns, as radiance from
    heaven thins;
Turquoise watchtowers looming and towering, they cross the
    dewy hunting park.
In the misty vapors of evening, atop a storied building, a purple
    phoenix sings;
Beneath triple-beaded trees, the blue ox eats.
Seen diffusely, the Nine Watchtowers face the Jade Illustrious
    One;
"Music to Equalize the Heavens" attracts the Gold Floriate
    Squire.
Lads scatter flowers—their crane cloaks short;
Bewitching girls play pitch-pot—moth eyebrows elongated.
They attend a feast in the Scarlet Courtyard on mats from the
    Turquoise Pond;
The old rabbit in springtime is lofty, the cinnamon palace white.
On the inferior state of P'eng-lai, he bestows a divided jade
    tablet;
From the Amah's golden peaches, she permits a small
    extraction.
Transcendents stream down myriad-corded texts: "Spring"
    written in bug-seal script.
The thirty-six grotto-heavens exchange wind and clouds.
A thousand years are just a small crack, like a cricket's chirp;
At the Cinnabar Platform, officials serve the Mulberry Ruler.
While the metal crow tests the bathing water at Blue Gate River,
How many times have the lower world's mayflies died?

                            (*CTS*, 4396)

After years of fasting and alchemical experiments, the Yellow
Thearch received a visit from a heavenly dragon who spirited him
away, leaving dragon whiskers, a talismanic pair of imperial sword
and mirror, and musical pipes behind. His beautiful but depressed
consorts are soon themselves whisked away by auspicious dragons
with shared wings. Together they view the sights of the Queen
Mother's paradise, such as trees with gems for fruit and the blue-
black ox ridden by Lao-tzu. Meeting high deities, they partake of a
ceremonial feast followed by music and games. All receive jade
tablets of feudal enfoeffment and eat the goddess's elixir peaches. As
the high point of the rites, they are awarded the textual transmis-

sions so essential to Shang ch'ing Taoists, including a talisman consisting of the life-prolonging graph for "spring" written in ancient, magical script and a map of sacred geography including the thirty-six grotto-heavens and the secret underground passages connecting them. The whole event passes in a flash in heaven, but lasts eons of earthly time.

The narrator of the poem called "Wandering in Transcendence" by Liu Fu, who became an advanced scholar in the period 766–80, departs from the earth to join the Yellow Thearch and the Queen Mother in celestial flight:

> Halting my carriage, I lean on the supporting mulberry tree;
> Footloose and fancy-free, I gaze off at the nine isle-lands.
> When the two ancients assisted Hsüan-yüan,
> He shifted his halberd and slew Ch'ih Yu.
> His victorious attack completed, he abandoned the world and
>   departed;
> Riding a dragon, he ascended the heavens to wander.
> Above the heavens, he was granted an audience with the Jade
>   Illustrious One;
> His longevity will only cease with heaven and earth.
> Looking down, I view the palaces of K'un-lun:
> Five city walls and twelve storied-buildings.
> The Queen Mother—how secluded and cloistered!
> Her jade substance pure as well as yielding.
> Flourishing her sleeve, she breaks off a rose-gem branch,
> And sends it to me at heaven's eastern head.
> We will think of each other for a thousand myriad years:
> Great cycles—their vastness so hard to perceive.
> Of what use is it to know my Way?
> Even the sun and moon cannot make a full circuit.
> So I entrust my good news to the blue bird's wings,
> And say parting words to you beside the Cyan Sea's flow.
>   (CTS, 1835)

This poem is a farewell message to friends and family from a departed immortal.[3] Like the ancient Chinese shamans in the hymns of the *Elegies of Ch'u*, his travels begin at the mulberry tree on the eastern edge of the world, where the sun climbs to heaven each morning. Wandering over the nine divisions of the original territory of China, he speculates on the mythical battle for control of the cosmos and on the Yellow Thearch's victory. Two old ones, primal forces of creation known as yin and yang, serve him. The Yellow Thearch visits the high court of the Jade Illustrious One, supreme deity of the Realm of Jade Clarity and teacher of the Queen Mother. Like the emperor, the narrator flies down to Mount K'un-lun to sit at the feet of that goddess. Liu names divinities and heavens revered by Shang ch'ing Taoists. When the goddess gives him a mineral elixir that transforms him, the narrator leaves, following the Yellow Thearch's example. He sends his final poem via the Queen Mother's post: the blue bird. The Yellow Thearch's achievement is also a victory for humankind since he opened the path to immortality through study with a divine teacher.

Liu Fu describes the Queen Mother's beauty much as Tu Kuang-t'ing does, comparing her basic substance to jade. The old poetic image of jade as a beautiful woman's flesh contains a contradiction central to the Queen Mother as a powerful deity who is also the ultimate embodiment of yin, the dark female force: she is hard and pure as that gemstone, and just as immortal, yet also pliant and yielding as befits the responsive nature of yin.

The four poems considered above glorify the Yellow Thearch. Like Tu Kuang-t'ing, they assign the Queen Mother a central role in his story. The Thearch gains power only after she advises him and immortality only after he visits her. Since Han times the myth and cult of the Yellow Thearch has always emphasized ruling power supported by religious sanctions. The Yellow Thearch is a political and military deity as much as a hero of the cult of immortals. His worship in the T'ang mixed Taoism and politics. His old and independent cult was potentially disruptive both to the state and to the Taoist church. Medieval Taoists of the Shang ch'ing school cultivated aristocratic followers and sought imperial patronage. They took great pains to bring the Yellow Thearch into their fold through identifying him with their lineage of divine masters and texts.

T'ang poets grant the Thearch his due as cosmic victor and first recipient of divine sanction for ruling China, a man supremely worthy of the mandate of heaven. But they focus on his contribution as the first human to become immortal. Rather than dwelling on the Queen Mother's legitimizing visit to him, they concentrate on his quest of the goddess, his studies under her, and his successful practice of her teachings. The Yellow Thearch provides a rare model of successful quest for both poet and adept to consider.

Shun

The second Chinese ruler the Queen Mother encounters is the sage emperor Yü Shun, more often simply called Shun, believed to have governed China a few centuries after the Yellow Thearch. Shun exemplified the virtuous ruler to Warring States rhetoricians and later Confucian scholars.[4] In Tu Kuang-t'ing's version, the parable of Yü illustrates the Taoist argument of the value of religion to the state. He receives the mandate of heaven in response to his virtue. The Queen Mother gives him maps and season-marking pipes that signify dominion over space and time. Tu furnishes a brief account of the goddess's visit to her second imperial pupil:

> After that Yü Shun took the throne. The Queen Mother sent an envoy to bestow on Shun a white jade bracelet. She also bestowed on his advisor I some territorial maps. Consequently Shun extended the Yellow Thearch's territory of nine isle-lands to twelve isle-lands. The Queen Mother also sent her envoy to bestow on Shun an illustrious tube, which he blew to harmonize the eight winds.   (*CMYC*, 24159)

In addition to the political power of religion, T'ang poems on the Queen Mother and Shun stress teaching and communication between the divine and mortal realms. The minimal plot of these poems contains three acts: the goddess visits the emperor, brings him gifts, and departs.

Pao Jung (fl. 820), in his "Song Embracing Transcendence," emphasizes the Queen Mother's legitimizing power:

> K'un-lun's nine-storied platform:
> On top of the platform, her palace walls are steep.
> The Queen Mother grasps territorial charts;
> Coming east, she submits them in tribute to Yü Shun.
> After the ceremonies in Yü's palace are completed,
> She reverses her rig; a transcendent wind follows her.
> Someone atop a twelve-storied building
> Plays a conductus on his mouth organ that bubbles up to heaven.

I pace aimlessly back and forth on Mulberry Tree Road;
The white sun brings up my parting resentments.
The blue bird will not come again;
Ma Ku has stopped writing.
Although I recognize the waters of the Eastern Sea
May be clear and shallow, who can I ask?

(*CTS*, 2919)

The Queen Mother leaves her inaccessible palace atop Mount
K'un-lun. Attracted by Shun's virtue, she brings him territorial
charts. These symbols of legitimation verify his possession of the
mandate of heaven. Her visit has a ritual character; Pao Jung speaks
of "ceremonies." Transmission completed, the Queen Mother departs. The person on the high building is Wang Tzu-ch'iao, a transcendent who called phoenixes with his syrinx. The Mulberry Tree
Road leads to where the sun rises in the east. The narrator feels
deserted; his anger comes up with the sun. Even the blue bird, the
Queen Mother's messenger, brings no news. And Ma Ku, a goddess
associated with the Eastern Sea who often figures as the Queen
Mother's counterpart, has severed communication. Although the
narrator wants to ask about the cosmic cycles of time defined by
alternations of mulberry fields and water in the Eastern Sea, he is all
alone. No one answers, or no one knows.

"On the Supreme Prime Day, I Dream of the Queen Mother
Submitting a Jade Bracelet," by Ting Tse (fl. 775) is set at New
Year's, which Taoists call the Supreme Prime Festival and count as
one of the three principal holidays (Three Primes) of the year. Ting
records a New Year's dream in which the Queen Mother submits a
jade bracelet to Yü Shun. Impressed with his charisma, the goddess
presents the ruler with this symbol of feudal enfeoffment to signify
his control over space. She also gives him a divine calendar, symbol
of control over time. In T'ang China, the calendar for the year was
published on New Year's Day and was the jealously guarded pre-
rogative of the ruling emperor.

> In my dream, it was the day we went to court for the Supreme
>   Prime Festival;
> Beneath the watchtowers we were saluting the celestial
>   countenance.

It seemed that I observed the Queen Mother,
Clearly discerning that she offered in tribute a jade bracelet.
With numinous appearance, she hurried to the head tent;
Awakened to the Way, she has opened the Mysterious Barrier
    Pass.
I seemed to see the white of her frost-like figure—
As though I looked at the moon's variegated arc.
With a rainbow-skirt dance, she went back outside perceptible
    phenomena,
But her phoenix calendar illuminates our human domain.
Transcendents and paragons are not far from one another;
They show up clearly between waking and sleeping.
                                                    (CTS, 1698)

Medieval Chinese people saw dreams as communications from
the spirits. Their messages were omens favorable to or critical of the
ruling dynasty. Ting Tse's dream compares the T'ang emperor's
New Year's celebration, when he published the annual calendar, to
that auspicious occasion on which the goddess visited Shun. Instead
of emphasizing separation of the divine and human realms, the poet
suggests that contact can occur. But his poem locates such contact in
special and limited mental states: the world of dreams or the twilight
zone between waking and sleeping.

T'ang poems and Tu's account of Yü Shun share a theme with
stories of the Yellow Thearch: a worthy ruler receives an epiphany
that grants him power to rule. Neither poets nor hagiographer
claims transcendence for Shun, a hero of the imperial ancestral cult
rather than the cult of the immortals. Unlike the Yellow Emperor,
we have no information on his afterlife. Perhaps for this reason the
tale of Shun meeting the Queen Mother held less attraction for
poets, appearing only twice in the Complete T'ang Poetry. With no
lesson on transcendence to expound, Tu emphasizes the Queen
Mother's importance, whereas poets speculate about time and relations between humans and gods.

Lao-tzu

One sage who meets the Queen Mother in Tu Kuang-t'ing's hagiography does not appear in earlier stories about the goddess. Lao-tzu

lived, or so T'ang people believed, around the time of Confucius in the sixth century B.C. But Tu does not write about the historical master; that man was just one manifestation of the eternal god, Lord Lao, who had met the Queen Mother centuries before in 1028 B.C. Lao-tzu became a major Taoist deity during the Han and Six Dynasties periods. During this era, he was often worshiped together with the Yellow Thearch; their cult, which joined the concerns of political legitimation and individual immortality, had a popular as well as an elite following. The god Lao-tzu was the source of revelations to the founder of the Celestial Masters school during the Han dynasty; these were later accepted into the Shang ch'ing canon. During the T'ang dynasty, Lao-tzu received even more attention as the originating ancestor of the royal Li clan. Tu may include the sage in an attempt both to honor and to co-opt the imperial progenitor. The cult of Lord Lao was especially active around the Blue Walled-city Mountain in Szechwan, the site where people believed he had appeared in the second century A.D. to the first Celestial Master, Chang Tao-ling, and where Tu Kuang-t'ing composed his biography of the Queen Mother. Tu's account opens with Lao-tzu traveling together with his companion Yin Hsi, elsewhere in Taoist lore a guardian of the western passes who became the recipient of the classic known as the *Tao te ching*.[5] They wander outside the eight longitudinal markers of the night sky to the goddess's paradise.

In the twenty-fifth year of King Chao of the Chou dynasty [1028 B.C.], when Jupiter was in B-hare [*i ch'iu*], Lord Lao and the realized person Yin Hsi went traveling to look around the eight cords. They wandered west to the Tortoise Terrace. On their behalf, the Queen Mother of the West explicated the Scripture of Constant Purity and Quiet. Thus the Transcendent Sire Ko Hsüan of the Left Palace of the Grand Bourne, in his preface to this scripture, says: "Formerly I received it from the Thearchic Lord of the Eastern Florescence. The Thearchic Lord of the Eastern Florescence received it from the Thearchic Lord of the Golden Watchtowers. The Thearchic Lord of the Golden Watchtowers received it from the Queen Mother of the West. In every case it was transmitted orally from one to the next, without recording the words or graphs. At this time, I am writing it down and making a record for the generations." (*CMYC*, 24159)

Tu Kuang-t'ing presents the Queen Mother as Lao-tzu's teacher, placing her in a superior role. Tu also credits her with ultimate

authorship of one of Lao-tzu's most famous works. Tu places Lao-
tzu and his revelations squarely in the line of Shang ch'ing textual
transmission when he quotes the introduction by Ko Hsüan, an
important early transmittor of Shang ch'ing sacred scriptures, as
well as the granduncle of the famous Taoist alchemist and author Ko
Hung.

The Queen Mother's meeting with Lao-tzu appears only once in
T'ang poetry, with the goddess taking the inferior position. This
suggests that Tu Kuang-t'ing's view of her as Lao-tzu's master may
be eccentric, discomforting to the imperium, or simply uninterest-
ing to poets. The single poem is Li I's (748–827) "Climbing the Altar
to Heaven and Viewing the Sea at Night." This piece is occasioned
by Li's visit to the Altar of Heaven Peak at Mount Wang wu, a
mountain sacred to the cult of the Queen Mother; the goddess
nevertheless takes an inferior role to the god. The author refers to
Lao-tzu by the title of his highest manifestation: Primordial Lord.
The goddess attends his court, a sign of her inferior status. Apparently, not all T'ang writers accepted Tu Kuang-t'ing's definition of
the relative positions of Lao-tzu and the goddess.

> In the morning I wander among cyan peaks—numbering thirty-
> six;
> At night I climb the Altar to Heaven and lodge beside the moon.
> A transcendent person takes me by the hand, to gather jade
> blossoms;
> Above the altar, at midnight, the eastern quadrant brightens.
> Transcendent bells clang and clang, as sun approaches sea;
> Right in the middle of the sea—far, far away—three mountains
> emerge.
> Auroral cloud staircases and blood-red city walls become
> distinct in the distance,
> Rainbow standards and vermilion tallies entrusted to cinnabar-
> red clouds.
> Eight simurghs and five phoenixes harnessed in variegated
> profusion,
> The Queen Mother is about to ascend to the court of the
> Primordial Lord.
> A flock of transcendents points to this spot and explains to me,
> How many times they have seen dust fly as the Glaucous Sea
> drains.

> Standing up straight, they depart from me—they have an
>   appointment at the Cinnabar Palace;
> In the empty mountains, they leave behind a pure wind.
> On the nine isle-lands, they look down to inspect the darkness
>   before sunrise.
> One-half of this floating life is all in the middle of a dream.
> I begin to understand why the Martial Illustrious One, seeking
>   not to die,
> Sent off men to pursue transcendent Hsien Men-tzu from Ying
>   Isle-land.
>   (*CTS*, 1708)

On a questing journey, the narrator ascends the holy mountain and gathers elixir blossoms. At midnight, he gazes east over the sea to view the islands of the immortals with their visionary palaces. The goddess's procession arrives, pays homage, and departs. Li's final remark alludes to a master who convinced Ch'in shih huang ti in the third century B.C. to send ships to search for magical islands in the Eastern Sea.

This little-known encounter of the Queen Mother and Lao-tzu, mentioned briefly in Tu's account and in one T'ang poem, carries different significance for hagiographer and poet. Each writer assumes dominance of one deity over another. Tu Kuang-t'ing provides us with the Shang ch'ing version, in which Lao-tzu submits to the Queen Mother, the source of all holy texts. As he did in the case of the Yellow Thearch, Tu attempts to incorporate Lao-tzu into the pantheon of Shang ch'ing Taoism and to assert control over his cult. In contrast, Li I's poem assumes a more popular story in which the goddess pays homage to the sage. But Li really pays little attention to the deities' proper respective places in the Taoist hierarchy; he devotes his attention to the adept's flight through the heavens in pursuit of wisdom and divine company. Doing so, Li elevates the individual's search for transcendence above the hagiographer's need to arrange deities in proper order and present correct information about his subject.

King Mu of the Chou

One of the most popular and best-known Chinese stories about contact between a goddess and a mortal features King Mu of the

Chou dynasty (r. 1001–946 B.C.). King Mu (his name means "tranquil") is the tragic hero who tries to have it all: to conquer death, find divine love, and rule China. Like the heroes of classical Greek tragedy, he attempts to win both worldly power and the love of the gods, but fails through his own flaws and the contradictions between his ambitions.

Medieval readers could find colorful treatments of King Mu's tale in the *Lieh-tzu* and the *Transmissions Concerning Mu, the Son of Heaven* (portions of both works are translated in Chapter 1). T'ang writers knew these texts well, citing them by name and using many of their words and images in poems on the Queen Mother and King Mu. The same books provide Tu Kuang-t'ing's most important sources for the meeting. He summarizes them in his account, shaping them to suit his needs. Tu makes everything that has gone before lead up to the encounter of the Queen Mother and King Mu, in which he emphasizes several key themes. The main issues are the search for the mandate of heaven, for eternal life, and for divine communication.

Tu Kuang-t'ing's Account

A long time later, King Mu gave the command to harness his eight fine steeds in two teams of four. In the team drawing the imperial chariot, the inside pair of horses consisted of Flowery Bay on the right and Green Ears on the left. The outside pair of horses were Red Thoroughbred on the right and White Sacrifice on the left. In the main chariot, Father Ts'ao was holding the reins. Shang was to the right. In the team of the next vehicle, the inside horses were Big Yellow on the right and Faster-than-Wheels on the left, while the outside horses were Robber Black on the left and Son of the Mountain on the right. Po Yao was in charge of the chariot. Ts'an Pai acted as rein-holder. P'ai Wu was to the right.

Riding full speed ahead for a thousand *li*, they reached the nation of the Great Sou Clan. The Great Sou Clan head then offered as tribute the blood of white swans for the king to drink; he set out ox and horse milk to be used for washing the king's feet. After the men from the two vehicles drank, they proceeded along the road.

They spent the night in a fold of K'un-lun on the sunny side of the Red Water River. On another day, they ascended K'un-lun Hill, in order to inspect the palace of the Yellow Thearch. They heaped up dirt to make a mound on it, in order to hand down knowledge of it to later generations. Subsequently he was a guest of the Queen Mother of the West. As they toasted each other with drinks at the side of the Turquoise Pond, the Queen Mother of the West composed poems for the king. The king matched them. Their lyrics were sad. Then he observed where the sun set. In a single day, it had gone ten thousand *li*. The king sighed and said, "I, the Unique Person, am not overabounding with virtue. Later generations will certainly trace back and count up my excesses!" It is also said that the king grasped a white jade tablet and heavy multi-colored damask, offering them in order to acquire the secrets of the Queen Mother's longevity. She sang the "Poem of the White Clouds." On top of Cover Mountain, he carved a stone to record his traces, then returned home.   (*CMYC*, 24159–60)

T'ang Poems

Tu Kuang-t'ing narrates the story known to the T'ang dynasty poets. The same basic plot lies behind both biography and poems. The plot structure has five essential parts: questing journey, meeting in paradise, communion feast, exchange of poems, and permanent separation. Several types of poem refer to King Mu's encounter. These include narrative renditions of the tale, both complete and partial, along with works that derive from one detail of the plot. Among derived types we find poems about the king's horses, royal processions, the Turquoise Pond, imperial feasts, and palace gardens. King Mu's valiant attempts to achieve immortality and union with a goddess deeply affected T'ang dynasty poets; he represented wishes and sorrows that remained current. The *Complete T'ang Poetry* contains over thirty major treatments of his story.

T'ang poets contract or expand the story of King Mu and the Queen Mother found in canonical sources such as Tu Kuang-t'ing's hagiography, enriching our understanding of contemporary perceptions of the goddess. The basic plot remains the same, while emphasis and details differ subtly but importantly. We can attribute such differences to the divergent functions and goals of hagiography and poetry. The hagiographer concentrates on the goddess; the poet on the human men who love her. The hagiographer emphasizes faith; the poet emotions such as hope and despair. The difference in interest leads to a difference in focus. For example, poets focus on a part of the older legend that Tu Kuang-t'ing dismisses: the lovers' exchange of poems. Tu leaves the outcome of the king's search for immortality vague; the poets follow older sources that assure us he failed. Poets emphasize another element Tu ignores: the king's unbalanced and ambitious character. His personality contains the tragic flaws that make his failure to achieve transcendence inevitable. The king's personality and struggles are the source of his appeal to T'ang writers, many of whom were officials trying to achieve a balance between personal religious goals and public duty. They mulled over his story in many types of poems, including both narratives and works focusing on decisive moments or characters. *Narrative poems: the whole story.* Some poets who draw on the story of King Mu and the Queen Mother of the West relate the whole narrative in condensed form, for example, Ch'en Tzu-ang, Li Chün-yü, and Ts'ao T'ang. Ch'en Tzu-ang (661–702), in the twenty-sixth poem of a series called "Heartfelt Encounters," emphasizes the king's obsession with the goddess that leads him to neglect his own mortal wives:

> How wild! Mu, the Son of Heaven
> Longed to arrange a "white clouds" appointment.
> Among the palace women, many resented his neglect;
> Storied city walls locked up their moth eyebrows.
> Daily growing more addicted to the pleasures of the Turquoise
>   Pond,
> How could he be wounded by the seasons of peach and plum?
> The green moss only withers away,
> As their white hair engenders netted gauze curtains.
>   (CTS, 507)

Eyebrows, made up in the fashion of the day to resemble moth's wings, represent the women. When the goddess casts her spell on King Mu, he ignores his wives, whose human beauty has a season as brief as spring flowers. They sit despondently as their hair turns white and grows long, covering them like the gossamer curtains of their lonely beds. These ghostly, spiderweb women present a nightmare image of the guilt haunting a neglectful husband in a patriarchal society. Ch'en's poem expresses a poignant and emotional side of the story Tu Kuang-t'ing, with his rejection of sensuality, is unlikely to embrace.

In "Mu, the Son of Heaven," Li Ch'ün-yü (fl. 847) also perceives King Mu as wild and ambitious. Despising his position as world ruler, Mu heads west to the Turquoise Pond. Deserted palace ladies speculate on his fate. Did he follow the Yellow Thearch to transcendence?

> Mu Man, addicted to unrestrained ambition,
> Moreover slighted his role as ruler of the subcelestial realm.
> One morning he obtained eight chargers,
> And, following the sun, went west to the Boundless Abyss.
> In the realm of utter silence, Thatched Hut Peak sequestered him;
> His tracks were cut off, but he left sky prints.
> Three thousand ravishing beauties, locked up in the palace,
> Resented being cut off; how could they help but speculate?
> Some said the Thearch Hsüan-yüan
> Had mounted a dragon to skim the purple vapors.
> At Bridge Mountain, they buried his bow and double-edged
>   sword.
> But all this is veiled in obscurity and confusion; finally it is hard
>   to distinguish the truth.
> Mu did not think of the five-stringed lute and zither,
> Or compose songs eulogizing the southern fragrant plants.
> He only had ears for the Queen Mother of the West,
> At the Turquoise Pond, singing of White Clouds.
>   (CTS, 3448)

Man is King Mu's personal name. Taking royal duties lightly, a sin to those whose primary concern is the state, is a virtue to Taoists. The sites Mu traverses on his quest include the Boundless Abyss of uncharted space; Thatched Hut Peak, where the sun goes in at night; and Bridge Mountain, where the Yellow Thearch (here called Hsüan-yüan) was buried. Indifferent to instruments of north and east and medicinal herbs of the south, the king is obsessed with the goddess. Their well-known love songs begin with her line "White clouds are in the heavens" and take the name "Songs of the White Clouds" from this line. This exchange of poems—so familiar to T'ang poets—survives in *Transmissions Concerning Mu, Son of Heaven* (see Chapter 1).

In "King Mu Feasts with the Queen Mother at the Hostel of the Flowing Auroral Clouds of the Nine Radiances," Ts'ao T'ang describes the scene on the banks of the Turquoise Pond. Nine Radiances is one epithet of the goddess, and Flowing Auroral Clouds the name of a transcendent wine. Ts'ao emphasizes the magic of the procession and the rapt absorption of the lovers:

> When mulberry leaves spread luxuriantly, obstructing the sun's
> glory,
> King Mu is commanded by invitation to a feast at the Flowing
> Auroral Clouds.
> Rainbow banners clothing the earth, only at the clouds does he
> make his first stop;
> His metal memorial tablet is raised to heaven just as the sun is
> about to slant downward.
> The fine wind of their rarefied songs blows powdery stamens;
> Clear dew leftovers from their drinking dampens the sand at the
> Turquoise Pond.
> They remain unaware that the white horse, its red reins released,
> Stealthily sips from the Eastern Field's cyan jade flowers.
>
> (CTS, 3828)

Mulberry leaves spread luxuriantly in the seventh month, the time of transcendent meetings. Summoned to the Queen Mother's side, King Mu flies upward. A metal memorial tablet reveals his status as her courtier and feudal inferior. In their pleasure, goddess and king ignore her white horse. Untended, he nibbles at forbidden elixir blossoms belonging to the King Father of the East, the goddess's heavenly consort. Perhaps Ts'ao suggests something illicit as well as hopeless about their union at the Turquoise Pond. He need not mention King Mu's departure; the reader already knows the sad outcome.

T'ang Yen-ch'ien (fl. 879) in "Transmissions Concerning Mu, the Son of Heaven," gently speculates on the reasons King Mu could never return to Mount K'un-lun: perhaps he still grieved over a dead wife.

> The Queen Mother's pure song makes the jade tubes sound
> depressed;
> There should have been a return appointment at the Turquoise
> Pond.
> But King Mu was unable to get an audience with her again—
> I suspect it was on account of his endlessly mourning Lady
> Sheng Chi.
>
> (CTS, 4004)

T'ang raises a lonely voice when he suggests the king stayed away because of grief over a human wife. King Mu married Lady Sheng Chi on his travels when he conquered her father. Most poets agree that King Mu's wild and extravagant personality led to his failure to achieve transcendence and return to Mount K'un-lun. Like the tragic heroes of classical Greek drama, despite his extraordinary deeds his own character brings about his inescapable defeat.

The eight chargers of King Mu. Among poems derived from King Mu's story, poems on the king's eight chargers—a favorite T'ang dynasty image of fine horseflesh—hold special interest. Poets, like the hagiographer, seem to love describing these animals. The horse provides a model of loyalty and ability in some poems, of equestrian speed in others. The chargers' speed is supernatural, making them kin with dragons and cranes as vehicles for heavenly flight, fit to carry shamans or transcendents. Li Shang-yin wonders why the king does not return, since his horses can go so fast:

> At the Turquoise Pond, the Amah's white damask window opens;
> Sounds of the "Yellow Bamboo Song" stimulate the earth to
>   mourning.
> His eight chargers could proceed thirty thousand *li* a day,
> So why does King Mu not return again?
>   (*CTS*, 3252)

She poses at the window, listening to the mournful song of her departing lover. If he fails to return, it will not be the swift horses' fault.

And Kuan Hsiu, writing about travel to a distant sacred mountain in "Mount Hao li," shows how thoroughly the horses were accepted as a standard of speed. The hare and the crow are the moon and the sun, symbols of the swift passage of time.

> The hare's not late, the crow even faster;
> I'm just afraid that even if I wield the whip, King Mu's chargers
>   won't get there.
>   (*CTS*, 4790)

The eight horses also provide a model for measuring equine beauty and talent. Lu Kuei-meng (d. ca. 881) compares them to Night-Shining White, the emperor Hsüan tsung's (r. 712–56) favorite, a dappled white stallion who danced to music while holding a

goblet of wine in his mouth. Lu's quatrain may refer to a painting of
the same name attributed to the famous T'ang horse painter Han
Kan (ca. 715–ca. 781), now in the Metropolitan Museum in New
York.[6]

> Snowy white tadpoles dapple the light charger, his paces like
>   flight;
> A single routine of soaring brilliance, flags that let moonlight
>   pass through.
> I smile in response to King Mu, who rejected the honor of ten
>   thousand vehicles,
> To tread on the wind and whip up the dew, heading for the
>   Turquoise Pond.   (CTS, 3771)

King Mu's famous ride calls forth images of adventure and excite-
ment for medieval Chinese writers and readers. The eight chargers
of King Mu also provided a popular theme for T'ang dynasty paint-
ers. Some of the greatest artists of the era, including Han Kan,
exercised their imaginations on the subject of these horses. Striking
poems by a number of T'ang dynasty poets describe contemporary
paintings of King Mu's eight chargers.[7]

Liu Ch'a (fl. 806–21) wrote in "Observing a Picture of the Eight
Chargers":

> King Mu's eight chargers go on without resting,
> Departing outside the seas to search for prolonged days and
>   months.
> In the five-colored clouds, cut off from even the farthest gaze:
>   the Amah's palace.
> Upon their return home, they automatically obtain new white
>   coats.   (CTS, 2349)

Both painting and poem show the animals racing outside time and
space, bearing the king ever westward on his search for immortality
until he reaches the heavenly palaces of the Queen Mother. Time in
heaven is not like time on earth: the team stays away so long that
when it returns the coats of the horses, like the beard and hair of Rip
van Winkle, suddenly turn ghostly white.

The poets Yüan Chen (799–831) and Po Chü-i (772–846) take
pictures of the eight horses as the occasion for political lectures in

poetic form. In his preface, Yüan explains that he intends to question contemporary representations of the eight horses. His lengthy poem details the traditional iconography of the horses. He describes their travels in lines reminiscent of shamans' flights in the hymns of the south. He grants their dragon nature, but points out that the artist must not neglect the divine rigs and charioteers, without which the trip would have failed. Citing a legendary wheelwright and charioteer of the Chou dynasty, he concludes that in his own time no one knows how to use divine mounts; that is, there are no men worthy of serving the ruler. Nor are there rulers capable of recognizing good men.

As for excellent horses, no generation has lacked them. Nevertheless, in the end none were as renowned as the eight chargers—why is that? I have heard that the eight chargers went thirty thousand *li* in a single day. Now the chariots also went thirty thousand *li*, yet they did not suffer the vexations of broken wheels or smashed carriage shafts. And the people who went the thirty thousand *li* daily, still without the vexations of decayed germinal essence or stripped-off earth souls, must have been divine people. Without all these three elements being divine, even if one obtained eight such horses, they would have smashed the chariots, obstructed the drivers, and made people's vehicles topple over. How could these men of the present generation even use them? Nowadays, when people paint this old subject, they paint the horses, but they do not paint the chariots and drivers. The reason they do not paint those things by which the horses were used is that they are not familiar with the old story. Accordingly, I have composed this poem in order to dispute with them.

> Mu Man, ambitious for space and breadth,
> Wanted to go to the wildernesses of the nine isle-lands.
> Divine rigs: four came his way,
> And heaven gave him eight chargers.
> They progress like dragons, without even temporarily settling.
> In the morning they say farewell beneath the Mulberry Tree;
> In the evening they spend the night below Mount K'un-lun.
> When their nostrils breathe, they snort out spring thunder;
> The trampling sound of their hooves cracks the bitter cold tiles.
> Tails switching: the black of glaucous waves.
> Their sweat dries: the red-brown of streaming clouds.
> Floriate shafts—tapering and drawn out.
> Kingfisher canopies—quite seductively adorned.

The drivers' wrists don't transfer the reins,
There's no leisure time for the riders to sleep.
Nowadays we have no Lun P'ien to chisel the wheels of our
     chariots,
And no Wang Lang to take hold of the reins.
Although a myriad chargers were to come,
Who is there that would dare to mount them?
                                                    (CTS, 2363)

Yüan Chen's friend Po Chü-i also takes a painting of the chargers of King Mu as a starting point for social criticism. Po argues that the ruler should not cherish extraordinary phenomena such as the eight coursers, since these were actually ill-omened freaks that presaged the decline of the royal house. They caused King Mu to neglect his royal duties of conducting sacrifices in the ancestral temple and state business in his audience hall, wasting his time and resources in the pursuit of sex and immortal life. The horses led the king to undo the virtue accumulated by generations of worthy Chou ancestors. Po calls the poem "A Picture of the Eight Chargers" and appends a moral to his title: "This is a caution against peculiar phenomena and a warning against idle wandering."

King Mu's eight chargers: the colts of heavenly horses.
Men of later times loved them and delineated them to make
     pictures.
Backbones like dragons—ah!—necks like elephants,
Bones prominent and sinews lofty, fat and flesh in fine form.
Daily they progressed a myriad *li*, as fast as flying;
King Mu alone drove them, and where did they go?
To the four wildernesses and the eight extremities, they trod
     almost everywhere—
Thirty-two hooves with no time to rest.
The dependent chariots' axles broke; they could not keep up.
Around the imperial yellow coach grasses have grown; it was
     discarded and apparently abandoned by the wayside.
He headed west to the Turquoise Pond, where the Queen
     Mother was holding a feast;
Years passed at his Seven Ancestral Temples without his
     sacrificing there himself.
South of the Jade Disk Platform he wandered together with
     Lady Sheng Chi;

At the Brilliant Audience hall, he did not again bring the feudal
   lords to court.
The "White Clouds" and "Yellow Bamboo" songs moved
The one man to wild pleasure, and the myriad people to grief.
The Chou dynasty, from Lord Millet to Kings Wen and Wu,
Accumulated virtue and piled up accomplishments; for
   generations they toiled and suffered bitterness.
How could they know that when the royal succession reached
   their fifth-generation descendent,
He would take the royal duties lightly to heart, like so much
   ashes and dirt?
Accordingly, such odd phenomena should not count as great;
If they can shake a ruler's heart, they can act so as to harm him.
The Literary Thearch discarded them and refused to ride them;
And when the thousand-*li* horses departed, the way of the Han
   dynasty arose.
So shouldn't King Mu's obtaining them serve as a warning?
The eight charger colts came, and the Chou royal house went
   bad.
Even now, these phenomena are held up and praised as rare
   treasures—
People don't realize that when the essence of the Chamber Star
   descends, it becomes an uncanny influence;
Pictures of the eight chargers should not be cherished by rulers!
                                                      (*CTS*, 2497)

Such poems assume the reader's familiarity with the King Mu
story, demonstrating its popularity among educated people of the
T'ang. Liu Ch'a summons up the tale with a few impressionistic
lines; Yüan and Po skillfully manipulate the well-known legend
along with the reader's expectations to criticize contemporary social
life.

King Mu's journey to the west. T'ang dynasty poets use another
image drawn from the King Mu cycle, the westward procession
culminating in a supernatural feast, to glorify T'ang dynasty imperial processions and picnics. Records of such occasions still survive,
together with poems written to celebrate them. For example, Yao
Ch'ung (651–721) and Chang I-chih (d. 705) commemorate a summer visit by Empress Wu Tse-t'ien (r. 690–705) to the Rocky

Springs Mountains, a range near the capital city of Lo yang that included Mount Sung, the holy mountain of the center. The Rocky Springs flowed from the eastern side of Mount Sung. The two poems answer an imperial composition. In "Offered to Match the Imperially Composed 'Wandering on a Summer's Day to Rocky Springs Mountain,' " Yao asserts that the empress's rule has restored long-vanished glories to the landscape:

> Two chambers and three mountains shed radiant light on earthly precipices,
> Adjusting the frost, calculating the sun, located at the center of the heavens.
> Rocky Springs' stone mirror always retains the moon;
> Mountain bird and mountain flower compete to follow the wind.
> Long ago, a Chou king declined the bounty of the Turquoise Pond,
> And a Han ruler felt anxious and ashamed at the Jade Tree Palace.
> Now, on the other hand, we have auspicious mists paired with beautiful breaths,
> Which can follow the light palanquin: altogether profuse.
>
> (CTS, 435)

Yao implies that perhaps here at Rocky Springs, with its beneficent vapors, conditions are right for the Empress Wu to succeed where King Mu of the Chou and Han Wu-ti failed.

Chang I-chih, the empress's youthful lover in her old age, depicts a divine retinue moving through a heavenly landscape to a divine feast:

> Six dragons rear up their heads, racing forward in the dawn light.
> Seven Paragons accompany the high chariot, perching on the shady side of the Yin River.
> One thousand yards of pine lichen join kingfisher hangings;
> A single hillock of this landscape matches a sounding zither.
> Blue birds and white clouds are the Queen Mother's messengers;
> Suspended rattan vines and severed kudzu creepers: the wild man's heart's desire.

> In the midst of the mountains the sun moves toward evening,
>   descending behind a secluded cliff;
> Lightly, their fragrance blowing, falling flowers deepen.
>
>   (CTS, 494)

The Queen Mother and ancient kings carry political overtones in these poems: they sanction the empress's rule. Legitimacy was a sensitive topic during the reign of Wu Tse-t'ien, the only Chinese woman ever to assume the full rank and title of emperor and to found a dynasty (the Chou dynasty, 690–705). Unlike other T'ang rulers, she was no serious patron of Taoism, favoring Buddhism. But Wu Tse-t'ien encouraged support wherever it appeared. Some of her followers identified her with Maitreya, the future Buddha. Others, like the courtiers Yao and Chang, flatter Wu in poetry, asserting that unlike her male predecessors she will attain transcendence and even comparing her to the Queen Mother herself.

On another occasion, the fifteenth day of the twelfth lunar month in 709, the emperor Li Hsien (r. 705–10) or, as he was posthumously known, Chung tsung, and his courtiers proceeded from the Floriate Clear Palace on Black Horse Mountain to the nearby White Deer Belvedere. When the emperor proposed a literary competition, several members of his retinue responded in verse. The T'ang shih chi shih (Records of anecdotes about T'ang poetry) preserves six of these poems; two allude to King Mu's travels.[8] Liu Hsien's (fl. 705) offering, "Composed on Imperial Command: Offered up in Competition on the Occasion of an Imperial Visit to the White Deer Belvedere," compares the T'ang dynasty outing to a feast in the Queen Mother's paradise, where fortunate courtiers drink elixirs and watch cranes dance.

> In mysterious wandering, we ride the falling light;
> At transcendent eaves, enveloping mists thin to a fine drizzle.
> A stone bridge winds around the torrent;
> Beaded banners sweep the altar and fly.
> Mushroom lads offer up oil and fluid elixirs;
> Cranes dance in ranks among the pines.
> Once again, as at the Turquoise Pond,
> Our songs completed, we wheel around and drive our chariots
>   home.
>
>   (CTS, 450)

Shen Ch'üan-ch'i's (ca. 650–713) entry on the same occasion, "Composed on Imperial Command: An Imperial Visit to the White Deer Belvedere," also flatters the imperial cortege:

> At the Purple Phoenix Realized Person's Archives:
> A mottled dragon from the household of the Grand Supreme.
> From the Celestial Stream, mushroom parasols descend;
> In the mountains' switchbacks, cinnamon flags slant.
> From the incomparable one's fine grass mats, bitter cold dew
>   drips;
> From transcendent cups drop rosy clouds of evening.
> I just need to ask the Queen Mother
> About her peaches: How many times have they flowered?
>
> (CTS, 578)

The Purple Phoenix Realized Person's Archives, named for an ancient Taoist holy person, formed part of the White Deer Belvedere. The dragon, vehicle of the gods and symbol of the emperor, emerges from the winter hotsprings palace at Black Horse Mountain. Transcendents descend from the Milky Way, and imperial standards line the mountain roads. The company enjoys two ingredients of the elixir of immortality: cold dew and auroral clouds. Chung tsung's charisma attracts the Queen Mother, and she brings a feast for all. Shen enquires politely, as one transcendent to another, about the number of thousand-year peach cycles the goddess has witnessed. In other words, he asks her age and that of the universe, since she and her peaches appeared just before creation. In a society that revered age and looked back to antiquity, her great longevity was a source of pride. The poet suggests that for a moment on this special day, the holy presence of the timeless touched a T'ang emperor and his retinue.

Two centuries later, Li Shun-hsien (fl. 910) wrote "Following the Riders, I Ramble to Blue-walled City," an example of the royal procession topos. Li Shun-hsien visited Tu Kuang-t'ing at the Blue Walled-city Mountain in the company of Wang Chien (847–918), king of the state of Former Shu. Li served as consort to Wang Chien, a monarch who venerated Tu. Li compares climbing Blue Walled-city Mountain to joining the westward excursion of King Mu to the Turquoise Pond:

> Following behind eight horses, I ascend the transcendent
>   mountain;
> Abruptly separated from dust and dirt, semblances of
>   phenomena locked up inside.
> I only fear that once we've gone west, seeking out the Queen
>   Mother's feast,
> Finally we'll grieve that returning among humans is too hard.
>
> (*CTS*, 4629)

Li Shun-hsien imagines a sudden separation from this world of dust and dirt when they climb Tu's mountain, which she characterizes as a grotto-heaven or Taoist microcosm, a complete and perfect world containing images of all created things. She fears that once they have experienced the bliss of paradise, they will change and find it difficult to go back. The last line admits a poignant ambiguity: the poet grieves either over the obstacles preventing her from returning home or over the pain of separating from paradise.

The Turquoise Pond. The Turquoise Pond, meeting place of King Mu and the Queen Mother of the West, appears repeatedly in T'ang poetry as the destination of royal processions and site of divine feasts. A figure of speech evoking the primal meeting of goddess and king, the pond itself became a subject of poems. It provides an image of paradise: perfect, eternal, complete. Poems about the original Turquoise Pond might tell the tale of King Mu, as does one by Li Ho. Li describes the king's elaborate procession to the heavens, adding such details from T'ang dynasty Taoism as elixir drugs and adept's vows—anachronisms in the original story of the Chou dynasty king, but true reflections of the Shang ch'ing milieu in which the story had been transmitted. Here is "Turquoise Pond Music":

> Mu, the Son of Heaven, sets going his dragon-decoys;
> Clink, clink! Eight sets of horse trappings make a circuit
>   following heaven.
> Five essences sweep the earth; congealed clouds open.
> Right and left of Highgate Peak, the sun and moon circle.
> Engraved and inlaid in all four directions, with beams and tiers
>   opulently decorated;
> Dancing auroral clouds coil round and round.
> River-limpid and sea-pure: the Divine Mother's features.
> Decorated with red, dotted with iridescent kingfisher, she
>   illuminates Yü's spring.

Pulling along clouds and dragging jade, she descends Mount
    K'un-lun,
Arrayed pennants like pine, stretched-out canopies like wheels.
The metal wind establishes autumn;
The Clear and Bright Festival produces spring.
Eight sets of harness bells and ten vehicles extend like a cloud
    mass.
Rose-gem bells, turquoise mats with sweet-dew pattern.
Mysterious frost and scarlet snow: how can one adequately
    speak of them?
Smoked plums and dye-willows, I'm about to give them to you.
Water of lead florescence, to wash your bones;
Together, facing each other, let us make the stuff of realization!

(CTS, 2339–40)

Mu sets forth on his questing and reign-asserting journey, using
steeds so noble that they attract dragons. Lords of the five directions appear as the king storms heaven, reaching Highgate Peak on
Mound K'un-lun. There in the west, as the sun sets, he spies the
Queen Mother, serenely beautiful and clothed in wondrous garb.
She descends in splendor to lay out a celestial feast. The rite culmi-
nates in her gift of elixir drugs and her vow to reach perfection
together with the king: to become his divine mate.

Poems about the Turquoise Pond assume familiarity with the
underlying story of King Mu. Usually such poems express the
king's longing for the goddess, but "The Turquoise Pond" by Li
Shang-yin ends with her plaintive question: "Why does King Mu
not return again?" (CTS, 3252). Poems on the goddess's pond may
evoke, from the point of view of separated human lovers, memories
of happier times spent together, memories that become heavenly in
retrospect. Time at the Turquoise Pond is divine time, distinct from
human time: a year there may equal centuries on earth. As Hu Tseng
writes in "The Turquoise Pond":

How moving! When the eight chargers, proceeding like
    lightning,
Returned home and arrived among humans, his state had
    already perished.

(CTS, 3873)

T'ang poets employ the image of the Turquoise Pond in several
ways. In the works of even a single poet, the image may take on

different meanings in different contexts. Tu Fu, for example, sometimes uses the phrase "Turquoise Pond meeting" as a trope for an elegant gathering. In "Together with Various Worthies, I Climb the Temple of Mercy and Comparison," Tu compares a drinking session of successful examination candidates to an immortal assembly beside the celestial pond. In secular terms, the graduates had reached heaven by passing the imperial exam, which opened the doors to a career in government. Tu captures the sadness at the end of the big day, in a moment when time seems to stand still:

> Alas! for the Turquoise Pond drinking session—
> The sun rests over K'un-lun Mountain.
>
> (CTS, 1223)

Elsewhere Tu glorifies a numinous pool known as the Dragon Pool, a royal bathing spot near the Floriate Clear Palace, by comparing it to the Turquoise Pond. The palace was a favorite winter destination of the T'ang emperor Hsüan tsung and Precious Consort Yang. By comparing the imperial and the heavenly pool, the poet compares a meeting of the emperor and his consort to that of the goddess and the king:

> Suspended upside-down: an image of the Turquoise Pond;
> On a twisted course, it flows into the Glaucous River's stream.
>
> (CTS, 1226)

A more pessimistic piece about the same imperial resort, fallen into disrepair after the rebellion of 756, again compares the earthly bathing pond to the Queen Mother's celestial one. This time Tu notes breaths emanating from the landscape as evidence of spiritual presence: "At the Turquoise Pond, the vapors are dense and impenetrable" (CTS, 1226). Perhaps the ghosts of Hsüan tsung and Lady Yang Kuei-fei still linger there.

In poems celebrating dynastic conquests, Tu Fu employs the Turquoise Pond as a metaphor for extreme distance from the center of the empire: a place as far away as one could go, even in imagination. Of the Nine Times Perfected Palace, a Sui dynasty royal compound destroyed and rebuilt by the T'ang, Tu writes:

> Although the imperial circuit did not reach the Turquoise Water,
> Still divine traces are right here, behind these carved walls.
>
> (CTS, 1223)

That is: although the rulers may not have gone to the Western Paradise, even their residence shows a holy aura.

Tu Fu's use of the Queen Mother's pond in poems about emperor and imperium shows the intimate relation between government, religion, and poetry in medieval China. Tu also demonstrates how flexible and rich with associations the image of the Turquoise Pond had become in his day.

Other T'ang poets mention the pond in works celebrating processions that never left the imperial gardens. Such poems present the palace grounds as a microcosm of the macrocosm, including all of time and space within their boundaries. Sung Chih-wen (d. 712), depicting a spring feast in the Lotus Flower Enclosed Garden in the capital city of Ch'ang an, compares the royal grounds to the Queen Mother's parks on Mount K'un-lun, and the occasion to a transcendent meeting.

> Lotus blossoms in the pond on Ch'in grounds;
> Golden tangerines in the Han house's gardens.
> The valley revolves: a slanting basin's diameter;
> The river returns, twisting to encircle the plain.
> Wind comes; flowers naturally dance.
> Spring enters; birds can talk.
> We've attended a feast: a Turquoise Pond evening.
> On our return journey, single-reed woodwinds blow over and
>   over again.
>   (CTS, 380)

Hsü Hsüan (916–91), known for his poems on pacing the void, likens a winter scene in the imperial grounds to the Queen Mother's paradise. The occasion is an all-night New Year's party in Ch'ang an; the emperor has just published the calendar for the coming year. The Queen Mother's association with the calendar reflects her roles as maintainer of the cosmos and bestower of political legitimacy. Falling snowflakes remind the poet of the willow catkins that will come next spring. Palace trees, encrusted with snow, hung with icicles, call to mind the cold, perfect mineral kingdom of the Queen Mother, where plants are made of precious stones and everything lasts forever. Guests at the Flower and Perianth Storied Building in the palace compound drink and recite from the classics as they view the frozen ponds and icy vistas of the garden. Here is Hsü's "Poem on Approaching Snow":

> About to start using the newly rectified calendar, we recognize
>   another good year of harvest is coming;
> Consequently, the whirling, light catkins match spring's return.
> Inspected at close range, rose-gem trees encage silver
>   watchtowers;
> Imagined far away, the Turquoise Pond girds the Jade Barrier
>   Pass.
> A healthy sheen follows, on wheat and barley crops spreading
>   out across the green wilderness.
> Geniality follows cups of wine, ascending vermilion faces.
> Morning comes to the feast inside the Flower and Perianth
>   Storied Building,
> Where they have been counting tunes and competing over songs
>   among the Elegies and the Odes.
>   (CTS, 4455)

Winter paradise imagery appears again in a poem attributed to
three different authors, entitled "Ascending the Pavilion of Clear
Brilliance, We Encounter Snow." This quatrain commemorates a
New Year's Eve when emperor Chung tsung ("the rein-holder")
climbed the pavilion for a night of drinking and stargazing. Snow
suddenly fell, transforming the night landscape:

> A myriad cups of incomparable wine—the rein-holder's mats
>   unrolled;
> Six-fold emerging auspicious blossoms in confusion surround
>   the branches.
> Right here divine transcendents face the rose-gem orchard;
> Why must we head our wheel-tracks to the Turquoise Pond?[9]

Liu Fan (Advanced Scholar, 747) compares the imperial palace
gardens in Ch'ang an during the eleventh month to the Western
Paradise at Mount K'un-lun:

> I remember Ch'ang an at the time of the embryonic moon;
> A thousand officials offering congratulations came right up to
>   the cinnabar walls.
> In the imperial hunting preserve, snow opened on rose-gem trees;
> At the Dragon Audience Hall, ice formed a Turquoise Pond.
> The animal-bone charcoal-burning felt stoves were exactly right,
> And our sable cloaks and fox-white capes went together well.
>   (CTS, 1845)

The warmly dressed officials who come to the emperor's audience to congratulate him on the occasion of the winter solstice carry small metal braziers wrapped in felt, a custom derived from northern nomads. The hunting park matches the goddess's gardens; the ornamental pools her sacred pond. The cold stillness of winter in the palace compound seems to freeze time, calling to mind the goddess's home. These winter garden poems depict a clear, pure, eternal world, using the same language found in canonical descriptions of Shang ch'ing Taoist paradises. The microcosmic palace grounds, planned to embody the universe in miniature, appear to become the reality of what they represent.

Since the Turquoise Pond suggested both paradise and eternity, going there became a euphemism for dying. Ch'u Kuang-hsi (fl. 742) performs a sacrifice at the altar of Liu Pei (162–223), a famous hero who was ruler of Shu during the Three Kingdoms period. Liu, a descendent of the Han dynasty imperial family, was known to Taoists as the Sire of Mysterious Virtue. In "Sacrifice at the Ancestral Temple of the Sire of Mysterious Virtue," Ch'u compares the commemorative altar at the spot where Liu Pei died to the Queen Mother's holy meeting place. The death shrine, located at White Thearch's Walled City on a spectacular site above the gorges of the Yangtze River, becomes equivalent in mythic geography to the location of the goddess's feast. The poet praises the dead, notes how his spirit continues to bless the living, and asks for his help, praying:

> The divine Way is basically endless;
> Completions and transformations are also spontaneous.
> You, Lord, dwell above the rarefied heavens,
> Yet your virtue still resides at the Jade Floriate Spring.
> Wandering in verity, you walked in the steps of kingly
>   preparations,
> Drawing out your days, slow to become a cloud-mounted
>   transcendent.
> Now I represent my slender designs to accomplish the Way,
> Intending with this bright sacrifice to pray for a good harvest
>   year.
> While numinous mountains look down on a new city,
> Variegated mists arise above the pines.

How do we know that Mu, the Son of Heaven,
Went so far away, to the side of the Turquoise Pond?
(CTS, 769)

Poems about the Queen Mother and King Mu have contributed to the Chinese language. Even today, in funeral processions in San Francisco's Chinatown, mourners carry banners that read "See you again beside the Turquoise Pond." "Turquoise Pond meeting," an expression T'ang poets frequently employ, refers to the story of the goddess and the king. The often-used term "white clouds appointment," sometimes abbreviated simply to "white clouds," refers to the same meeting. Specifically, it calls to mind the exchange of melancholy songs. T'ang poets use both phrases to suggest assignations in paradise between mortals and goddesses. These are images of both hierogamy and death. Such figures of speech as "Turquoise Pond meeting" and "white clouds appointment" allow writers to allude to the tale of King Mu and the Queen Mother of the West in a highly concentrated way. This device of concentrated allusion by key phrase helps give T'ang dynasty poetry its multivalence, suppleness, and density.[10]

T'ang poets subtly reinterpret the story of the Queen Mother and King Mu found in such canonical sources as Tu Kuang-t'ing's account. They also knew older versions of this tale. Compared to the hagiographer, medieval poets take a more pessimistic view of the meeting. They emphasize the king's personal faults and his tragic failure to achieve transcendence, aspects Tu neglects. King Mu becomes for these writers a heroic symbol of struggle against the limitations of the human condition. He represents our longing for divine love, immortality, and perfection. The hagiographer, on the other hand, concerns himself with narrating accurately the acts of a great goddess as she intervenes in human history, to reveal her power and glory and to show why people worship her. His ultimate message is hopeful, since as a Taoist master he believed that transcendence is possible. But Tu and the poets agree in presenting the Queen Mother as a potent deity through whom humans can gain access to transcendence and to the world of the gods.

4

❖ *Eating the Peaches of Immortality:*
Emperors and Immortals

Only one story matches that of King Mu of the Chou for passion
and tragedy: that of Han Wu-ti, the Martial Thearch of the Han. To
medieval Chinese people, the Chou dynasty was ancient history,
and the Han was more recent and familiar. Of all earlier eras, people
of the T'ang most identified with the Han, another long native
dynasty during which China reached its previous height of wealth,
power, and territorial expansion. The Han saw the growth of the
Silk Route, bringing people, goods, and ideas from west to east and
initiating a period of foreign influence and openness unequaled until
the T'ang. During the Han, no reign outshone that of Han Wu-ti for
military conquest, new government institutions, and religious innovations. The *Records of the Historian* chronicles the rituals and sacrifices as well as the conquests and acts of government he undertook.
In 110 B.C., at the height of his reign, legend tells us that Emperor
Wu was visited by the Queen Mother of the West.

This chapter focuses on the visit of the goddess to Emperor Wu,
the longest single story in Tu Kuang-t'ing's hagiography and the
meeting most often mentioned by T'ang poets. The encounter repeats the themes of communication, legitimation, and search for
eternal life that characterize King Mu's meeting. Another Chinese
ruler seeks the goddess's secrets but fails to achieve immortality because of tragic flaws in his character. Emperor Wu's goal approaches
the ideal of Shang ch'ing Taoism even more closely than that of King
Mu: he tries to become an adept and practitioner of religious asceti-
cism rather than a wandering shaman. Following the *Esoteric Trans-*

missions Concerning the Martial Thearch of the Han, Tu inserts a great deal of specifically Shang ch'ing ritual and teachings into the Martial Thearch's story. The main issues of the story for Tu are political and personal: the proper relation between ruling power and religion, and the correct path for the individual adept to follow to immortality.

Tu Kuang-t'ing precedes his story of the Queen Mother's visit to Han Wu-ti with a lecture on stages of transcendence and an account of Chang Tzu-fang, an earlier immortal from the time of the first emperor of all China, Ch'in shih huang ti. Although Tu fails to mention Ch'in shih huang ti, T'ang poets have something to say about the Queen Mother and the First Illustrious Thearch of the Ch'in dynasty. Tu Kuang-t'ing follows his account of Han Wu-ti with that of the Shang ch'ing Taoist patriarch, Mao Ying or Lord Mao. Tu purposely surrounds his long narrative of Emperor Wu with shorter tales that serve as opening and closing statements. Following Tu Kuang-t'ing's order, we will introduce the tale of Han Wu-ti with brief records of Chang and the first emperor and close it with Lord Mao. The chapter takes on a certain symmetry: two royal failures balanced by two transcendent success stories.

Chang Tzu-fang

Before he tells us about the goddess and the emperor, Tu Kuang-t'ing celebrates an early hero of the cult of transcendence: Chang Tzu-fang, who departed in 187 B.C. Chang's story follows an explanation of classes of transcendents. Tu inserts this exposition between the stories of King Mu and Han Wu-ti, warning the reader that every adept must follow the prescribed stages to immortality. Even riches and royalty do not provide a shortcut.

As for the transcendents of the world who have ascended to heaven: in general they fall into nine classes. The first are the supreme transcendents, called Realized Kings of the Nine Heavens. The second or next transcendents are called Realized Illustrious Ones of the Three Heavens. The third are called Grand Supreme Realized People. The fourth are called Realized People Who Fly Through the Heavens. The fifth are called Numinous Transcendents. The sixth are called Realized People. The seventh are called Numinous People. The eighth are called Flying Transcendents. The ninth are called Transcendent People.

None of these ranks may be skipped or superseded. So it is that at the time when one ascends to heaven, first he must salute Wood Sire; afterwards he must pay a ceremonial visit to Metal Mother. Only at that moment when the business of receiving transmission and ordination is finished does one ascend to the Nine Heavens. One enters the Three Realms of Clarity, salutes the Grand Supreme, and is received in audience by the Celestial Worthy of the Primordial Commencement.

Thus it is that at the beginning of the Han dynasty there were four or five children playing in the road. One child sang: "Wearing a blue apron, I enter heaven's gate. I bow to Metal Mother and then salute Wood Sire." Among the people of the time, no one recognized him. Only Chang Tzu-fang recognized him. Chang saluted him, saying: "This is none other than the jade lad of the King and Sire of the East. A transcendent person who has attained the Way and ascends to heaven must bow to Metal Mother and then salute Wood Sire. Anyone who is not himself a master who skims the void and climbs to realization cannot recognize the ferrying-over [liberation] of a transcendent." (*CMYC*, 24160)

This little essay reveals the author's concern with hierarchy, lineage, and ceremony. Tu employs the voice of Chang Tzu-fang, a popular hero of the cult of immortality that had flourished since the Ch'in and Han dynasties—before the era of Shang ch'ing Taoism— to explain the doctrines of his school. This lends the teachings both primacy and legitimacy, as well as demonstrating the school's tendency to absorb and reshape when it could not eliminate deities and beliefs of popular origin.

The song of the child recognized by Chang as the goddess's consort in disguise belongs to a class of prophetic ditties, often put in the mouths of madmen or children, that Han officials collected and scrutinized for their significance to the ruler.[1] The use of such folk songs and sayings by the Taoist establishment as well as the imperium provides a good example of absorption of popular culture by the literate elite. The Queen Mother functions in this incident as one of a pair of authority figures whom the transcendent must greet ceremoniously on beginning his ascent to the Clear Realms. Once there, he is received by the highest gods of the three heavens, including the Queen Mother's teacher. Tu places the goddess over the popular immortal Chang Tzu-fang in the hierarchy of the Shang ch'ing pantheon. Not sharing Tu Kuang-t'ing's sectarian concerns,

T'ang poets showed no particular interest in a connection between Chang Tzu-fang and the Queen Mother. Poems on that immortal never mention her.

The First Illustrious Thearch of the Ch'in

Although no canonical sources mention a meeting of the Queen Mother and the first emperor of all of China, historians agree that Ch'in shih huang ti, the First Illustrious Thearch of the Ch'in Dynasty, avidly pursued the cult of immortality. They also agree that his efforts ended in failure, a failure attributed to his ambitious and cruel personality. Chinese historians give the first emperor a mixed review. On the one hand, he made great contributions such as unifying China and standardizing the language. On the other hand, extravagant public works projects such as the Great Wall and his own huge tomb near Sian stretched the nation's resources and manpower to their limits, creating many hardships.[2] His legacy is enormous: some claim the Great Wall is the only human construction visible from the moon, and even today viewers gasp in awe at the vast pits of life-sized pottery warriors guarding his tomb. Later ages have both hated and revered him. Writers used him as a negative example, but sympathized with his desires. Thus it is not surprising to find the early ninth century author Chuang Nan-chieh writing poetic words of warning about that emperor, in a work entitled "Wounded Song Lines":

> The rabbit walks, the crow flies; they don't see each other.
> Human affairs are vague and uncertain—rapid as lightning.
> While the Queen Mother's bewitching peach flowers open a
>   single time,
> In the jade storied buildings, pink variegated blossoms have
>   changed a thousand times.
> Chariots and racehorses once traversed the Hsien yang road;
> Former dwellings of the stone households—now empty
>   wilderness grasses.
> Without passions, autumn rain does not regret the flowers;
> One by one, lotus blossoms turn upside down, their fragrance
>   startled.

I urge you, Milord, do not mistakenly plant briars and thorns,
Or, like the Illustrious One of the Ch'in, vainly waste strength
sufficient to move a mountain.
His flourishing breath once departed, he never more will speak;
His white bones buried deep, the evening mountains turn cyan.

(*CTS*, 2836)

Chuang's song expresses grief over the passage of time; the sun
crow and moon rabbit chase each other endlessly, and human lives
are short. All the bustle on the road to the Ch'in capital of Hsien
yang near modern Sian led only to bones entombed in royal burial
grounds. Life passes as quickly as the sun sets, leaving the mountains dark blue against the sky. Nature is eternal and indifferent to
the suffering of mortals. The Queen Mother here represents the
temptation to pursue eternal life and divine passion, to transcend the
human condition. The narrator urges an unnamed emperor, perhaps
the Martial Thearch, not to follow the example of the Ch'in emperor and waste his brief life on a hopeless search for drugs and arts
of immortality. The cautionary tale of Ch'in shih huang ti has parallels in both character and action with that of Han Wu-ti.

The Martial Thearch of the Han

About a thousand years—which represents one cycle of the Queen
Mother's peach trees—after King Mu of the Chou dynasty enjoyed
his appointment at the Turquoise Pond, the goddess's next great
royal pupil and lover, the Martial Thearch of the Han, assumed the
throne. Commensurate with its importance, the story of the Martial
Thearch and the Queen Mother is the longest in Tu's hagiography.

Tu Kuang-t'ing's Account

The Filial and Martial Illustrious Thearch of the Han, Liu Ch'e, was fond of
the Way of extending life. During the original year of the Primordial
Enfoeffment reign period [110 B.C.], he climbed the heights of Marchmount
Sung and there built a terrace for seeking realized ones. He fasted, observed
abstinence, and made his thoughts seminal. In the fourth month, on the
E-dragon [*wu ch'en*] day, the Queen Mother sent the Jade Girl from the
Fortified City, Wang Tzu-teng, to come and talk with the thearch. She said:

"I have heard that you are willing to slight the emoluments of the four seas and keep at a distance the noble rank of a myriad vehicles in order to seek the veritable Way of extended life. How diligent! On the seventh day of the seventh month, I will certainly come for a little while." The thearch inquired of Tung-fang Shuo to find the proper response to this divinity. Then he purified himself and fasted for one hundred days, burning incense in the palace.

On the night in question, after the second watch [9–11 P.M.], a white cloud arose in the southwest. Dense and thick, it arrived and crossed over the courtyard of the palace. It gradually drew near; then came clouds and evening mists of nine colors. Pipes and drums shook empty space. There were semblances of dragons, phoenixes, men, and horses, with a guard mounted on *ch'i-lin* and harnessing deer. There were ranks of chariots and heavenly horses. With rainbow banners and feathered streamers, the radiance from a thousand vehicles and myriad outriders illuminated the palace watchtowers. Celestial transcendents, both followers and officials, arranged in ranks, numbered one hundred thousand multitudes. All were ten feet or more tall. Once they had arrived, the followers and officials disappeared.

The Queen Mother rode an imperial carriage of purple clouds, harnessed with nine-colored, dappled *ch'i-lin*. Tied around her waist, she wore the whip of the Celestial Realized Ones; as a pendant she had a diamond numinous seal. In her clothing of multi-colored damask with a yellow background, the patterns and variegated colors were bright and fresh. The radiance of metal made a shimmering gleam. At her waist was a double-bladed sword for dividing phosphors. Knotted flying clouds made a great cord. On top of her head was a great floriate topknot. She wore the crown of the Grand Realized Ones with hanging beaded strings of daybreak. She stepped forth on shoes with squared, phoenix-patterned soles of rose-gem. Her age might have been about twenty. Her celestial appearance eclipsed and put in the shade all others. She was a realized numinous being.

She ascended the dais and sat down facing east. The thearch saluted her, kneeled, and inquired how she fared. Then he stood in attendance. After a good long while, she called the thearch and allowed him to be seated. She laid out a celestial fast consisting of fragrant flowers, a hundred fruits, purple mushrooms, and magic mushrooms, as variegated as prismatic shellfish. Their seminal essences were rare and odd; they were not what regularly exists in this world. The thearch could not even name them.

She also ordered a serving girl to fetch peaches. A jade basin was filled with seven of the fruits. They were as large as bustard's eggs. She took four and gave them to the thearch. Mother herself ate three of them. When the thearch had eaten the peaches, he hastily put away the pits. Mother asked him why he was doing this. He said, "I just want to plant them." Mother said, "These peaches only bear fruit once in three thousand years. The land is poor in middle earth; even if you plant them, they will not grow. So what is the point?"

Thereupon the Queen Mother commanded the serving girl Wang Tzu-teng to play the eight-orbed chimes, Tung Shuang-ch'eng to blow the Cloud Harmony Mouth Organ, Shih Kung-tzu to strike the jade sounding stone from the courtyard of K'un-lun, Hsü Fei-ch'iung to sound the Thunder Numen Flute, Wan Ling-hua to hit the musical stone of Wu-ling, Fan Ch'eng-chün to strike the lithophone of the grotto yin, Tuan An-hsiang to make the "Harmony of the Nine Heavens," and An Fa-ying to sing the "Tune of the Mysterious Numen." The whole ensemble of sounds was exciting and distinct; their numinous timbres startled empty space.

When the song was finished, the thearch got down from his mat, kow-towed, and asked about the Way of extending life. The Queen Mother told him: "If you can consider glory cheap and delight in humble living quarters, if you can become addicted to the void and acquire a taste for the Way, then you will naturally revert to excellence. But if your passions are licentious and your body desirous, if your lewd behavior is unbalanced and your excesses extreme, if you kill and attack in battle without the right to do so, then you will waste and squander your vital energies. Excessive licentious-ness becomes a vehicle to rip open your body, and lust becomes an ax to smash your body. Killing produces an echo in response; profligacy wastes the heart. If you store up desire, then your spirits will fail. If you accumulate all these pollutions, then your lifespan will be cut short. With your own unworthy body, you provide lodging for thieves who will annihilate your frame. It is just as if you were to take a piece of wood a little over a foot long, and attack it with a hundred knives. If you want in this fashion to sever and cast off the three corpses and to make your body whole and permanently enduring, it cannot be done. It would be the same as a wingless quail wanting to drum with its wings on the Heavenly Pond, or a mushroom born in the morning wanting to enjoy whole springs and autumns.

"Cleanse yourself of this whole multitude of disorders; reject annihila-tion and change your intentions. Protect your spirits and vital energies in the scarlet archives; lock up the palace of debauchery and do not open it. Still your profligacy and extravagance in a quiet room. Cherish all living beings and do not endanger them. Observe compassion, devote yourself to charity, refine your vital energies, and hoard your seminal essence. If you behave in this fashion, you will be close to ideal. If you do not act like this, it would be like trying to cross the Long River [Milky Way] carrying rocks."

The thearch received the Queen Mother's admonitions on his knees, and said: "I, Ch'e, the untalented one, am plunged into a capricious mode of life. Having inherited the work of my predecessors, I am impeded by worldly ties. In my punishments and government, I rely on error and falsehood. My sins pile up, making hills and mountains. After today, please allow me to practice your words of instruction."

The Queen Mother said: "As for the Way of nourishing your nature and the essential requirements of regulating the internal order of your body, by now you already have a solid understanding of these. But you must practice diligently without being remiss. In a former time, on the Lofty Empyrean Terrace, my master, the Celestial Worthy of the Primordial Commencement, bestowed on me the core of his words: Whoever wants to extend his life must grasp it within his body before going outside his own body. Make firm and preserve the three ones. Protect the numinous root [the tongue]. Take the floriate vintage of the mysterious vale [saliva] and force it into the deep treasure passage. Irrigate and extend the pure seminal essence; have it enter the celestial gate [the mouth]. At the golden apartments, have it turn and then go inside the central barrier [the nose]. Then divide the bright light into blue and white, and have it reach the mud ball [in the center of the brain].

"Nourish the fluids and lock up the seminal essence, and you will make the body and spirits whole. Keep the spirits of the three palaces in good order and well defended; then you will preserve the scarlet palace. The unflowing source of the E-snake [*wu ssu*] organ from the yellow courtyard [spleen] will penetrate and pass through the five viscera and twelve threads. It will be exhaled from and inhaled into the six archives [lesser viscera]. Then the cloud-souls and earth-souls will be delighted. You can drop the hundred afflictions of the present place and block extremes of heat and cold. You will protect your seminal essence, retain your lifespan, and permanently extend and preserve your life.

"This is what is called the Veritable and Requisite Way of Exhaling and Inhaling the Grand Harmonies to Protect and Preserve the Spontaneous. Even when ordinary people do it, all of them automatically extend their lives. They also can control and make messengers of ghosts and divinities, and can wander and play on the Five Marchmounts. All they cannot do is fly through empty space or ascend into the void. If you can practice it, that will be adequate to allow you to escape this world. Of those who have studied transcendence, there has never been one who did not start with this.

[Here Tu interpolates a list of mineral and vegetable drugs of immortality in order of their efficacy and status, along with their effects.]

"Those who seek the Way must first follow these steps, then gradually they can reach distant victories. If you can exhale and inhale, and rein in the seminal essence, you will protect and make firm the spirits and breath. When the seminal essence is not cast off, then you will permanently endure. If the breath is extended and preserved, then you will not die. These methods do not require using the expense of drugs and minerals, nor will you have the hard work of scheming to lay hands on them. Just grasp it in your body. The common folk of a hundred surnames use this method daily without recognizing it. This therefore is the Way of the supreme class, the requisite essential of naturalness.

"Furthermore, as for a person's single body: heaven stores it with spirits, the earth stores it with a shape, and the Way stores it with breath. If the breath is preserved, then you live. If the breath departs, then you die. The myriad creatures as well as herbaceous and woody plants are also all like this. The body takes the Way as its basis. So how could you not nourish its spirits and make its breath firm in order to complete your frame? For a person's corporeal frame and spirits together to be whole: that is what the supreme paragons valued. If the frame is annihilated, the spirits are cut off. How could this not be painful? Once you have lost your present body, for a myriad kalpas it will not return. Don't you think you should treasure it? What I have been saying is in fact the words bestowed on me by my master, the Celestial King of the Primordial Commencement. Afterward I will command the jade girl, Li Ch'ing-sun, to write it out and grant it to you. You are to put it skillfully into practice."

The Queen Mother, having commanded that her vehicles be harnessed, was on the point of departing, when the thearch got down from his mat, kowtowed, and requested that she stay. The Queen Mother then commanded her serving girl to summon the Lady of the Supreme Primordial to descend and join them at the thearch's palace. After a good long while, the Lady of the Supreme Primordial arrived. Again they sat. She provided a celestial feast. After a long time, the Queen Mother ordered the Lady to bring out the Writ of the Eight Unions, the Veritable Shape of the Five Marchmounts, the Talismans of the Six Cyclicals of the Five Thearchs, and the Numinous Flying Beings: altogether twelve items. She said: "The texts may be transmitted from above the heavens only once in four myriad kalpas. Once they are among humans, every forty years they may be bestowed on a gentleman who possesses the Way."

The Queen Mother then commanded the serving girl Sung Ling-pin to open the cloud-patterned multi-colored damask bag and take out a fascicle to bestow on the thearch. The Queen Mother stood up holding the text. With her own hands, she granted it to the thearch. As she did so, the Queen Mother recited an incantation:

> Heaven is high and earth low;
> The Five Marchmounts fix their configuration.
> Spurting breaths of the Primordial Ford,
> Mysterious seminal essences of the Great Conduits,
> Nine paths encircling the heavens,
> Extended peace of the six harmonies,
> Eight unions of the Grand Supreme,
> Accomplishments of the flying celestials:
> All are credentials of realized transcendents.
> On the basis of these you communicate with numinous beings.
> Leak them and you will fall into annihilation and putrescence;
> Treasure them and you will return home to long-toothed old
>   age.
> You, Ch'e, be careful of them!
> I'm telling you, disciple Liu!

When the incantation was finished, the thearch saluted and bowed to receive the Queen Mother's words: "Now that you are beginning to study the Way and have received talismans, it would be appropriate for you to perform special sacrifices to various veritable numina of the rivers and marchmounts and to purify yourself and fast before hanging the talismans on your belt. After forty years, if you are going to transmit and hand down what you possess, then Tung Chung-shu [ca. 170–104 B.C.] and Li Shao-chün [2d c. B.C.] may be bestowed with it. You should be all the more diligent since you are the thearchic king. Sacrifice to the rivers and marchmounts in order to pacify the state and the households. Cast tallies to the veritable numina in order to pray for the black-haired masses."

Her words finished, together with the Lady of the Supreme Primordial, she commanded the chariots, giving the word to depart. Her followers and officials collected in the dark.

When they were about to ascend to heaven, she laughed, pointed to Tung-fang Shuo, and said: "This is the little boy from my neighbor's household. His nature is very mischievous. Three times he has come and stolen my peaches. Formerly he was a transcendent official of the Grand Supreme, but because he sank into drunkenness on jade wine, and caused a loss of harmony among the bureaucrats, he was banished to serve you. He is not of the common run of men."

After that, the Martial Thearch could not make use of the Queen Mother's admonitions. He abandoned himself to strong drink and good looks. He killed and attacked without respite. He invaded the Liao Peninsula to strike Korea, and he opened communications with the southwestern barbarians. He constructed terraces and kiosks, raising them up out of earth and wood. Inside the realm bounded by the four seas, the people were depressed and angry. From this time on, he lost the Way. He made an imperial visit to Hui chung in the northwest and then presided over the three shrines at the Eastern Sea. The Queen Mother did not come again. The texts he received, he arranged on the Cedar Beam Terrace, where they were burned by a celestial fire. Li Shao-chün discarded his form and departed. Tung-fang Shuo soared up in flight and did not return. The affair of the shamans and their dangerous potions arose. The thearch grew more and more regretful and resentful.

In the second year of the Primordial Commencement reign period [87 B.C.], he died at Five Oaks Palace and was buried at the Fertile Tumulus. Later, the Taoist texts that had been deposited in the Fertile Tumulus—fifty or more scrolls filling a golden box—came out one day at Mount Pao tu. There was also a jade casket and jade staff that emerged at Fu feng market-town. When people examined the Fertile Tumulus, they found it undisturbed as of old, and yet the casket and staff had come out among men. This might be evidence of the liberation of the corpse by entrusting it to shapes.   (*CMYC*, 24160–63)

Tu's account is based on the classic rendition of the tale in *Esoteric Transmissions Concerning the Martial Thearch of the Han*, a work well known to T'ang writers.[3] Tu includes interpolations from other popular Six Dynasties works such as *Han Wu ku shih* (Old tales concerning the Martial One of the Han) and the encyclopedic *Monograph on Broad Phenomena*.[4] Writing a religious account of the goddess's intervention in human history rather than the official record of a Chinese ruler, Tu himself relies little on the detailed accounts of the reign of Han Wu-ti in the dynastic histories. His sources did use the official histories as a chronological framework. Those histories contain some of the same information, verify elements of the tale, and supply a familiar form for its writing.

Liu Ch'e is the emperor's clan and given name. His sacrifices at holy mountains, including Mount Sung, are recorded in the "Monograph on the *Feng* and *Shan* Sacrifices" in the *Records of the Historian*. His zeal attracts the goddess, who sends the serving girl Wang Tzu-teng, a frequent intermediary between deities and humans in Shang ch'ing texts, to announce her pending arrival. Tu does not mention the blue bird, the Queen Mother's usual messenger. Forewarning is typical of the visits of great Taoist deities.

Wu asks his courtier Tung-fang Shuo, whose biography appears in Pan Ku's *Book of Han*, a man rumored to be a transcendent and credited with authorship of many books of marvels during the Six Dynasties period, about the proper etiquette for the situation.

The Queen Mother, described as an imposing presence, arrives at the Han palace with a large entourage at the bewitching hour of midnight. Seating arrangements and order show her precedence over the earthly ruler. An elixir feast commences. Communal eating is a central part of these meetings, as we also saw in the case of King Mu. The goddess is simply called Mother in this section, stressing the fictive kinship relationship of teacher and pupil. The term suggests intimacy as well as authority, as when modern Indian women saints are called Mother by their disciples. A musical performance, always an important part of Shang ch'ing rituals and transcendent meetings, follows the food. Then the emperor requests teaching, using the rites of disciple and master.

The Queen Mother of the West responds with an introductory lecture on the general principles of Taoist religion, another of Tu's carefully inserted lectures to the reader. The Queen Mother explains that her Way requires devotion and self-restraint, leading to purification, good works, and meditation. Han Wu-ti responds with gratitude and an expression of his own worthlessness. This confession of unworthiness together with a request to a deity for a saving gift is found in other religions: before receiving communion in the liturgy of the Mass, Catholics say: "Lord, I am not worthy to receive you, but only say the word and I shall be healed."

The emperor's confession of guilt is followed by more serious and detailed instruction from the goddess. After admonitions, she tells him she will give him the core of her master's teaching, that is: the essence of Shang ch'ing Taoism. Through dietary restraint, sexual abstinence, and refraining from violence, the adept prepares himself for meditation and visualization. His exercises promote the circulation of *ch'i* (breaths) through his body, in turn preserving his vital essences (including sperm) and protecting his indwelling body gods. These practices lead to health, longevity, and control of deities.

Tu provides a long list of vegetable and mineral elixirs together with their effects as revealed by the Queen Mother to Han Wu-ti and then has the goddess deliver another sermon. She tells the emperor that the same effects of immortality and miraculous powers can be achieved through meditation, allowing one to avoid the expense and danger of drugs. One who complies with the Way of nature will save his own body, spirits, and breath. Tu is an early advocate of internal alchemy, *nei tan*, a Taoist practice of meditation and visualization directed to compounding the elixir of immortality within our own bodies.

Just when the Queen Mother is about to leave, the Lady of the Supreme Primordial arrives with a set of revelations of her own. Here the transmission changes from oral to written form. The Lady hands over actual texts and talismans, all part of the Shang ch'ing canon. Taoists of the Shang ch'ing lineage saw the Queen Mother as too elevated to serve directly as spouse to a human, yet they had inherited many stories such as those of King Mu and emperor Wu where she was apparently just that. Perhaps Tu intends the Lady to be a divine bride for Han Wu-ti, to replace the Queen Mother who would then move off to a safe distance as matchmaker and ultimate source of teachings. The Queen Mother appears in many Shang ch'ing works such as the *Declarations of the Realized Ones* as the ultimate source of texts bestowed on adepts by their divine spouses. The primary example is Lord Mao and Lady Wei Hua-ts'un, whose story Tu relates a little later.

The goddesses give Han Wu-ti a final poem of investiture and warning before departing. The Queen Mother will allow him to transmit her teachings only to Li Shao-chün, a famous magician, and Tung Chung-shu, a renowned Confucian cosmologist, men who represent the two poles of Han thought. She tells Emperor Wu to put his beliefs into practice with wholesome rituals to benefit the state and himself. As she ascends, she notices Tung-fang Shuo and indulgently accuses him of stealing her peaches. She reveals that he is an immortal in disguise. As this episode shows, the mischievous peach thief Tung-fang Shuo provides one basis for the character of the monkey-king so beloved in Chinese legend and literature up to the present.

After this holy feast, which is also the emperor's last supper with the deity, he utterly fails to keep her commandments. He falls into drink and debauchery in his personal life, violence and excess in his public acts. He loses everything: the sacred texts literally go up in flames, his magician and resident immortal desert him, and scandals shake his government to the quick. Finally he dies in bitter disillusion.

The last paragraph notes miraculous occurrences after the emperor's death. Tu records local traditions of extrusions of holy texts and jade objects as evidence of the spiritual power of the Shang ch'ing scriptures and teachings they contain. The last line doubtfully recounts the possibility that Han Wu-ti only appeared to die but in fact achieved immortality through liberation by means of the corpse. Liberation by means of the corpse is a Shang ch'ing technique of transcendence in which the realized person seems to die and receive burial but actually rises to heaven in secret. Should his coffin later be opened, only some object like a book or shoe will remain; his body will be gone. In his preface to the collection of biographies of female transcendents, Tu Kuang-t'ing mentions liberation by means of the corpse as a way of reaching the Realms of Clarity, a means inferior only to ascending to heaven in broad daylight. Tu records this possibility for the Han emperor because it had currency in his day and because the rulers he served identified with the Han imperial family; the rest of the story makes it clear that he does not believe that Han Wu-ti achieved transcendence.

Tu Kuang-t'ing devotes the largest section of his hagiography to the Queen Mother's most spectacular failure. Sheer space as well as the detailed attention dedicated to this tale reveals its importance to Tu. Han Wu-ti is a great hero of Chinese history and the model of a successful monarch; yet he failed in Taoist terms because he did not achieve the proper balance between political and religious concerns. Tu's account draws on central works of the Shang ch'ing canon. He also incorporates sermons on the correct way to pursue immortality, iconographically exact descriptions of the goddess and her followers, and attractive depictions of the celestial pleasures and powers awaiting the worthy adept.

T'ang Poems

The story of the goddess and the emperor, with its human interest and tragedy, appealed deeply to people of medieval times. It appears over and over again in T'ang poetry. The plot of Han Wu-ti's meeting with the Queen Mother of the West narrated in Tu Kuang-t'ing's hagiography matches the tale told by poets. This plot has seven basic parts: the religious practice of the emperor, arrival of the goddess, communion feast, music, Taoist revelations, departure of the goddess, and death of the emperor. Poems about the story of the Martial Thearch are the most numerous category of T'ang poems portraying the goddess. These poems divide into two main types: narrative poems and treatments of isolated or associated themes. The latter include historical reflections, celebrations of holidays and feasts, descriptions of palaces, and praises of the Queen Mother's peaches.

Narrative poems: the whole story. Ts'ao T'ang presents a concentrated version of the entire narrative, extended over two poems. He calls the first "The Martial Thearch of the Han Waits for the Queen Mother of the West to Descend":

> K'un-lun—he fixes his imagination on the loftiest peak;
> The Queen Mother comes, riding a five-colored dragon.
> Songs are already heard while only her purple simurgh is
>   hauntingly faint in the distance;
> Chattering as it comes, her blue bird appears quite casual and
>   relaxed.
> Wind returns and water falls—the moon in the Three Clear
>   Realms;
> A clepsydra covered in bitter frost transmits the fifth watch bell.
> Trees' reflections become distant and tenuous, flowers quiet and
>   still;
> It seems he hears the syrinx pipes—that's evidence that she's on
>   her way!
>   (*CTS*, 3827)

The second he calls "The Martial Thearch of the Han Gives a Feast in His Palace for the Queen Mother of the West":

> Clouds from Sea Turtle Mountain descend to the Grand Unity
>   Altar;
> The Martial Illustrious One fasts and purifies himself, unable to
>   overcome his joy.
> Their appointment was personally set in "long life" cyan graphs;
> He lets her see in detail his Extended Longevity Cinnabar
>   Springs.
> The double-edged sword hanging at her waist sounds; palace
>   trees become still.

> The Starry River has no reflection; flowers of the forbidden
>   interior grow bitter cold.
> Autumn wind curls around like smoke; the moon is clear and
>   distinct;
> With the jade girls' pure song, the whole night comes to an end.
>
>   (*CTS*, 3827)

The first poem shows the emperor visualizing the goddess's mountain paradise at the bewitching hour of midnight, as she sets out on a simurgh, the favored avian vehicle of Taoist deities. Ts'ao emphasizes music in the epiphany, beginning with the Queen Mother's nearly imperceptible entrance hymn. When her messenger arrives, a lull of hushed anticipation follows; then syrinx notes attest her approach. The second poem describes the actual feast. The emperor waits for the goddess at his altar; she comes from her throne on Sea Turtle Mountain. He gives her a guided tour of the palace; she shows him her demon-slaying sword. In her presence, all becomes still and cold. Even the Milky Way ("Starry River") loses its reflection. Ts'ao draws a veil over the exchanges between the emperor and goddess, and the pair of poems concludes with the musical finale of the ceremony. Ts'ao T'ang echoes Tu Kuang-t'ing in his attention to iconographic detail and emphasis on music.

Wei Ying-wu (737–ca. 792) presents a colorful synopsis of the tale in two long poems. These contain details of the meeting as reported in the *Esoteric Transmissions Concerning the Martial Thearch of the Han* and Tu Kuang-t'ing's hagiography of the goddess. Wei further enriches his narrative with references to religious innovations instituted by that emperor as recorded in sacrificial treatises of the official histories of the Han dynasty. The goddess examines the monarch, gives him her peaches, and imparts religious instruction with a Shang ch'ing flavor. She teaches that immortality depends on the Way rather than elixir drugs. In the end, believing he will succeed as a transcendent, she disappears. Heaven remains mute in answer to human questions. Here is the first of Wei's "Assorted Songs on the Martial Thearch of the Han":

> The Martial One of the Han longed for divine transcendents;
> He made a platform of yellow gold, to draw closer to heaven.

Once the Queen Mother, having plucked her peaches, was
   returning from beside the sea;
Moved by him as she passed westward, she proposed to
   question and examine him.
About to come but not yet come, the night still not over,
Before his basilica the blue bird preceding her wheeled and
   soared.
Her green-glinting side-locks intertwined with clouds, her
   sleeves dragging mists,
Paired tallies twirling and whirling, she descends with
   transcendent paces.
As clearly distinguishable as in broad daylight, she arrives in this
   world;
Where in the cyan void is the route by which she comes to this
   appointment?
In a jade basin she offers up peaches, intending to submit them
   to the ruler;
Uncertain and hesitant, not yet departed, she retains her
   variegated cloud vehicle. [She speaks:]
"The sea's waters and mulberry fields, how many times have
   they alternated?
In the midst of their cycles, these peaches have ripened four or
   five times.
How moving! King Mu attended the Turquoise Pond feast;
It happened that the flowers opened just then, but he did not
   obtain the gift.
For flowers to open, and fruit to ripen, how can one set a
   time?
What a surprise if precisely at the time of the Martial One of the
   Han,
Their cheeks resemble fragrant flowers, washed pure like jade!"
But in her heart she thinks, "My Illustrious One has too many
   addictions and desires.
Although I leave the peach pits behind, and the peaches contain
   numina,
This shit and dirt among humans—planted in it they cannot
   grow.
Originally it depends on the Way, how could it depend on
   drugs?
Toiling in vain, recipe masters proceed along the sea."

Putting down her fan and giving a single word, she takes leave
of him;
Like mist and yet not mist, she disappears.
(*CTS*, 1093)

The second of Wei's songs adds more details:

Solitary tips of golden stalks—ah!—they skim the purple mist.
Beauties from the Han palace look far off into obscurity.
Above the Platform Communicating with Heaven, the moon
has just emerged;
In the basin for receiving dew, beads are just now rounded.
If one can drink the beads, his longevity may be prolonged.
The Martial Illustrious One faces south, as dawn light is about
to become distinct.
Descended from the void, jade cups are cool;
Green kingfisher feathers from this world are made into a tally-
bag.
As for the "First Day of the Eighth Month" Transcendent
Person's prescription:
This transcendent prescription is considered a supreme drug.
If one takes it when quiet, he will become as continuous as
unraveling thread.
But at the Cedar Beam Terrace, his deep drinking gradually
harmed his spirits.
Similarly I hear that one who preserves youthful features at
seventy springs,
Is someone who recognizes that all sweet, strong wine is
putrefied and stinking stuff.
It is only bland and calm water that can benefit humans.
His "myriad years metal basin": where is it now?
As for metal cast at that time, I fear it is not solid.
As creeping herbaceous plants arise, and spring is replaced by
autumn,
What do the cyan heavens have to say? The dew falls from the
void.
(*CTS*, 1093)

Wei's "golden stalks" were bronze pillars topped by statues of
transcendents holding basins for receiving the dew. According
to the "Monograph on the *Feng* and *Shan* Sacrifices," Han Wu-ti

erected these pillars at the Cedar Beam Platform in his palace compound at Ch'ang an. The platform is the same as the Cedar Beam Terrace where Wei says Han Wu-ti harmed his spirits and Tu Kuang-t'ing reports he stored the texts received from the Queen Mother that ultimately burned. Ssu-ma Ch'ien also records a Platform Communicating with Heaven, called "a platform of yellow gold" in the first poem, that Han Wu-ti constructed at his Sweet Springs Palace after an advisor informed him that spirits love high buildings and might come if he built one. The "myriad years basin" was cast after the alchemist Li Shao-chün told the emperor to use eating and drinking utensils of alchemically obtained gold in order to communicate with transcendents and obtain immortality. The message seems to be that despite his great efforts and vast resources, the emperor died. His ignorance and attachment proved fatal. Nature remains constant and indifferent: plants grow, the seasons revolve, and the same dew falls silently from heaven.

Li Ch'i (fl. 725) tells the whole story in the long "Song of the Queen Mother":

> The Martial Illustrious One fasted and observed abstinence in his Receiving Florescence Basilica.
> He stood upright with folded hands; in an instant the Queen Mother came to grant him an audience.
> Rainbow standards luminously flashing: *ch'i-lin*-drawn chariots,
> Feathered parasols streaming and pheasant fans.
> Fingers of her hands holding intertwined pears, she sent them along for the thearch to eat.
> By means of them, one can prolong life and preside over the cosmos.
> On top of her head she wore the nine-starred crown.
> She led a flock of jade lads, then sat facing south.
> "Do you want to hear the essential words? Now I'll report them to you."
> The thearch thereupon burned incense and requested such discussion.
> "If you can rarefy your earth-soul and dispatch the three corpses,
> Afterwards you will certainly have an audience with me at the Celestial Illustrious One's palace."

Turning her head back, she told the serving girl, Tung Shuang-
ch'eng,
"The wine is finished; you may perform on the Cloud Harmony
Mouth Organ."
Red auroral clouds and white sun, in strict attendance, did not
move.
Seven dragons and five phoenixes in variegated disarray greeted
them.
How regrettable! He was too ambitious and arrogant; the
divinities were not satisfied.
They sighed and lamented over his horses' hooves and chariots'
wheel tracks.
In his covered walkways, song bells became hard to discern in
approaching evening;
In the deep palace, peach and plum flowers turned snowy.
But now I just look at my blue jade five-branched lamp;
Its coiled dragon spits fire; the light is about to be severed.

(CTS, 750)

Li Ch'i's poem parallels Tu Kuang-t'ing's account quite closely.
One original feature: the Queen Mother gives him pears of immortality, twisted auspiciously, rather than peaches. She wears
the nine-starred crown of a priestess as she explains the basic teachings of Taoism. After the feast and instruction, the minor goddess
Tung Shuang-ch'eng, one of the celestial musicians mentioned in
Tu Kuang-t'ing's account, performs heavenly music on her divine
pipes. Inevitably, war and adventure ("horses' hooves and chariots'
wheel tracks") seduce the emperor into abandoning the goddess's
teachings. Dying, he leaves the ladies of the inner palace, his "peach
and plum blossoms," to grow old alone. In the final couplet, after a
night of reflection on legend and mortality, the narrator stares at the
oil-burning lamp as it sputters out.

Shang ch'ing Taoist teachings popular among the T'ang dynasty
literati are projected back into the story of Han Wu-ti and the
goddess by these poets. For example, Ts'ao T'ang stresses visualization and music, Wei Ying-wu condemns normal food and praises
elixir alchemy, and Li Ch'i speaks of dispatching the three corpses:
all practices that entered Taoism after the Han dynasty. Another
anachronism occurs in a poem by Li Shang-yin entitled "The Han
Palace." The *chiao* or cosmodrama, a rite of cosmic renewal per-

formed at regular intervals on behalf of the community by the Taoist clergy, a piece of liturgy not instituted until the Six Dynasties period, takes place in the Han palace.[5] Li Shang-yin emphasizes by this means the ritual nature of the meeting. The poem ends on a melancholy note: communication with deities and transcendents is severed and the emperor is teased by a fleeting vision of his dead mistress, Li Fu-jen.

> On the night for communication with numina, the cosmodrama
>   lasts until pure daybreak.
> Basins for receiving the dew dry in the sun; it's spring at the
>   head tent.
> The Queen Mother doesn't come, and Fang Shuo has departed,
> But in a flash he again sees Lady Li.
>   (CTS, 3249)

Decisive moments. Poets treated key incidents of the story of Han Wu-ti, such as the musical performance, in varied and often idiosyncratic ways. In much the same way as the early twentieth-century photographer Cartier Bresson sought to capture on film the "decisive moment" when all the elements come together to make the perfect picture, the T'ang poets with great skill and patience sketch the telling details that make us see to the heart of the story.

Lu Kuei-meng writes about stone chimes called "square resonators" that announce the Queen Mother's arrival to the Han palace, incidentally underlining the importance of music in Taoist ritual. Sounding stones hung in graduated series on wooden frames; they were struck with a wooden mallet to provide music for court and religious ceremonials. Their use goes back to antiquity; Chou dynasty sets have been excavated in recent years. In answer to the frost-covered sounding stones, the goddess's jade ornaments make their own music:

> Someone strikes the frost-covered, bitter cold jades—a confused
>   "clink, clink!"
> Flowers lower, as autumn winds brush the seated masters.
> The Queen Mother is coming in leisurely fashion to see the Han
>   Son of Heaven.
> Filling everything!—in the Orchid Basilica, the sound of her belt
>   pendants and jade rings.
>   (CTS, 3770)

The poet might choose a minor incident and elaborate on it: Han Yü writes a humorous and irreverent account of incidents involving the Queen Mother and the mischievous trickster Tung-fang Shuo, who makes brief appearances near the beginning and end of Tu Kuang-t'ing's account. The biography describing his unconventional court career in Pan Ku's *Book of Han* contains the shocking incident depicted here of his urinating on the pillars of the emperor's office (*HS*, 65).[6] In "Various Things—On Reading Tung-fang Shuo," Han Yü (768–824) depicts Tung-fang as a spoiled brat who irresponsibly lets loose thunder chariots and behaves rudely to lesser deities but in the end evades punishment. The goddess, portrayed as his indulgent godmother, dares not discipline her charge.

> Straight and lofty peaks—the Queen Mother's palace.
> Below are only the myriad transcendents' households.
> When she sucks in air to yawn, it makes the whirling wind.
> When she rinses her hands, a great rain streams down.
> When Fang Shuo was a lad in her service,
> She spoiled him despite his arrogant behavior and did not
>   restrict or criticize him.
> Stealthily he entered the thunder and lightning office;
> Rumble, Rumble! He lost control of the ungovernable chariots.
> The Queen Mother, hearing of this, smiled about it;
> Her guards and officials went right along with her: "Yuk, yuk."
> Unconcerned about the myriad myriad human beings,
> Whose living bodies were buried in mud and sand,
> He dallied and trifled as the Five Mountains tumbled,
> Floated and drifted as the eight weft threads slipped loose.
> She said, "My son, you are at fault;
> What can I do when you joke like this?"
> When Fang Shuo heard this, he grew displeased;
> He turned and used a net to catch a twisting serpent.
> Looking across at the handle of the Northern Dipper,
> He spontaneously rubbed it together in his two hands.
> Then the flock of transcendents rushed to say to the Queen
>   Mother:
> "How can his hundred transgressions be allowed without
>   prejudice?
> We have just seen things we cannot countenance.
> This affair has come to the point where he cannot be forgiven."

She did not want to spread and publish word of his crimes,
But outside folks really got in an uproar.
The Queen Mother could not do anything.
Features frowning, her mouth released a sigh.
Nodding to show she agreed,
She sent the plaintiffs horse-ornaments of purple jade.
But Fang Shuo was not corrected by punishment;
Supported by imperial compassion, he became even more brash
    and arrogant.
He insulted and cheated the Liu Son of Heaven;
In broad daylight, he urinated at the basilica offices.
Then one morning, without even parting words of instruction,
Carrying away his body, he skimmed auroral pink clouds in a
    watchet sky.   (*CTS*, 2022)

In a somewhat skeptical and satirical tone, Han Yü writes an allusive poem concerning a complaint brought by sensitive and self-important middle-level deities to the Queen Mother about her spoiled favorite, Tung-fang Shuo. When he usurps the privileges of the weather gods and causes the death of thousands of innocent people just to enjoy a prank, the Queen Mother first laughs, then pleads with him to stop causing trouble, and finally is reduced to attempting to placate the other gods with fine words and expensive gifts of jade. Tung-fang Shuo, entirely unrepentant, plays with dragons and constellations, and insults the Martial Thearch. But nothing can interfere with his divine destiny: as befits a transcendent of the highest order, he ascends to heaven in broad daylight in corporeal form. Han Yü implies that even though Taoist immortals exist, they have no respect for human feelings or imperial authority. Like Tung-fang Shuo, they transmit no teachings that would allow future adepts to follow them.

Some poets focus on another significant moment in the story: the dance of the departing goddesses. Dance and music were a central part of Taoist ritual. Wang Chien describes the Queen Mother taking her leave in a poem called "Rainbow Chemise Lyrics." The dance of the "Rainbow Chemise and Feathered Robe" is first mentioned in Po Chü-i's long poem of 806 entitled "Song of Everlasting Regret," which narrates the ill-fated love story of the T'ang emperor posthumously known as Hsüan tsung and his beloved consort, Yang Kuei-fei. The dance was performed in the T'ang palace in the 730's by Yang Kuei-fei and other actors of the Peach and Pear Garden Troupe. Stories tell us that Hsüan tsung, who was also known as Ming huang—the Brilliant Illustrious One, for the radiant culture of his court—brought the music back from the moon after a visit in a dream; more likely it was a Sogdian tune adapted for Taoist rites. The feathered robe represents the wings of the goddess, the rainbow chemise her dress of shimmering, many-colored clouds. We can speculate that the "Rainbow Chemise and Feathered Robe" was a music and dance performance staged at the Taoist court of Hsüan tsung that used tunes from the Silk Route to celebrate the departure of the Queen Mother and her entourage from the Han palace as described in the *Esoteric Transmissions Concerning the Martial Thearch of the Han*. Here is Wang Chien's rendition:

> Silk-thread stringed instruments thrum and thrum, separated
>   from us by variegated clouds.
> It first issued forth at the fifth watch; the whole palace listened.
> The Martial Illustrious One himself sends off the Queen Mother
>   of the West,
> Newly changed into a rainbow chemise and moon-colored
>   jacket.
>   (*CTS*, 200)

Po Chü-i's own famous poem on the same subject, called the "(Dance of the) Rainbow Chemise and Feathered Jacket," describes a performance of the dance popular at the T'ang court in the mid-eighth century.[7] Po spent many of his years as governor of Hang chou trying to reconstruct the work and then to collect and train a troupe to perform it. Dancers enacted the departure of the goddess and her attendants from the Han palace:

> The Lady of the Supreme Primordial, dotting her hair coils,
>   summons Perianth Green;
> The Queen Mother, shaking her sleeve, sends off Flying Rose-
>   gem.
>   (*CTS*, 2644–45)

Perianth Green and Flying Rose-gem are minor attendant goddesses. Poems eulogizing this incident emphasize the importance of dance in medieval Taoist ritual.

A number of poets turned their attention to the actual night of the holy feast of the emperor with the Queen Mother: Double Seven, the seventh day of the seventh month, an important Taoist holiday and the perfect night for divine meetings and ascents. The night was especially sacred to the Queen Mother of the West as the anniversary of her feast in the Han palace. Double Seven was also the time of the meeting of the Herd Boy and the Weaver Girl stars, heavenly lovers who crossed the Milky Way once a year to spend a night together. This ancient and important folk festival is sacred to Taoists, who have connected it with the Queen Mother since the Six Dynasties. Ts'ui Kuo-fu, a scholar official active during the reign of Hsüan tsung (712–56), enumerates associations and customs that characterize the holiday. In the "Seventh Night," he addresses his musings to a governor who is a member of the imperial family (the "Transcendent Lake Clan"):

> The Grand Conservator is of the Transcendent Lake Clan;
> On the seventh night, his suppressed passions are many.
> Wind from fans activates the jade clepsydra;
> Its channeled water depicts the Silver River.
> Beneath the pavilions, men spread out books and registers;
> Within the chambers women sun white damask and gauze net.
> Distant thoughts of the Martial Thearch of the Han;
> Her blue bird—when will it pass by?
> (CTS, 661)

Ts'ui wonders passively when a messenger will come by. In "Cyan Walled City," no. 3, Li Shang-yin, on the other hand, actively invites a goddess for the night of Double Seven:

> For the time when the seventh night comes, we have had an
>   appointment from early days.
> My grotto-like chamber's hanging curtains and screens, until
>   now have been hanging down.
> The back-glancing rabbit in the jade wheel begins to grow an
>   earth-soul;
> In the iron net, the coral does not yet have branches.
> I gather together divine prescriptions that teach how to stop at
>   the phosphors,
> Collect and take up phoenix-patterned paper, to write out
>   mutual thoughts.

> In the *Esoteric Transmissions Concerning the Martial Illustrious One*,
> these matters are distinct and clear.
> Don't say they have never been known among humans.
>
> (*CTS*, 3246)

The Taoist goddess will teach Li how to create and nurture his immortal embryo like the waxing moon or cultivated coral growing in the sea in iron baskets. He requests instructions on how to pace the void. The *Esoteric Transmissions Concerning the Martial Thearch of the Han*, which anyone can read, prove that goddesses may make assignations with humans and reveal secrets to them.

A poem by Hsü Yin (Advanced Scholar, 894–98) called "Night," of a type known as *yung wu* "eulogizing things," contains a series of riddle-like allusions to Double Seven, the most important night of the year in Taoist lore. One line presents this clue: "At the Han basilica, when the moon arises, the Queen Mother comes" (*CTS*, 4254). Hsü's assumption that readers would identify his reference shows that the trope of the goddess's arrival at the Han palace had joined a group of allusions clustered around that sacred night, becoming part of the T'ang dynasty poet's grab bag of clichés and formulas.

Historical reflections. Another type of poem, known as *yung shih*, "eulogizing history" or perhaps "historical reflections," often provided a setting for the story of the Queen Mother and Han Wu-ti. Some of these poems recollect the cherished past with sadness and regret. For example, in "Thoughts Arising in Autumn," Tu Fu relates a dream of the Queen Mother's visit to the Han palace—a gentle reverie of past splendors. The poet recalls a time during the reign of Hsüan tsung when both he and the T'ang dynasty were young and vigorous.

> P'eng-lai palace watchtowers face the Southern Mountains;
> Golden stalks for receiving dew from the Empyrean Han River
>   are spaced like pillars.
> Gazing far westward to the Turquoise Pond, he causes the
>   Queen Mother to descend;
> As she comes, a purple vapor fills Envelope Pass.
> Clouds shift pheasant tail fans and open palace screens.
> Sun glints off dragon scales—I recognize the incomparable
>   countenance.

Once again I've fallen asleep by the Glaucous River—startled by
the year's growing late;
How many more times will I be on the dot for morning audience
at the Blue Gemstone Gate?

(*TSYT*, 468/32E)

In another poem of the same type, "Dwelling on the Past," Tu Fu
again remembers the good years during the reign of Hsüan tsung.
This one starts where the last left off, by the blue gates to the
imperial palace in Ch'ang an. The poet presents a glimpse of an
intimate moment in the private life of the T'ang emperor ("the
dragon") and his beloved consort, the Lady Yang, comparing them
to the Martial Thearch and the Queen Mother. The last couplet
contains a double meaning: "musical secrets" could also be "secrets
of pleasure"; the graphs are the same and either meaning would suit.

I dwell on the past, when inside the Blue Gates,
The P'eng-lai palace guard was frequently shifted.
Floriate bewitchers beckoned from a motley of trees;
The dragon rejoiced, emerging from the flat pond.
The falling sun detained the Queen Mother;
In the faint wind she leaned on a young child.
Inside the palace they practiced musical secrets;
Rarely did outsiders know about them.

(*TSYT*, 461/9)

"Historical reflections" draw lessons from past events. In "Old
Moth Brows' Resentment" by Wang Han (fl. 713), a former palace
woman laments Han Wu-ti's neglect. Her understanding is that
he deserted his harem after becoming infatuated with the Queen
Mother. The Taoist adept, who forsakes sexual intercourse for
transcendence, would have another interpretation. A subtheme of
Wang's poem is the unfair competition between human and immortal beauty. And yet the goddess's promise of immortality and eternal
love can be deceptive; the emperor's efforts have only led him to the
grave. When he finally meets her, the goddess is coming to welcome
him in death. Having an appointment with the goddess signifies
both death and eternal life, like the expression "gone to a better
place" in a modern Christian context. His former palace woman,
named "Old Moth Brows" after her brows made up in the shape of
moths' wings, sings to his spirit on the very morning of his funeral.

His chariot leaves the palace for the final time. He is to be buried in the Southern Mountains, in the Fertile Tumulus. The T'ang royal burial grounds were located nearby; Wang Han surely intends a comparison between Han Wu-ti and the contemporary T'ang ruler.

> You made a basin of yellow gold, a stalk of bronze,
> Received white dew from the heavens in open hands.
> The Queen Mother, captivated and moved by your intentions,
> Is coming to welcome you with cloud chariots and feathered standards.
> Before the Flying Incorruptibles Belvedere, I feel vain resentment and longing.
> Oh small ruler, why did you have to be so misled?
> This single morning, you'll be buried in the Fertile Tumulus field;
> Considering your handmaiden's moth brows worthless, you don't even turn back your head.
> As the palace chariots go out late to head for the Southern Mountains,
> Transcendent guards meander off, departing never to return.
>
> (CTS, 882)

A reflective poem entitled "Eulogizing History," no. 6, by Li Hua (d. ca. 769) describes Mount K'un-lun and the charmed life the immortals (called "feathered people" because of their wings) lead there. But the narrator cautions that you cannot grab the Way by pursuing it and warns against imitating Han Wu-ti. All his ostentatious devotions and expensive plans could not prevent his death.

> As the sun shines on top of K'un-lun,
> Feathered people don their feathered garments.
> Riding dragons, they harness clouds and mist,
> About to go off, their hearts are without transgressions.
> This mountain is located in the northwest;
> It is, in fact, the divine transcendents' nation.
> Numinous breaths are all spontaneously thus:
> If you seek them, you won't be able to obtain them.
> Why act like the Martial Thearch of the Han,
> Who made his thoughts essential and went to a whole flock of mountains?
> With waste and extravagance, he aggrandized a myriad schemes,
> But his palace chariots in the end did not return.

Glaucous green—the trees at the Fertile Tumulus
Are enough to serve as a warning to humans.

(CTS, 872)

The Taoist master Wu Yün wrote fourteen poems entitled "Viewing the Old." His conventional title leads the reader to expect didactic lessons from history; normally such poems express predictable Confucian wisdom. Wu Yün toys with the reader's expectations by making Taoist points. In the sixth poem of the series, he explores the reasons the first emperor of the Ch'in and the Martial Thearch of the Han, despite enormous efforts, failed to attain immortality. Overweening ambition and arrogance, together with ignorance, anger, and lust, destroyed their character and resolve. Reflected mercilessly in the mirror of history, they are seen as greedy, impatient, sensual, and bloodthirsty. Although they made promising starts, in the end gods and transcendents deserted them.

Once I searched for the Way of the realized transcendents;
Purifying and quieting myself, I drove off the flock of
    annoyances.
The Illustrious One of the Ch'in, along with the Martial One of
    the Han:
How were they able to roam its frontiers?
Their passions tamed, a myriad crises disintegrated;
Their positions surpassed the honor of all within the four seas.
But then they wanted to precede all space and time,
And to regulate the succession of the hexagrams.
To be revered and lofty, equal of the ancient and distant:
Created phenomena can never maintain both aims.
How much more so since they indulged their addictions without
    restraint,
While the seductions of the wilderness cut down their numinous
    roots?
Golden oil elixir requires an extended waiting period,
But jade complexions repeatedly moved their cloud-souls.
Punishing and attacking, they exhausted all the outer territories,
While killing and injuring covered the central plain.
The celestial mirror is faithful—hard to accuse of falsifying;
The divine inner structure cannot be considered deceitful.
[The transcendent] An Ch'i went back to P'eng-lai;
The Queen Mother returned to K'un-lun.

Strange arts were finally reported in neither case.
How depressing! What can I say in the end?

(CTS, 4943)

Li Po's "Old Airs," no. 43, presents the same Taoist character lesson, blaming the failure of King Mu and the Martial Thearch on their personal flaws:

Mu of the Chou had ambitions for the Eight Wildernesses;
The Illustrious One of the Han had a myriad vehicles' honor.
But in lust and pleasure the heart should not go to extremes;
As for courage and bravery—how are they even worth
    discussing?
At the Western Sea, Mu feasted the Queen Mother;
At the Northern Palace, Wu invited the Lady of the Supreme
    Primordial.
By the Turquoise Water—hearing the song left behind;
Over jade cups—in the end empty words.
Numinous traces have become creeping grasses;
They just depress the thousand-year-old cloud-souls.

(CTS, 921)

The old cloud-souls are unquiet dead who disturb the poet—ancient ghosts of kings howling for the goddess.

T'ang poets question neither the value of immortality nor the grandeur of the royal heroes. Mere contact with the Queen Mother reveals how closely they approached divinity. Writers seem to derive two opposite lessons from the kings' stories: first, since immortality is impossible to achieve, the reader might as well not even try; and second, the ancients came so close that with a little more effort the modern adept might be able to succeed. Authors writing in the second vein cautioned the Taoist adept not to rest with following the example of Mu and Wu but to strive for still greater perfection.

Celebrations. Just as they cite King Mu's western journey in poems on royal processions, T'ang poets mention Han Wu-ti's visit from the goddess in poems celebrating contemporary holidays and sacrifices. They honored the glory and legitimacy of the reigning monarch by references to the Queen Mother's feast in the Han palace. The present ruler's virtue has attracted the goddess once again, they imply. Such formulas could become tired and predictable; in the hands of a master the challenge was to render the standard phrases new and surprising. When Tu Fu submitted a poem on Hsüan tsung's birthday, the "Thousand Autumn's Holiday," he depicted deities participating in the celebrations along with the ruler's favorite horse, Night-shining White, and acrobats from his performing academy:

> Driving forth clouds, his storied buildings are spacious.
> Gulping in wind, his variegated insignia are high.
> Transcendent people draw out their esoteric music;
> The Queen Mother submits as tribute her palace peaches.
> In netted gauze stockings—the sensuous charm of pink lotus
>   blossoms.
> With golden bridle—his fur coat like white snow.
> The one dancing on the steps, holding Longevity Wine in his
>   mouth;
> The other walking on a tightrope as if borne on the tip of an
>   autumn hair.
> But those the incomparable ruler considered precious in other
>   years,
> Are now pushed aside in his heart, and this day considered
>   irksome.
>   (TSYT, 549/23B)

Tribute of peaches reappears in a poem by Li Ho eulogizing the intercalary month of 809. When the emperor publishes the official calendar, as he alone has the right to do, divinities respond to his charisma:

> As our thearch multiplies his brilliance, so the years multiply
>   their seasons;
> Seventy-two periods return, pushing in cyclical order.
> Ash remnants fly around in celestial officials' jade tubes.
> This year, how it extends! The coming year is correspondingly
>   delayed.
> The Queen Mother transports her peaches, offering them as
>   tribute to the Son of Heaven,
> While Mr. Hsi and Mr. Ho take the dragon reins far afield.
>   (CTS, 2325)

The seventy-two periods are an ancient division of the calendar year; T'ang people believed that in antiquity the officials had observed ashes in measured tubes to determine the seasons.[8] As she did in days

of old, the Queen Mother grants a virtuous emperor control over
the calendar, which in turn grants him power over time and the
workings of the cosmos. Hsi and Ho are old gods who rule celestial
movements. Li Ho flatters the ruler with so many fawning comparisons from classical times that to the modern reader the poem
seems servile, demonstrating the dependence of poets on the crown
for their livelihood. Among the host of allusions, the association of
the Queen Mother and her peaches with the calendar, time, and
legitimacy stands out clearly.

In "Remembering the Suburban Sacrifice to Heaven," Pao Jung
recalls the splendors of the T'ang imperial suburban sacrifice to
heaven in days gone by, comparing that ritual to the ceremonies of
Emperor Wu. As a sign of divine approval of the emperor's performance of the rites, the goddess presents maps, signifying control
and legitimacy. These charts demonstrate the Queen Mother's control over space; the appearance of auspicious shrubs called calendar
plants that told the day of the moon's cycle demonstrates her control
over time as well. The last couplet compares the T'ang emperor to
Han Wu-ti, his sacrificial music to the music of Shun, and his dances
to the heavenly steps witnessed by King Mu beside the Queen
Mother's pond. Yin and yang harmonize in the suburban sacrifice
under the leadership of the emperor as they do in heaven under the
guidance of the Queen Mother.

> My memories return to the suburban sacrificial altar where I
>   gazed from afar at the Martial Illustrious One;
> His nine armies' flags and tents descended to the southern
>   quadrant.
> Six dragons, the sun holding their reins, moved across the
>   heavens with vigor;
> The Divine Mother presented charts with the earth's paths
>   shining forth clearly.
> Amid dense and genial breaths were engendered calendar plants;
> Within the mists of so and not-so, he cherished turquoise broth.
> Even now I fill my ears with syrinx tunes of the ancients,
> And crave in vain the dance of the male and female phoenix by
>   the Turquoise Pond.
>   (CTS, 2932)

In one of four pieces entitled "Conductus on the Pavilion for
Attending the Court of the Primordial" (no. 1), Ch'en T'ao com-

pares another T'ang ceremony to the Queen Mother's visit to the Han palace. The rite called Attending the Court of the Primordial took place at the pavilion of the title, an altar inside the palace where the T'ang royal family worshiped the deified Lao-tzu as their clan ancestor. The most famous Pavilion for Attending Court of the Primordial was located in the Floriate Clear Palace compound at Black Horse Mountain, but the imperial compound in the capital city of Ch'ang an had one as well.[9] In Ch'en T'ao's quatrain, Lao-tzu and the Queen Mother of the West appear to corroborate the ruler's legitimacy and the ritual correctness of his ancestral sacrifice.

> The thearch's candle glitters and flashes, descending from the
>   Nine Heavens;
> In dawn light at the P'eng-lai palace, the jade stove smokes.
> Inexhaustible numbers of simurghs and phoenixes, following
>   the Queen Mother,
> Come to offer congratulations in the incense-permeated wind:
>   "A whole myriad years!"
>   (CTS, 4402–3)

Palaces. Medieval writers refer to the story of the Martial Thearch in descriptive pieces on palaces and other structures. Poets glorify buildings to glorify the dynasty. The story lent itself well to this purpose because the goddess came to visit the emperor in his own home, rendering the place permanently numinous. Just as the Turquoise Pond was the sacred spot of the meeting for the King Mu story, so the Han palace represents holy ground in Emperor Wu's tale. The image can become formulaic; the challenge is to keep it vivid and relevant.

In "The Palace of Supreme Yang," Wang Chien, for example, describes a T'ang dynasty imperial complex in the capital city of Lo yang. He quotes a biography (no longer extant) of the Queen Mother to support his claim that she prefers this earthly palace to her own celestial home.

> At the Palace of the Supreme Yang, flowers and trees do not
>   experience autumn;
> The Lo River's waters thread through the palace, flowing
>   everywhere.
> In painted pavilions and red storied buildings, palace women
>   smile;
> Jade syrinx and metal pipes make the passerby sad.

Screening walls enter the ravine; orange tree flowers issue forth.
A jade palanquin climbs the mountain; cinnamon trees' leaves
  grow dense.
I once read, in "Transmissions Concerning the Queen Mother"
  from the "Arrayed Transcendents":
"The Nine Heavens don't surpass wandering in the midst of this
  place."

(CTS, 1805)

The same poet wrote about the ancient site of the Warm Springs Palace, predecessor of the Floriate Clear Palace. Ruined buildings, once the scene of an epiphany, now stand abandoned; small deer called elaphure play there. The meeting of emperor and goddess that sanctified the place is now only a memory: "The Martial Illustrious One has obtained transcendence; the Queen Mother has departed" ("Lines on the Warm Springs Palace," CTS, 1785).

Li Yü-chung, in contrast, captures the impression of a building at the exact moment of receiving divine grace. For that instant, the structure is paradise. "When the Sun First Illuminates the Phoenix Storied Building" gives luminous tribute to the palace compound in Ch'ang an. This intensely visual and light-filled poem renders the effects of the rising sun on the building and compares the transient beauty of dawn to the passage of a deity:

Daybreak at the basilica of mist and clouds;
The morning sun provides a candle for the thearch's dwelling.
Cutting through auroral clouds, it gives rise to peaked eaves;
Passing through pavilions, it beautifies the clear spaces.
Flowing and multi-colored on joined vermilion balconies,
Its mounting brilliance illuminates a white damask spread.
Just appearing through glittering obstacles—seen within dawn
  phosphors,
Visible and invisible in alternation, the radiance of dawn's full
  light begins.
By doors and windows, transcendent mountains draw near;
At balcony railings, phoenix wings spread out.
Again it seems the Queen Mother is passing—
Crossing far away: her five-colored cloud chariot.

(CTS, 2889)

A comparison to the Queen Mother's residence might also glorify Taoist structures. Several poets record an incident of the Primal

Accord reign period (806–21). A transcendent maiden visited the T'ang Prosperity Belvedere, a Taoist compound built for the royal princess of the same name, a daughter of emperor Hsüan tsung. Princess T'ang Prosperity had planted jade stamen flowers in the garden. According to Chang Chi (ca. 776–ca. 829), their profuse spring blossoms, just at the point of releasing pollen to the wind, tempted a little transcendent to desert Mount K'un-lun.[10]

> Within a thousand branches of flowers, jade dust flies;
> Even inside Amah's palace, one sees it's also thinly dispersed.
> She should be contending with various transcendents over the
>   hundred grasses;
> Instead she's come alone, stealthily, to obtain a single branch and
>   return.
>
> (CTS, 2299)

Chang compares the garden of the Taoist close favorably with heavenly parks, playfully honoring the convent, the princess—like the little transcendent, a client of the goddess—and the dynasty. In the poet's imagination, the immortals are always with us, gracing special places with their secret presence.

Peaches. Poems about the Queen Mother's peaches arise from Han Wu-ti's story. Those twisted trees on Mount K'un-lun set a standard of beauty for the peach tree, flower, and fruit. An efficacious elixir, the numinous peach also signifies immortality. Starting in the T'ang dynasty, the peaches, rather than the *sheng* headdress of earlier eras, become the most important iconographic sign of the Queen Mother of the West. Peaches become the favorite symbol of the goddess in poetry, repeated so often that the association is automatic. The image can seem hackneyed and mechanical; it takes special creativity on the part of a poet to make those old peaches fresh.

Peach poems composed on imperial command might praise the emperor to the point of toadying, comparing his party to the goddess's feast. In "Attending a Feast in the Peach Tree Flower Garden, We Enjoy Peach Flowers," Chao Yen-chao admires seductive peach blossoms in the imperial orchard, ending on a self-deprecating note:

> Pink perianths compete in allure just before sunrise at the spring
>   hunting park.
> Powdery down tufts are newly spat out; imperial feast mats open.

> We've wanted to make an offering to the Queen Mother of the
> West, for the sake of extended years,
> But intimates and attendants alike are ashamed of lacking Tung-
> fang's talent.
>
> (CTS, 269)

Chao's concluding couplet compares the speaker to King Mu, who gave the Queen Mother gifts to learn her secrets of longevity, and to the mischievous Tung-fang Shuo, who stole her peaches.

One recorded banquet in the peach orchard elicited a number of poetic effusions, all entitled "Lines on Peach Blossoms." When the thearch threw a feast for the conquering northern general Chang Jen-t'an in the Western Hunting Preserve, he ordered the assembled officials to compose commemorative quatrains. Some survive, laden with inevitable references to the peaches, intended to please both emperor and general. Li I, for example, makes the traditional connection between military conquest, death, west, autumn, and the goddess. He links the spring banquet with the goddess's autumn visit to the Han palace, suggesting that she might like to attend this occasion:

> White silk perianths make a path—everywhere in the fenced-off
> imperial hunting park are fragrant plants.
> Pink blossoms spread the ground—filling the feast mats with
> fragrance.
> Don't pass on the news of this autumn feast to the Queen
> Mother,
> Lest she come to compete with the spring flowers, making
> offerings to the incomparable illustrious one.
>
> (CTS, 269)

The Queen Mother's fruit also provided T'ang writers with a measure for cosmic time: the peach cycle. This period—the time it takes her peach trees to flower and fruit—lasts one, two, or three thousand years, depending on the source. The cycle of the numinous tree provided a native Chinese figure of speech to replace the Chinese translation of the Sanskrit word *kalpa*, an equivalent term measuring vast eons of cosmic time, which had come into popular use through the influence of Buddhism. In poetry, the peach cycle often appears in parallel construction with another native Chinese measure for long periods of time, one favored by the Taoists—the cycle of alternations of mulberry fields and water in the Eastern Sea. In the poem by Wei Ying-wu translated above, the Queen Mother asks: "The sea's waters and mulberry fields, how many times have they alternated? / In the midst of their cycles, these peaches have ripened four or five times" (CTS, 1093). And Huang-fu Jan questions an immortal: "At what seasons have you planted peach seeds? How many times have you seen the mulberry fields?" (CTS, 1499). Poets use the Queen Mother's peaches as an emblem of longevity, contrasting their immortality with the brevity of human life. In "Late Flowers Open in Front of My Courtyard," Li Po compares a late-blooming peach he planted in his garden, never expecting to see it flower during his lifetime, to divine trees. Friends mock him for tending such a bothersome plant, but he enjoys its rare blossoms and reflects on the transience of beauty.

> I planted peaches from the Queen Mother of the West in my own household;
> Every three thousand sunny springs they blossom only once.
> Their setting fruit is so toilsome and tardy that others laugh at me;
> I draw one down and break it off—oh me, oh my—I breathe a long sigh.
>
> (CTS, 5081)

Li Ho contrasts the futile and anxious efforts of ambitious young men to the infinite cycles of the universe. While human heroes die over and over again, "the Queen Mother's peach flowers redden for the thousandth time" (CTS, 2325). The narrator of "Wounded Song Lines," translated above, contrasts human time with that of the goddess in these terms:

> While the Queen Mother's bewitching peach flowers open a single time,
> In the jade storied buildings, pink variegated blossoms have changed a thousand times.
>
> (CTS, 2836)

The narrator contrasts cycles of divine and earthly blossoms, a figure of speech for immortal versus human lifespans. Deities can afford a lofty indifference to the passage of time; humans must seize the moment or lose it forever. Earthly flowers like the pink variegated blossoms in the poem contrast poignantly with the divine peach flowers and provide a favorite T'ang metaphor for lovely young women—beautiful, fruitful, fragile, and short-lived.

Li Po, Li Ho, and Chuang Nan-chieh contrast the longevity of the peach tree to the short span of human life. On the other hand, Wen T'ing-yün (ca. 812–70) praises the peaches as reminders of immortality in this world. Wen borrows the voice of an old monk in "The Return-to-life Peach Blossoms Come Out; So I Take Them as the Subject for a Poem":

> My sick eyes encounter spring—four walls of empty space.
> Coming at night, mountain snow breaks the east wind.
> Not yet recognizing the Queen Mother's thousand-year-
>   ripening peaches,
> I'm about to share a laugh with Squire Liu.
> Already falling, they open again and cross the late evening
>   kingfisher;
> It seems there's not, then again there seems to be a belt of
>   morning pink.
> For the monks' reverences, our tallow candles are three feet
>   high;
> Let's not regret the shining dewy thickets of the linked
>   empyreans.
>   (CTS, 3535)

Outside on a spring night, a monk with failing vision mistakes suddenly blooming flowers for snow on the branches. Like Squire Liu of Taoist legend who met a goddess and ate peaches of immortality, the narrator will soon have divine fruit to eat. The rare and treasured flowers already have a restoring and warming effect, like an elixir. Falling blossoms cross the brilliant deep blue of late night mountains, making a band of pink color that drifts across the sky, like auroral clouds. The candles, still with hours to burn, illuminate his nocturnal rituals. A visiting immortal would have no reason to miss paradise.

As King Mu's chargers did for horses, the Queen Mother's peaches set a poetic standard of quality against which to measure other plants. Po Chü-i, in his ode to the peony, shows the universal currency of the peach standard by deftly twisting it in the peony's favor. In comparison to the peony, he asserts, "the Queen Mother's peaches are small and without fragrance" (CTS, 2497).

Li Shang-yin uses the comparison in an unexpected way when he writes a sensual eulogy to the pomegranate, likening the plant to a soft, yielding, and fertile woman:

> Pomegranate branches are sinuously winding, pomegranate
> fruits dense;
> Pomegranate membranes are light and iridescent, pomegranate
> seeds fresh.
> One might covet the cyan peach trees by the Turquoise Pond,
> But the cyan peaches redden their cheeks only once in a
> thousand years.
>
> (CTS, 3238)

One may wish for the Queen Mother's magical peaches, but they are rarely met. On the other hand, the lush pomegranate fruit, with its plentiful red seeds a universal symbol of fertility, is both appealing and available here and now.

Ku K'uang (ca. 725–ca. 814) compares the Queen Mother's peach flowers to a painted blossom in his "Song of a Flower Painting by Liang Kuang." The painting by Liang, a T'ang dynasty artist known for realistic depictions of flowers, attracts Flying Rose-gem Hsü, an attendant of the Queen Mother who is also the youngest daughter of the Lady of the Supreme Primordial. Descending to assist in ceremonies at the Han palace, she sees Liang's skillful work, which demonstrates his potential to become a transcendent. The young goddess abandons her post as attendant in the divine procession to follow a higher calling as a spouse-instructress according to the dictates of Shang ch'ing Taoism and marry Liang.

> The Queen Mother was about to pass Liu Ch'e's household;
> Flying Rose-gem entered her cloud-canopied chariot by night.
> Purple writs and allotted portions entrusted to the blue bird,
> They dropped down toward our world, seeking excellent flowers.
> The Lady of the Supreme Primordial's smallest daughter,
> Head and face correct to the smallest detail, is an able
> conversationalist.
> She takes Master Liang's painted flower in her hands and looks.
> Knitting her brow, she hides a smile; her heart pledges him.
> Her heart pledges him,
> To explain to her mom that she'll follow him in marriage!
>
> (CTS, 1574)

King Mu and the Martial Thearch

King Mu of the Chou and the Martial Thearch of the Han were closely associated in the minds of medieval Chinese poets. Their personalities and goals were similar, as were their failures. Thoughts of the goddess would bring them both to the mind of a medieval Chinese literatus. The same authors wrote about both rulers; they often appear together in the same poems, frequently in paired couplets or parallel lines. Li Po wrote: "Mu of the Chou had ambitions for the Eight Wildernesses. / The Illustrious One of the Han had a myriad vehicles' honor" (*CTS*, 921). Elsewhere, Wei Ying-wu regrets that King Mu did not live when the peaches ripened and that Han Wu-ti managed to eat them but could not benefit (*CTS*, 1093). They made a natural pair in the poems on the Queen Mother's shrine translated in the first chapter.

In one of a series of poems from court theatricals of Shu, the Queen Mother herself associates the two men:

> The glaucous sea has become dust—for how many myriad
> autumns?
> Cyan peach trees issue forth, prolonging my spring
> despondency.
> It must be many thousands of years since I've come;
> Where have Mu of the Chou and the Illustrious One of the Han
> wandered to?
>
> (*CTS*, 5001)

Returning to this world after an absence of eons, the goddess misses the human rulers she met in the past.

No wonder images and themes from the stories of Mu and Wu become blended in poetry; the two share a single literary role. Both possessed unrestrained energy and ambition in temporal and religious pursuits; both held immortality in their grasp and then lost it. Both communicated with the goddess, but failed to maintain the connection. Contact with the deity brought the ruler divine sanction and powers; severance of contact ultimately brought death. Stories of the two kings were extremely popular among T'ang dynasty poets. In the *Transmissions Concerning Mu, Son of Heaven* and *Esoteric Transmissions Concerning the Martial Thearch of the Han*, they read narratives in beautiful language that appealed to their imaginations and love of detail. Images were there for the taking. The poet also held up the Chou king and Han emperor as mirrors to T'ang rulers. The poignant themes of pursuit of immortality in the face of inevitable death and hope for contact with divinity in the midst of the mundane proved attractive to medieval Chinese writers. Poems on the two emperors embodied the contradiction of human aspirations with reality in concrete stories.

The quests of Mu and Wu also lend themselves to comparison with the aim of the Taoist adept. Taoist literature depicts the adept as a ruler and hero whose foremost goal is transcendence. The adept, as we shall see in the story of Mao Ying, and in poems of the next two chapters, surpasses the worldly king because he succeeds in the ultimate conquest: immortality.

Mao Ying

One last human encounter with the goddess concludes Tu Kuang-t'ing's hagiography. The author presents his model for the ideal Taoist adept in this final tale. The person who serves as a positive example for Taoist believers of medieval times was the founder of the Shang ch'ing school of Taoism: Mao Ying or Lord Mao. The eldest of three brothers who lived in the south of China during the Han dynasty, Mao Ying received a visit from the goddess in 1 B.C., 109 years after her visit to the Martial Thearch. The Queen Mother gave Mao Ying, or ordered other deities to give him, texts and entitlements of a high transcendent official. She also bestowed on him a divine spouse and teacher, Lady Wei Hua-ts'un, beginning a pattern that all Shang ch'ing Taoist adepts in following ages longed to emulate. The final place in Tu's account is clearly the place of honor, and the case of Lord Mao in many ways sums up the lessons taught by the Queen Mother in her meetings with mortal men.

Again there was the Great Lord Mao Ying who ruled over Bucklebent Mountain in the south. In the second year of the Primordial Longevity reign period [1 B.C.], in the eighth month, on the F-Cock [*chi yu*] day, the Realized Person of the Southern Marchmount, Lord Ch'ih, and Wang Chün-feng of the Western Walled City, and various blue lads followed the Queen Mother and descended together to Mao Ying's chambers. In an instant, the Celestial Illustrious Great Thearch sent his messenger in embroidered clothing, called Ling Kuang-tzu Ch'i, to present Ying with a divine seal and jade emblem. The Lord Thearch of Grand Tenuity sent the Autocrat's Notary of the Left Palace of the Three Heavens, Kuan Hsiu-t'iao, to present Ying with an eight dragon multi-colored damask carriage and purple feathered floriate clothing. The Grand Supreme Lord of the Way sent the Dawn Assisting Grandee, Shih Shu-men, to present Ying with the Veritable Talisman of the Metal Tiger and a folly bell of flowing metal. The Incomparable Lord of the Golden Watchtower commanded the Realized Person of the Grand Bourne to send the Jade Squires of the Rectified Unity and Supreme Mystery: Wang Chung, Pao Ch'iu, and others, to present Ying with swallow wombs of the four junctions and divine fungi of flowing brightness.

When the messengers from the four had finished the bestowals, they had Ying eat the fungi, hang the seal at his belt, don the clothing, straighten his crown, tie the talismans at his waist, grip the folly bell, and stand up. The messengers from the four told Ying: "He who eats concealed fungi from the four junctures takes up the position of a Steward of Realized Ones. He who eats jade fungi of the Golden Watchtowers takes up the position of Director of Destiny. He who eats metal blossoms of flowing brightness takes up the position of Director of Transcendent Registers. And he who eats the paired flying plants of extended luminosity takes up the position of a Realized Sire. He who eats the grotto grasses of night radiance will always have the responsibility of governing the autocrat's notaries of the left and right. You have eaten all of these. Your longevity will be coequal with heaven and earth. Your place will be situated as the Supreme Realized Person who is Director of Destiny and Supreme Steward of the Eastern Marchmount. You will control all divine transcendents of the former kingdoms of Wu and Yüeh, and all the mountains and water sources left of the Yangtze River."

Their words finished, all the messengers departed together. The Five Thearchic Lords, each in a square-faced chariot, descended in submission to his courtyard. They carried out the commands of the Grand Thearch, presenting to Ying a purple jade plaque, writs carved in yellow gold, and patterns of nine pewters. They saluted Ying as Supreme Steward of the Eastern Marchmount, Realized Lord Who Is Director of Destiny, and Realized Person of the Grand Primordial. The affair finished, they all departed.

The Queen Mother and Ying's master, Lord Wang of the Western City, set forth drinks and a feast from the celestial kitchen for Ying. They sang the "Tune of the Mysterious Numen." When the feast was over, the Queen Mother took Lord Wang and Ying to examine and inspect Ying's two younger brothers. Each had bestowed on him the requisite essentials of the Way. The Queen Mother commanded the Lady of the Supreme Primordial to bestow on Mao Ku and Mao Chung the Hidden Writs of the Supreme

Empyrean, the Seminal Essence of the Way of Cinnabar Elixir and the Phosphors, and the like, comprising the Precious Scriptures of the Taoist Canon in Four Sections. The Queen Mother held the Hidden Writs of the Grand Empyrean and commanded her serving girl Chang Ling-tzu to hold the oath of exchanging faith, while she bestowed them on Ying, Ku, and Chung. The affair concluded, the Queen Mother of the West departed by ascending to heaven.

After this, the Primordial Ruler of the Purple Heavens, Lady Wei Hua-ts'un, purified herself and fasted on the Hidden Primordial Terrace at the Mountain of Yang lo. The Queen Mother of the West and the Incomparable Lord of the Golden Watchtower descended to the terrace. They were riding an eight-phosphor carriage. Together they had visited the Supreme Palace of the Pure Void and had received by transmission the Hidden Writs of the Realm of Jade Clarity in four scrolls in order to bestow them on Hua-ts'un. At this time, the Lady of the Three Primordials, called Feng Shuang Li Chu, along with the Left Transcendent Sire of the Purple Yang, Shih Lu-ch'eng, the Lofty Transcendent Sire of the Grand Bourne, Yen Kai Kung-tzu, the Realized Person of the Western City, Wang Fang-p'ing, the Realized Person of the Grand Void, Ch'ih Sung-tzu of the Southern Marchmount, and the Realized Person of Paulownia-Cedar Mountain, Wang Tzu-ch'iao, over thirty realized beings, each sang the "Tune of the Yang Song and the Yin Song of the Grand Bourne." The Queen Mother composed the lyrics for it:

> I harness my eight-phosphor carriage;
> Like thunder! I enter the Realm of Jade Clarity.
> Dragon pennants brush the top of the empyrean;
> Tiger banners lead vermilion-clad men-at-arms!
> Footloose and fancy-free: the Mysterious Ford separates me
>   from the human world;
> Among a myriad flows, I have no temporary resting place.
> Grievous—this alternate departing and lingering of unions.
> When a kalpa is exhausted, heaven and earth are overturned.
> She must seek a phosphor with no center,
> Not dying and also not born.
> Embodying the spontaneous Way,
> Quietly contemplating and harmonizing the great stygean
>   realm.
> At Southern Marchmount she displays her veritable trunk;
> Jade reflections shine on her accumulated essences.
> Having the responsibility of office is not your affair;
> Empty your heart—you will naturally receive numina.

> The "Scarlet River Tune" of your auspicious meeting—
> The joy you give each other is neverending.

When the Queen Mother had finished the song, and the answering song of the Lady of the Three Primordials also reached its end, the Queen Mother, along with the Lady of the Three Primordials, the Left Transcendent Sire of the Purple Yang, and the Transcendent Sire of the Grand Bourne, as well as Lord Wang of the Pure Void, departed together with Wei Hua-ts'un. They went to the southeast and all visited Mount Huo in the Heavenly Terrace Mountains. When they passed the Golden Altar on Bucklebent Mountain, they gave a feast for the Grand Primordial Realized Person Mao at the Grotto-heaven of the Floriate Yang. Leaving Hua-ts'un behind, beneath the jade eaves of the grotto palace at Mount Huo, all the flock of the realized ascended following the Queen Mother and returned to Tortoise Terrace.   (*CMYC*, 24163–64)

Tu Kuang-t'ing derives his account from a lost fourth- or fifth-century biography of the Mao brothers, now preserved in the *Mao shan chih* (Monograph on Mount Mao) which appears in the present Taoist canon. In doing so, Tu adapts the very text that formed the basis of the *Esoteric Transmissions Concerning the Martial Thearch of the Han*, the book he relies on in his narrative on that emperor. The author of the *Esoteric Transmissions* had already borrowed the Mao brothers' biography, and in effect Tu tells the same story twice, giving the protagonists different names and their encounters with the goddess different outcomes. Where Han Wu-ti fails, Mao Ying triumphs.[11]

The Queen Mother's visit to Mao Ying and his younger brothers occurs in 1 B.C., during an era of political and economic crises for the Han dynasty. At this time, the peasant cult devoted to the Queen Mother of the West was strong and the great founding schools of the Taoist religion, the Ways of the Celestial Masters and Great Peace, had not yet arisen. By placing Mao Ying's meeting so early, Tu claims Shang ch'ing precedence over the two schools that actually started the Taoist religion.

Bucklebent Mountain is Mao shan, in modern Kiangsu province. The Queen Mother is accompanied by famous heroes of the cult of transcendents and by high gods and celestial officials of Shang ch'ing Taoism. Lord Ch'ih is Ch'ih Sung-tzu, Master Red Pine, a popular immortal who figures in many stories of the Six Dynasties and

T'ang. Wang Chün-feng is Lord Mao's master. The Celestial Illustrious Great Thearch, the Lord Thearch of Grand Tenuity, and
the Grand Supreme Lord of the Way are high celestial deities of the
Shang ch'ing pantheon.

All the gift givers are members of the celestial imperium. The
gifts Mao Ying receives are protective talismans, elixir drugs, registers of deities' names, texts revealing teachings of the Way, and
symbols of divine office. The Queen Mother's visit is, in fact, his
investiture as a member of the heavenly bureaucracy, and Tu spells
out his future title, privileges, and duties. The Five Thearchic Lords
of the directions submit to Mao, indicating his rule over nature, and
bestow sacred Shang ch'ing texts on him. The Queen Mother also
grants titles, talismans, elixirs, and texts to Mao Ying's younger
brothers.

After the initial encounter, the gods deem Mao Ying worthy of a
divine bride and prepare the Lady Wei Hua-ts'un for him. The
Queen Mother of the West visits Mao Ying a second time; this time
she leaves behind a goddess to marry and instruct the adept: the core
of Shang ch'ing revelations was believed to have resulted from their
union. [12]

Surprisingly enough, poets of the T'ang dynasty did not dwell on
the story of Mao Ying. Meng Chiao (751–814) appears at first to be
an exception: the editors of the *Complete T'ang Poetry* anthology
credit him with authorship of the "Song of the Metal Mother Flying
in the Void," which Tu repeats almost verbatim in his account
translated above, naming it the "Tune of the Yang Song and the Yin
Song of the Grand Bourne." But the same song also appears in the
Esoteric Transmissions, which precedes Meng Chiao's work by a few
centuries. [13] It is an earlier work of the Shang ch'ing school and
belongs together with the songs of the great goddesses collected in
such other texts as the *Declarations of the Realized Ones*.

The song is performed by the Queen Mother while dancing, with
replies given by the Lady of the Three Primordials. Since the
complete cycle should number nine yang and six yin chants, and
only nine couplets remain here, the Lady's replies may have been
dropped out, leaving only the Queen Mother's words. The words
are typical of Shang ch'ing ceremonial introductions of a goddess
to her prospective human bridegroom. The song opens with the

Queen Mother's ecstatic flight through space as she descends to arrange a marriage that will destroy the barriers between gods and humans. The Queen Mother acts as a divine matchmaker between Wei Hua-ts'un and her intended spouse and pupil, Mao Ying. Her song is both a hymn to the beauty and accomplishments of the divine bride and an evocation of future bliss for the wedded couple. Their meeting is no mere tryst, however heavenly, but a union of instructress and adept, with revolutionary consequences for the future of Taoism. The encounter of Lady Wei and Lord Mao provides a model of transcendent marriage between goddess and mortal that Shang ch'ing adepts will try to repeat in their own practice as they strive to attain immortality.

Only one T'ang poem celebrating the Queen Mother's visit to the founder of Shang ch'ing Taoism remains today: Pao Jung's "Song of the Transcendents' Meeting":

> Light, light—indistinct, indistinct:
> Dragon words and phoenix chatter.
> How informal and relaxed!
> There's a resonance in the ears—Ah!
> But no traces in the eyes.
> Dark, dark—silent, silent:
> Flowers stretch out like a multi-colored damask weaving.
> When the Queen Mother first came from K'un-lun,
> Mao Ying and Wang Fang-p'ing by her side.
> The blue-downed transcendent bird, holding in its beak a multi-
> colored damask talisman,
> Promised to send up news of Ah Huan's records of arising and
> settling, and the Queen Mother's texts.
> Then I first began to know about transcendents' affairs; also
> there were many stories.
> Since the separation by the Scarlet River, it has been over a
> thousand years.
> The auspicious jade graphs will increase our happy pneuma!
> At the Turquoise Platform, the bright moon comes and falls on
> the ground.
> With caps and double-edged swords, as they look down on the
> dawn, their trampling dance becomes urgent.
> Their ceremonious comportment completely appropriate for an
> affair between prince and vassals,
> They request word on the lesser transcendent arts.

One with the given name and surname of Flying Rose-gem
  Hsü,
Plays the Grotto Yin jade chimes, striking up a celestial
  resonance,
Delighting the Queen Mother in one single, long send-off.
In jade cups—long-life wine;
By cyan flowers, their drunken numina are flaunted.
Laughing, she bestows on the two masters the recipes for
  extending life.
Before the two masters have reached the point of salutations and
  words of thanks,
She's above the Glaucous Sea, beneath the flashing glitter of the
  firmament—on her way home.

                                       (*CTS*, 2918)

Pao Jung's song rejoices in the beauty of the ceremony of conferral of divine knowledge. Its simple plot of arrival, exchange, and departure of the goddess follows the scheme familiar from poems on King Mu and Emperor Wu. But Pao's poem contains one crucial difference: the seeker's pursuit of immortality meets with success instead of failure. In this, it resembles poetic treatments of the Yellow Thearch.

Perhaps Mao Ying's very success made his tale less interesting to poets than the moving failures of King Mu and Emperor Wu. Writers may also have felt that the Shang ch'ing texts could not be improved upon. The central events of Mao Ying's victory are esoteric and not subject to words, making them less amenable to poetry than the richly documented stories of royal defeat. Although the story of Mao Ying and the goddess only rarely makes a direct appearance in poetry, writers found inspiration in his example for their treatments of contemporary men and women who were specially blessed by the presence of the Queen Mother in their lives. Poems devoted to them appear in the next two chapters.

❖ *Coming to Her Court to Receive the Way: Men of the T'ang*

Roughly a thousand years, or, in the Queen Mother's time, another peach cycle, after the goddess left the Han palace, the T'ang dynasty ruled China. During these centuries poets wrote about the Queen Mother as never before. They described her visits to great men of the past but particularly savored her appearances to their contemporaries. This chapter is devoted to T'ang epiphanies: the goddess's appearance to blessed men in the poetic present. T'ang writers continued to connect the goddess with immortality and death, love and separation, her permanent province, but the special immediacy of poems about contemporary people strikes the modern reader as it must have struck the medieval audience.

Tu Kuang-t'ing, concluding his hagiographical account of the Queen Mother of the West, explains why successful adepts continue to meet the goddess even in his own day. Summarizing her duties and significance, Tu remarks in closing:

The Grand Realized Metal Mother is master and maker of the myriad classes of beings, teacher and leader of the whole flock of realized ones and paragons. Her position is honored and lofty; she holds central control of registration of both the secluded and the revealed. Now, in the matter of approaching the grotto mystery, one must come in person to her court to receive the Way. And as for thanking the spontaneous: effulgent ones attend her and then climb to transcendence. Therefore transmissions of grotto mysteries and the spontaneous are said to be from Master Metal Mother. This is in fact the Queen Mother. In affairs of which evidence is given in the mysterious scriptures, her traces are certainly numerous. This is not a complete account. (*CMYC*, 24164)

Tu calls the goddess master and creator of all living beings, teacher and registrar of immortals, and source of the revealed scriptures of Shang ch'ing Taoism. The grotto mysteries are the essential teachings contained in the sacred texts of the Shang ch'ing lineage, hidden in the grotto-heavens and later revealed to humans to become part of the Taoist canon. Hardly an event recorded in the holy texts is without the Queen Mother's influence. Whoever receives the Way and ascends to transcendence does so through her. Tu Kuang-t'ing implies that readers might meet the goddess themselves by faithfully following Taoist precepts. T'ang poets devoted many works to men and women who encountered the Queen Mother in their own day. Tu's hagiography and the T'ang poems reflect the desire of medieval men to find a divine teacher who will show them the meaning of life, leading them to experience perfect fulfillment and to escape ignorance, suffering, and death.

Medieval Men

T'ang poems praising Taoist masters, adepts, and heroes by relating their meetings with the Queen Mother recall tales of the goddess's encounters with the two great rulers of old: King Mu and Emperor Wu. Her association with immortality and divine communication are continuing themes, but the poems glorifying medieval men are more optimistic and the results of the encounter more often successful. In outcome, these poems hark back to victories in the history of humankind's quest for contact with deities and for eternal life: tales of the Yellow Thearch, Shun, Lao-tzu, legendary transcendents, and Lord Mao. Here the Queen Mother figures as teacher, priestess, and high official of the celestial imperium. She may appear in meditative visions or in response to correctly performed ritual. The adept's power to summon her in person verifies his status and spiritual advancement.

Taoist Masters

One important group of poems involving the Queen Mother of the West consists of eulogies addressed to Taoist masters. In such poems, the narrator describes his own journey, celebrates the master's practice and attainments, and requests instruction. The great man's teachings and texts derive from the Queen Mother, and her arrival in vision or corporeal form confirms his lineage and possession of the Tao.

Lu Ching's (7th century) "Wandering at the Clear Capital Belvedere, I Seek out Taoist Master Shen and Obtain Transcendent Graphs" describes the author's visit to a Taoist alchemist who possesses texts of the highest order. Lu searches out Shen's temple to pursue the Queen Mother's secret writings:

> Intending to shove open the Inner Door of Numinous Charms,
> Slowly pacing, I enter the Clear Capital.
> A master of outer space from Blue Gorge,
> His mind fixed on the mysterious, follows the Pivot of the Way.
> From ten-bearded erianthus grass, he produces drug hampers;
> Seven flames issue forth from his cinnabar stove.
> In clear green book wrappers—the Paulownia Lord's registers;
> In vermilion writing—the Queen Mother's talismans.
> Palace pagoda trees scatter their green seed pods;
> Sun hibiscus lets fall its blue calyx buttons.
> Straightening their quills—Thunder Gate cranes;
> Coming in flight—wild ducks from Leaf County.
> Skimming the wind, they may be reined and kept under control,
> But what would it serve to force them down to the central
>   region?
> I've just overtaken my feather-transformed companion;
> Having followed him here, I obtain a Mysterious Pearl of the
>   Way.
>
> (*CTS*, 291)

Master Shen was Shen Shu-an, a contemporary of Lu Ching who lived in seclusion in the Clear Capital Belvedere, a temple named after the Supreme Clear Realm residence of a lofty Taoist deity known as the Heavenly Thearch. The temple was located by the scenic Blue Gorge near Nanjing, a Shang ch'ing center. Behind the closed door of his meditation cell, he practiced astral travel to the handle of the Big Dipper ("Pivot of the Way"). Outside he tends his garden of medicinal herbs. Master Shen's studies attract both the Paulownia Lord, a patron saint of elixir drugs, and the Queen Mother. Lu compares the recluse to a crane or wild duck, symbols of the freed soul, and rejoices in receiving the mysterious pearl of his teachings.

Going to see the Queen Mother on her cosmic mountain signifies going to study with her. Paying respects to her consort, sometimes called the Lord of the Eastern Sea, and her servants, the Lads of the Western Mountains, can mean a return to transcendent studies. In "Liu the Prior-Born Dwells in Seclusion," Ch'u Kuang-hsi welcomes Master Liu back to his temple in the capital after military service. The poem's preface explains that "Liu the Prior-Born, after passing the examination, dwelt as a Taoist Master in the Palace of the Realm of Supreme Clarity. Later he followed the military and then returned home."

> After a high ranking, he returned home to the Way,
> Dwelling thereafter in the Jade Floriate Palace.
> Footloose and fancy-free, among humans in this world,
> He was no different from the Worthy of Floating Hill.
> But how could he join his feathers in sweet sleep?
> He went out the gate and suddenly joined the military.
> Just about to wander to Mount K'un-lun,
> He tended to consider even the K'un-t'ung mountains small.
> "Approach or retreat in any case depends on oneself."
> Now he has come back to the center of Ch'ang an,
> Burned incense to the Lord of the Eastern Sea,
> Then attended the throne of the Lads of the Western Mountains.
> Skilled at proceeding without leaving traces of his wheeltracks,
> How then could I fathom him?
> I only see that his divine appearance is sequestered;
> He centers his heart as if on the barren void.
> I have an appointment with him, whose age is comparable to
>   that of heaven,
> Whose realized virtue is vast enough to assist the thearch.
>   (CTS, 781)

Master Liu, called "prior-born" or elder by the narrator as a mark of respect, is compared in one line to an ancient transcendent known as the Worthy of Floating Hill, who hailed from the immortal isles in the eastern sea, and is then admired in another line for his skill in warfare. He embodies the joining of military and religious wisdom that characterized Han dynasty Taoism of the Huang-Lao cult. The Queen Mother blesses this combination in the person of Liu, as she did in the Yellow Thearch. After passing the imperial exam to become a *chin shih* (advanced scholar), he entered a monastery rather than take bureaucratic office. Unable to sleep when the nation was in danger, he joined the army, where his Taoist arts brought him both detachment and success.

Finally Liu the Prior-Born purifies himself with incense, returns to his practice, and becomes unfathomable. The Taoist master meditates on the void, as contemporary Buddhists did on emptiness or *śunyata*, another case of the mutual approximation of the two rival faiths that appealed most to T'ang literati. The poem closes with the narrator's conventional difficulty in finding one so untraceable and with conventional praise of Liu as one worthy to serve the state. The implication, which would not be out of place in our own day, is that he has taken up religious life not as a means of escaping his own failure to compete in the real world but as a free choice.

The goddess also taught a famous T'ang recluse to whom a number of poets wrote. They marveled at his apparent youth in old age, attributing it to religious practice. In "Given to Transcendent Grandpa Mao," Yang Ssu-fu (fl. 795) calls him a jade squire, one of the goddess's boy attendants. Yang considers Mao an exiled transcendent, worthy companion of renowned immortals of old. Mao's teachings come directly from the goddess, whose personal visit practically guarantees the adept's success in creating an immortal embryo. Yang wishes to become Grandpa Mao's disciple, making his request in the manner prescribed by Taoist etiquette. In a conclusion reminiscent of the story of King Mu, Yang asks for immortality in the form of recipes of well-known mineral elixirs, such as the nine-times-recycled and *lang kan*, each of which is the subject of numerous canonical works, presenting in return ceremonial gifts. Giving gifts to a master in exchange for teaching is part both of stories of the Queen Mother's encounters with human aspirants and of Taoist ceremonial usage.

> A jade squire from above the heavens, astride a white crane:
> Beside his elbow a metal pot full of wondrous drugs.
> Temporarily wandering, he descends to our world's boundaries,
>   but scorns the five feudal marklords.
> Repeatedly he's looked at old city walls and fortifications from
>   those days.
> Wearing luxuriant and soft feathered garments, light like snow,
> Comes a pair of lads from above the clouds, grasping scarlet
>   tallies.

The Queen Mother herself sewed a bag of multicolored damask
    with a purple ground,
Ordering Mao to put it in his breast and treasure its secret
    instructions.
Ling-wei and Tzu-chin will both always be his peers and
    comrades,
At the Eastern Marchmount, together they seek out the Grand
    Realized Woman.
Collecting oddities, they make continuous rhymes to harmonize
    with "Sunny Spring":
Their literary compositions and emblems are not about
    humankind's chatter.
Drugs completed, he spontaneously makes firm his golden
    bones;
Equal to heaven and earth—Ah!—his body will not decay.
Inside the sun and moon palaces: that's right where his
    household is.
Below he inspects Mount K'un-lun: how it protrudes!
For boyish demeanor and jade appearance—who can compare to
    him now?
His dusky hair and green-glinting whiskers shine abundantly.
All morning generals and prime ministers are disciples at his
    gate,
All completely willing to cast away the world's dust and dregs
    to follow this master.
He must have a surplus of the nine-times-recycled and *lang kan*
    elixirs;
I wish to present a knife and a jade tablet in order to receive long
    life.
                          (CTS, 2805)

As the case of Grandpa Mao demonstrates, a visit from the goddess confirms an adept's achievement. Tu Fu presented the poem "Song of the Altar of the Mysterious Capital" to an old friend he calls the Primal Untrammeled Person. This recluse lives in a thatched hut alongside the Altar of the Mysterious Capital, a holy place located in Tzu wu Valley near the capital city of Ch'ang an. The altar named after the Queen Mother's capital was dedicated to high gods of Shang ch'ing Taoism. The Primal Untrammeled Person wears a magic sword and decocts a potent elixir, the same one mentioned in Yang's poem to Grandpa Mao. From his nearly inaccessible retreat, he cares for the sacred shrine. In recognition of his virtue, the Queen Mother makes an appearance, preceded by a hawk cuckoo's mournful cry, the voice of the King of Ch'u wailing for the goddess.

> A person from the old days formerly secluded himself at Eastern Meng Peak;
> Already hanging at his belt was a sword inscribed "Hold a phosphor in your mouth," with the image of a grizzled essential dragon.
> This person from the old days lives today in the Tzu wu Valley;
> Alone on Sandy Cliff, he has tied together a thatched dwelling.
> Before his dwelling: the Altar of the Mysterious Capital from grand antiquity,
> The blue stone sky so vast, constant wind bitter cold.
> A hawk cuckoo cries out at night; mountain bamboo splits open.
> The Queen Mother descends in broad daylight, cloud standards swirling.
> She recognizes the perfection in milord's plans will be of long duration.
> Mushroom plants and *lang kan* elixir must be growing daily.
> Iron locks reach so high, they can't be climbed to the top;
> Devoting all your life to a sacred spot—how austere and yet buoyant!
>
> (CTS, 1220)

The Queen Mother's appearance in visions confirms the correctness of a holy man's efforts. Yüan Chieh's (719–72) "Celebrating Grandpa Longevity" asks the old man how he has nourished his vital essences. Grandpa Longevity replies he simply imitated nature:

> I avail myself of this chance to ask Grandpa Increased Longevity:
> "With what recipes did you spontaneously perfect and nurture yourself?"
> He says only, "I have followed that which is so;
> To make my passions perish, I imitated grass and trees.
> When I began to know the arts of this world,
> With labor and bitter toil, I transformed gold and jade.
> I did not see how to fulfill what I sought,
> And heard in vain about regulating indulgences and desires.
> Then in the harmony of the Realms of Clarity I visualized the Queen Mother,
> Becoming submerged and diffused, without turmoil or blackening."

For whoever really is fond of extending life,
These words are worth wearing as a belt ornament.

(*CTS*, 1449)

Grandpa Longevity's instructions praise Taoist inner alchemy and visualization; he criticizes overreliance on expensive and obscure elixir drugs. His words support Shang ch'ing tenets. While practicing erroneous techniques and getting nowhere, he receives a merciful vision of the goddess during meditation that turns him around and confirms the truth of his words. From that point on, he remains submerged in the Tao, which he compares to the laws of nature, unsullied by the turmoil of the world.

In "Composed in Response to 'Sending Taoist Master Liu off to Wander on Heavenly Platform Mountain,'" Po Chü-i varies the usual form of the poem in praise of a Taoist master. Master Liu sets off to dwell in seclusion on Heavenly Platform Mountain (T'ien t'ai shan), a famous Buddhist pilgrimage center. Heavenly Platform was also a Taoist holy mountain, connected with Shang ch'ing Taoism since the fifth century at the latest. Tu Kuang-t'ing lived and studied there in the late ninth century.

Po describes Master Liu's trip in terms of the Taoist ritual known as pacing the void, a symbolic representation of the adept's ascent to transcendence. The new immortal takes his commission from the Honored Illustrious One, one of the loftiest Taoist divinities and teacher of the Queen Mother. Liu dresses in ceremonial garb and registers formally with the goddess and her consort. Then in the company of realized ones, he travels to the peak of K'un-lun called Lofty Whirlwind, home of the Queen Mother, to the portals of heaven known as the Golden Watchtowers, and to the constellation we call the Milky Way and the Chinese call the Silver River.

Throughout his travels, Master Liu never leaves his meditations. He continues his Taoist physical practices, ingesting elixirs formed of essences of the sun and moon as well as meteorological elements and thereby becomes one of the greater transcendents who see through the dreams and illusions of this world. In "Composed in Response to 'Sending Taoist Master Liu off to Wander on Heavenly Platform Mountain,'" Po Chü-i predicts that Liu will dominate the mountain center of the foreign religion with his native Chinese religious teachings.

I hear you've dreamed of wandering in transcendence,
Lightly lifting off and leaping over worldly miasmas.
Grasping the Honored Illustrious One's tallies,
Granting you supreme command over the guard: an army of
    envoys and armed men.
Their numinous standards—with star and moon images;
Your celestial garments—with dragon and phoenix figures.
To belt your clothes: cross-tied sash registers;
You intone and sing from a stamen-beaded text.
At the Lofty Whirlwind Palace, in the realms of the subtle and
    indistinct,
Harmonious music, thinly dispersed, is heard.
You purify your heart, to pay a formal visit to the Western
    Mother;
Saluting with the *anjali mudra*, you go to the court of the Eastern
    Lord.
Mist and smoke form Tzu-chin's apron;
Auroral clouds glisten on Ma Ku's petticoat.
Suddenly separating from your realized companions,
Sadly you gaze far away, following the returning clouds.
Human life is like a great dream:
Dreaming and waking—who can distinguish between them?
How much more so this dream within a dream?
How remote! What could be adequate to express it?
You seem to be at the summit of the Golden Watchtowers;
You might suppose yourself to be at the headwaters of the Silver
    River.
But in fact you have not yet emerged from the triple world,
And still must be residing within the five *skandhas*.
Drinking and gulping down essences of sun and moon,
Eating and chewing up fragrances of mist and fog.
There still remains here the scent and flavor of form,
Of that by which the six *gata* are scented.
Among transcendents, there are the greater transcendents;
They emerge ahead of the flock of dreams and illusions.
Their compassion radiates as a single illuminating candle;
Along with the impenetrable dharma, they are mutually
    generative vapors of heaven and earth.
If one does not recognize the evening of myriad teeth [old age],
He will not see the twilight of the three radiances.
If one's single nature is spontaneously clear and distinct,
The myriad karmic causes will accordingly fade out.

The Sea of Bitterness cannot bear him away;
The kalpa fire cannot consume him.
This place, in fact, belongs to the Indian teaching,
Where the prior-born will suspend the classics and the mounds.

(CTS, 2652)

Po Chü-i's poem praising a Taoist master in residence on a Buddhist holy mountain uses a striking number of Buddhist terms derived from Sanskrit. All these terms were current in the vocabulary of the educated person of the T'ang, but their concentration here is suggestive: the poet appropriates the language of the foreign religion as he imagines Master Liu conquering its stronghold. The *anjali mudra* is a humble gesture of greeting, made by joining the hands in front of the chest as if in prayer. The gesture, which originated in India, typifies Buddhist salutations. Po also uses the Sanskrit word *skandha* (heaps, bundles), a Buddhist expression for the five human attributes that give us the illusion of existing: form, perception, consciousness, action, and knowledge. Other Buddhist terms he mentions include the six *gata*, or paths of potential rebirth (deity, giant, human, animal, hungry ghost, and soul in hell); *dharma*, or true teachings of the Buddha; *karmic causes*, which create the bonds that keep us tied to this world of suffering; and *kalpa* or world age. Perhaps the Buddhist ideal of the compassionate bodhisattva lies behind Po's emphasis on mercy and teaching. Buddhist ideas and terminology were part of the common language of medieval religious thought. They permeated the works of Taoist authors during the T'ang dynasty, as Taoist notions colored Chinese Buddhist writing. Tu Kuang-t'ing, in his works including the hagiographical account of the Queen Mother, uses numerous words of Buddhist origin, as Po Chü-i does in this poem for Taoist Master Liu.

Competition between Buddhism and Taoism runs through the poem as it did through religious communities on Heavenly Terrace Mountain and through T'ang intellectual life as a whole. Po settles the debate in the last couplet in favor of Taoism. In his thought and practice, Master Liu unifies the two teachings by absorbing Buddhist elements into his Taoist system. Suspending "the classics and the mounds" provides the final coup for the native religion: the phrase refers to records of the Five Thearchs and Three Illustrious

Ones of Taoism. On the mountain renowned for its Buddhist establishments, Po implies, the Taoist Master Liu will prevail. The modern reader might also note that mutual influence and competition between Buddhism and Taoism prevails today in Chinese practice.[1]

In Po Chü-i's farewell poem, visiting the Queen Mother's court means beginning the actual ascent to transcendence: the adept has been formally accepted as a pupil of the goddess. When Wang Wei (701–61) wrote a poem of praise, "Given to Li Ch'i," a trip to the goddess's holy mountain likewise initiates the adept's flight to immortality. (Li Ch'i wrote the "Song of the Queen Mother" translated in Chapter 4.) According to Wang Wei, Li is also a feathered transcendent of long-standing, an alchemist and space traveler so eminent that the Queen Mother eagerly awaits him when he sets off on his celestial wandering:

> I hear milord makes tidbits of granulated cinnabar;
> You have extremely good countenance and complexion.
> I don't know how long ago
> You produced feathered wings.
> The Queen Mother, shaded by floriate mushrooms,
> Looks for you from afar by Mount K'un-lun's side.
> Patterned hornless baby dragons, followed by red leopards,
> Go eight thousand *li* in just a single breath.
> How sad! The people of this generation
> Find pleasant this stinking and putrescent food.
>   (*CTS*, 682)

Heroic Laymen

Poets might lend the Queen Mother's charisma to men of splendid although secular accomplishments. Their works resemble poems in praise of Taoist masters. In verses celebrating heroes of the T'ang conquest of the west, the Queen Mother stands for the distant and romantic occident. Parallels to the western victories of Han Wu-ti and the conquering journeys of King Mu of the Chou abound in these works. For example, in "After He Smashed Outlaws at the Yellow River's Source, I Gave This to General Yüan," Fa Chen (fl. 785) praises the general for suppressing a rebellion of Tibetan tribes at the source of the Yellow River (which traditional Chinese geographers located at Mount K'un-lun). The general and his conquering armies traveled so far west, reaching Split-leaf Land (located in former Soviet Central Asia), that he could have called on the goddess:

> White feathers at three thousand post stations,
> Neighing and whinnying—a ten thousand *li* line.
> Going out through the barrier pass, you deepened the Han
>   ramparts;
> Guided by the moon, you smashed barbarian encampments.
> Creepers and grasses were the same color as the Yellow River
>   plains,
> But mournful nomad flutes had the sound of Split-Leaf Land.
> On the point of going to court at the Queen Mother's basilica,
> By the forward road, you planted your lofty standards.
>   (*CTS*, 4708)

Tu Fu flatters his military friends with similar conceits. One poem compares General Wang to King Mu of the Chou dynasty: both left "hoofprints of entering horses" at Mount K'un-lun when they undertook pacification campaigns to the far west (*CTS*, 1282). Another, written in 756 near the end of the An Lu-shan rebellion, celebrates the western campaign of a General Wei. The general deploys his soldiers so far to the west that they see the goddess's dwelling place: "At the K'un-lun moon grottoes, the eastern side is steep cliffs" (*CTS*, 1287). Here Mount K'un-lun represents the ultimate west; the general who reaches the mythical mountains joins the ranks of heroes who have attained immortality in reputation if not in bodily form.

The Queen Mother of the West appears in poetry on Taoist masters and adepts to lead them along the path of transcendence or to certify their holiness. Laymen of superior achievements borrow her blessing from the adepts; poems on exploits of conquering generals use her distant paradise as an emblem of the exotic occident.

Numinous Objects

T'ang poets introduce the name of the Queen Mother to certify the transcendence of objects as well as of their owners. Some focus on bestowals by the goddess to charismatic people; others emphasize the objects themselves. These include means of transcendence such as elixirs, vehicles, and musical instruments. Medieval encyclopedias abound with tales of miraculously effective food and drink, blessed by the goddess. Such tales appealed particularly to poets.

Some time after 756 Li Po sent a farewell gift of uncut gemstones to his friend Ts'ui Huan. Ts'ui had left the capital to serve as Emissary Who Manifests the Thearch's Soothing for the Chiang nan region, a sort of viceroy for the south. He had taken up office at Tan yang near Nanjing, an important southern center of Shang ch'ing Taoism. Li Po accompanied his present with a poem claiming that the gems, left by a visitor from the Queen Mother's cosmic mountain, were her own magically efficacious food. Li admonishes his friend to value the uncouth southerners in his charge just as he values the uncut jade, discerning true worth beneath a rough exterior. He compares the jade to a famous stone of feudal times, unappreciated until Pien Ho (8th c. b.c.) recognized its value. The stone later became a prize sought by various warring states, providing the occasion for Lin Hsiang-ju's (3rd c. b.c.) demonstration of wise diplomacy in sensitive negotiations. Li Po urges his friend to accept the gift so that they may become divine transcendents together.

> A stranger came from Mount K'un-lun;
> He left me a pair of uncut jade gems.
> He said they were the leftover food of one who had obtained the
>   Tao of old: the Queen Mother of the West;
> If one eats it, he can skim the great void.
> If you cherish these, you may be called exceptional in both past
>   and present;
> If you seek out and recognize the people of the Yangtze and
>   Huai River region, they are the same as this type of stone.
> Now these present stones, even in the hand of Pien Ho,
> Might seem really burned out and dried up.
> Even if you recognized them clearly, what good would that do
>   you?
> But I have respectfully heard that among scholars there was a
>   certain Hsiang-ju,
> Who first returned from the capital city of Hao,
> Then wanted to go back to the capital city of Hao.
> If I could ascend the Prince of Ch'in's basilica,
> When in returning radiance could we gaze at each other even once?
> I want to send milord this boon to protect milord's blessing of
>   years.

Milord should grasp and take it; don't cast it aside or reject it.
Don't cast it aside, but take it,
And together with you, Milord, I'll become a divine
transcendent.   (*CTS*, 1037)

A T'ang dynasty poet wanting to praise a fine object might credit it with power to bestow immortality, associating it with the Queen Mother of the West. Ku K'uang does so in "Thanking Lord Wang Chung-chien for a Gift of Zither and Crane." Symbols of reflective life cherished by literati, the zither, comparable to legendary instruments of old, produces divine music, and the crane, a symbol of longevity, is the preferred vehicle of the immortals. The gifts also recall one Southern Ch'i (479–502) emperor's bestowal of a deertail whisk and zither on Ku Huan, a learned scholar whose canonical studies of Shang ch'ing texts were models for Tu Kuang-t'ing. They inspire Ku K'uang's imagination; he sees himself soaring through space to visit the Queen Mother in her Jade Capital on Mount K'un-lun, enjoying the company of great immortals of old:

This zither is in a class with Charred Tail;
This crane is actually womb-born.
Quickly tapping, how it goes back and forth!
Their inner structures responding, created phenomena
     spontaneously fall in line.
Standing alone, above river and sea,
With a single strum, heaven and earth become purified.
Vermilion strings move the turquoise flowers;
White feathers swirl up to the Jade Capital.
In response, I visualize Hsien-men's palanquin;
Subtly, my four limbs become light.
Tzu Ch'iao soars over the forests of Teng,
As the Queen Mother wanders at her tiered city walls.
Suddenly it seems I'm starting on numinous offices,
As simurgh and phoenix cry out in harmony with them.
How can I climb from a jade girl's bed,
And go off to eat blossoms of *lang kan* elixir?
                                    (*CTS*, 1571)

Thanks to his friend's numinous gifts, Ku K'uang attains all the goals of the Shang ch'ing adept. He wanders through space in the company of famous transcendents, achieves his own vision of the Queen Mother, receives transcendent office, shares a jade girl's bed, and ingests the elixir of immortality.

Realms of Clarity

The Taoist adept's project is to achieve immortality and celestial office. This goal toward which a lifetime of effort is directed may be prefigured in meditative visits to the realms of clarity. At the end of his earthly life, the adept makes a final ascent. The highest immortals ascend to heaven in broad daylight, the next class achieve "liberation by means of the corpse," a subterfuge whereby they appear to die and receive burial but in fact secretly rise to heaven, leaving behind such traces as a pair of shoes or a sword.

The Queen Mother, as Tu Kuang-t'ing takes pains to assert, governs entrance to the highest heavens of Shang ch'ing Taoism: Supreme Clarity, Jade Clarity, and Grand Clarity. Several T'ang poems describe the adept's meditative ascent to heaven. The ascent theme may appear independently or, as we have seen, in works on other subjects such as the Queen Mother's home, companions, or encounters with legendary kings and adepts.

Poems on the actual ascent often bear titles which reveal their content: "Lines on the Ascent to Transcendence," "Cantos on Pacing the Void," "Wandering in Transcendence," or "Lines on the Realms of Clarity." Many works with these titles refer to encounters with the Queen Mother; they comprise a subset of poems on the goddess. Several such poems are discussed in Chapter 2 because of their vivid descriptions of the Queen Mother or her realm. Their subject and language owe a great deal to the shamanistic hymns in the *Elegies of Ch'u*. At the same time, T'ang poems on wandering in the realms of clarity draw religious content and descriptive detail from visionary accounts of astral travel in the Shang ch'ing Taoist canon. The narrator's journey may start at a specific location in this world, usually a holy mountain. The cosmic pillar called Mount K'un-lun marks the takeoff point. After taking off, the adept narrates a travelogue of places visited, deities seen, and adventures encountered in paradise. The poem may close with separation from the gods and return to earth.

Ascent to Transcendence

Although all ascent poems belong to a single broad category, narrower groups, defined by separate titles, have special features. Poems entitled "Lines on the Ascent to Transcendence" begin with the adept's physical regimen, by which he attains a state of perfection allowing him to mount a divine vehicle and proceed upward. He leaves the terrestrial realm from Mount K'un-lun, where heaven and earth communicate. In one such poem by Chang Chi, the adept's body grows light:

> My body not submerged,
> My bones not heavy,
> I spur a blue simurgh,
> And harness a white phoenix.
> Pennants and parasols whirling upward, I enter the cool void.
> A celestial wind sighs and soughs; the Starry River moves.
> Turquoise watchtowers jagged and serrated: Amah's household.
> Playful and relaxed beside storied buildings and platforms:
>   congealed red lacquer clouds.
> Five sets of three little transcendents ride dragon chariots.
> Before her audience hall, they grind flowers of the coiling peach
>   tree into mush.
> Turning my head, I look back once more to the summit of
>   P'eng-lai:
> A single dot of thick mountain mist within a deep well.
>   (*CTS*, 217)

The adept lingers, entranced, in the Queen Mother's palace grounds. He partakes of an elixir compounded of her peaches of immortality before flying so high that the cloud-enfolded island of immortality in the Eastern Sea looks like a tiny speck at the bottom of a well.

A poem in the same vein by Ch'u Kuang-hsi describes another's ascent. Ch'u admires Liu Chien or Liu the Sixth, a contemplative dwelling in a Taoist belvedere in Lo yang known as the Jade Floriate Palace, after a celestial palace of the same title. Master Liu starts his journey from one of the three peaks of K'un-lun. His autumnal music attracting the Queen Mother, they play a duet.

A realized person lives at Lofty Whirlwind Peak;
Sometimes he performs the pure *shang* tuning.
Then his listener is in fact the Queen Mother;
"Thrum, thrum"—they harmonize on large and small fretted
   zithers.
He sits facing branches of a thrice-flowering tree,
Goes along following shadows of five-colored clouds.
As heaven extends, K'un-lun grows small;
As his days are prolonged, P'eng-lai sinks deep.
On high he comes from the Jade Floriate Palace;
Below he inspects Shou yang Peak.
Our divine isle-land is pure and still,
About to float and sink spontaneously.
How moving! My lines are so bitter;
"Ah, woe," this little wanderer intones.
At Lu I encounter Master Likeness,
Thinking that I will transform yellow gold.
Rain and snow submerge great mountains,
Who can have a non-returning heart?
Footloose and fancy free, you reside in the Cloudy Han;
Maybe I can come and seek you there.

(CTS, 771)

In his meditations, Liu visualizes elixir plants called thrice-flowering, the name of a tree in the Queen Mother's garden and also a type of palm from India whose leaves were used for inscribing scriptures. Then he travels the heavens. K'un-lun shrinks and the Isles of the Blessed sink as his sight grows cosmic. Above he hails from the celestial capital; beneath he spies Shou yang, highest mountain of the Mang range south of the eastern capital of Lo yang. In his apocalyptic vision, China itself (the "divine isle-land") seems to bob like P'eng-lai and may be approaching the end of a world age when the eastern sea will engulf it.

In contrast, the narrator searches for wisdom but only meets elusive transcendents who, like Master Likeness of old, refuse to share their secrets and flee his presence. His confidence in his own intention to seek enlightenment is shaken. The term "non-returning heart," derived from Buddhism, means a mind set on escaping this world of suffering by understanding the illusions upon which it is based. In the end, inspired by the example of Liu Chien, who seems to dwell high above him in the Milky Way ("Cloudy Han"), the narrator takes courage and resolves to question him. As in poems to other eminent Taoist masters, the narrator praises and hopes to study with his somewhat enigmatic subject.

Mount K'un-lun as the first stage in celestial flight appears in most ascent poems. A poem by Tu Kuang-t'ing's friend Wei Chuang (843?–910) celebrates a holy mountain called Moon Peak in present-day Szechwan province in southwestern China, not far from where Tu lived in his old age. The narrator compares the place to the goddess's home and his climb to a journey to heaven. Wei precedes his work with a preface:

Thirty *li* west of Hsin chou is a mountain called Walled City of the Transcendent People, beneath which is Moon Peak Mountain. Its form is beautiful and prominent: in its center is a mountain gate shaped like a full moon. I accordingly went along and passed beneath it, then composed a poem on the place.

> I urged my chariot past Min and Yüeh;
> The road goes out west of Abundant Yang.
> Transcendent mountains, iridescent kingfisher color like a
>   painting,
> Budding forth, give rise to male and female rainbows.
> The flock of peaks are like attendants and followers,
> Groups of mounds like babes in arms.
> Cliffs and precipices swallow each other and spit each other out;
> Passes and peaks follow and lead one another.
> In the middle is the moon wheel—full,
> White and washed pure, resembling a round jade disk.
> The Jade Illustrious One was addicted to wandering and
>   inspecting;
> Reaching here, his spirits must have become confused.
> Ch'ang Oh, dragging her cape of auroral clouds,
> Pulls me along as we clamber up together.
> Soaring and leaping, we climb to the halfway point of heaven:
> A jade mirror suspended from a flying stepladder.
> At the Turquoise Pond—how imperceptible!
> Simurgh and crane roost within the mist.
> Turning my head back, I look at the world's dust;
> As the dew descends, how piercing the bitter cold!
>   (*CTS*, 4183)

The narrator departs from a southern location he calls by the evocative names of two ancient states. He travels west of the sun, meeting with a vast mountain range, in the center of which he finds the moon gate, a place worthy of a visit from the highest gods. He climbs up to heaven from this spot, accompanied by moon goddess Ch'ang Oh, until he stands with divine birds at the Turquoise Pond and looks down at our dusty world. The flying stepladder is Mount K'un-lun, stretching from earth to heaven like Jacob's ladder in the Hebrew Bible (Gen 28.12). K'un-lun serves the same purpose as the Israelite patriarch's ladder: it marks a place where heaven and earth are not separated. As angels went up and down the ladder in Jacob's vision, so men and deities can climb up and down the goddess's mountain.

Pacing the Void

T'ang dynasty lyrics on pacing the void describe a Shang ch'ing Taoist rite in which the adept makes a symbolic flight through the heavens. Texts in the Taoist canon describe how to do this through meditation and map out the appropriate steps and itineraries. Several poems and series, often entitled "Pacing the Void," explore this subject.[2] The Taoist master Ssu-k'ung T'u receives instruction from the Queen Mother in performing this ritual:

> Amah personally instructing me, I learn to pace the void;
> The Lady of the Three Primordials prolongs her banishment to descend from P'eng hu.
> As her "Cloud Tune" harmonizes with common music, I stop my turquoise-inlaid zither,
> Simurgh and crane fly down, brushing my precious stove.
> (CTS, 3792)

The narrator calls the Queen Mother "Amah" (wetnurse), an intimate term of address claiming her as his surrogate mother as well as his teacher. With a single term of endearment, he asserts the two most important lineage connections with the deity: kin and discipleship. Her companion, the Lady of the Supreme Primordial, sacrifices her safe passage home to fly down from P'eng lai to help teach him. (Both lady and island are called by alternate names.) Ancient music forming a part of the ceremony silences the adept as holy birds, messengers and vehicles of the gods, touch his alchemist's stove.

Poems on pacing the void may emphasize ceremony. One of Ch'en Yü's (fl. 806) two "Cantos on Pacing the Void" traces the T'ang ritual back to Han Wu-ti and his preparations for the Queen Mother's visit:

> The Martial One of the Han purified himself, fasted, and read the tripod texts;
> His grand officials helped him ascend a painted cloud chariot.
> Atop his altar the moon shone brightly; the palace basilicas were closed.
> Lifting his head to gaze at the Starry Dipper, he performed rites to the empty void.
>
> (CTS, 2055)

Like other ascent poems, cantos on pacing the void show Mount K'un-lun as the starting point for celestial navigation. Ch'en Yü's second canto describes that way station:

> Storied buildings and basilicas, layer upon layer—the Amah's household.
> At the summit of the K'un-lun mountains, we stop in pink auroral clouds.
> Mouth organ players and singers come out to see Mu, Son of Heaven;
> Smiling as we pull each other along, we view flowers of snow gem trees.
>
> (CTS, 2055)

Here the goddess and her entourage greet King Mu of the Chou; the adept compares his joyous ascent in the company of divine maidens to the ancient king's westward journey.

Quatrains do not allow lengthy accounts of the adept's itinerary. A longer poem on pacing the void, the fifth in a series of ten by the Taoist priest Wu Yün, provides a fine description of the Metal Mother's Household, where the narrator wanders in the early stages of his dawn space flight:

> As the supporting mulberry tree bears the earliest phosphors,
> Feathered umbrellas skim rosy auroral clouds of dawn.
> Quick as a flash, I make it to the western regions,
> Wandering in delight to the Metal Mother's household.

At the Cyan Ford's deep swelling source,
Burningly brilliant—unfolding lotus blossoms.
Sparkling and flashing: blue-gem palaces.
Excellent and tasty: arrayed jade flowers.
Realized breaths fill the Scarlet Archives to overflowing;
Naturally I concentrate on having no heterodox thoughts.
I look down and pity the bureaucrats within the districts:
Bewitched and turbid—well might one sigh!
(*CTS*, 4944)

Wandering in Transcendence

Poems called "Wandering in Transcendence" cover a wide range of celestial adventures. Wu Yün describes a solar circuit that begins with a visit to the Queen Mother of the West in the tenth of his twenty-four poems with that title.

Then I visited Metal Mother,
My feathered canopies passing over the South Pole.
I subsequently entered Plain White Middle Heaven,
Stopping my wheels beside the Grand Meng.
Semblance flowers brushed flowing reflections,
Not allowing the white sun to be concealed.
Overturning daylight, once again we have reached noon;
In all six directions there is no stygean color.
Transformations of the Way: following and responding, one
transcends.
This inner structure—who can fathom it?
(*CTS*, 4941)

After his courtesy call to the goddess, the adept follows the sun's path: going first to the south pole, then to the apex of the heavens as viewed from earth, and finally to Grand Meng, the farthest point on the sun's westward journey. Semblance trees, sometimes called *fu-sang* trees, stand at the far east and west for the sun to ascend and descend. Racing the sun and winning, the adept sees no more dark colors from the underworld. He concludes in awe of the miraculous changes of the Way: he believes he can ascend to transcendence by following and responding, even if he does not understand it.

Poems on celestial wandering might reveal intimate glimpses of the immortals: glances stolen by the adept as he roams. The tran-

scendents lead charmed, pleasure-filled lives under the supervision
of the Queen Mother of the West, "on top of the K'un-lun Mountains, beneath the peach blossoms" (CTS, 3833). Their activities
reflect the highest happiness a T'ang poet could imagine: lives of
favored courtiers at the imperial palace. Their days given over to
music, feasting, and conversation, some may even enjoy dallying
with mortals. The Taoist Hsü Hsüan manages a secret tryst with a
transcendent called Little Jade. In a poem he calls "Wandering in a
Dream," Hsü brags:

> A lovely person from the southern nations called Little Jade:
> Lotus flowers for her pair of cheeks, distant mountains for
>   eyebrows.
> She's made a pact with her transcendent lover to remember each
>   other a long time.
> How could Amah suspect? She won't find out.
> We cross clouds in a dream, returning again in a flash,
> Holding hands in the dark: suddenly I suspect it's growing late.
> Following our thoughts after parting, beneath closed windows,
> She manages to weave a "returning pattern": how many poems?
>
> (CTS, 4488)

This love affair results inevitably in separation; afterward Little Jade
weaves into her fabric a poem that can be read in any direction. The
image of a solitary woman weaving is ancient, poignant, and evocative in Chinese poetry. The Queen Mother here is a duped duenna,
not the omniscient ruler of the immortals. Such poems humanize
and to a degree trivialize the goddess, making her share the fate that
had already befallen other ancient goddesses and offering a foretaste
of what happens to her in later eras.

Realm of Supreme Clarity

The same interest in personal details and divine gossip frequently
appears in poetic vignettes of the Taoist heavens. Chang Chi's
"Canto on the Realm of Supreme Clarity" complains about parking
problems of the immortals. Chang tells of a jade girl from the Purple
Yang Palace, home of the highest male deities, who offers a mineral
elixir to the Queen Mother. Commanded to take it to Han Wu-ti,
bad weather prevents her landing. In the end, people who have been

looking expectantly to the Isles of the Blessed are consoled by a glimpse of blossoms in their own garden—a sign of the goddess's passage.

> A woman from the Purple Yang Palace offered up granulated
>   cinnabar;
> The Queen Mother ordered her to go by the Han Thearch's
>   household.
> But the spring wind won't let her transcendent rig stop;
> Still facing P'eng lai, we see apricot flowers.
>
> (*CTS*, 1461)

Li Chiu-ling, in the second of five "Lyrics on the Realm of Supreme Clarity" (see Chapter 2), describes the Queen Mother's wedding feast. Such poems, belying their reverent titles, sound like accounts of lifestyles of the rich and famous in the modern popular press. They express the same wish for familiarity with cultural ideals and idols that we see today in mass market magazines, the same prurient interest, and the same desire to believe that those at the top suffer too. According to the hagiographer, everything is perfect in the realm of the immortals and we should all try to go there. According to the poets, there can be trouble in paradise, and the human world has its own bittersweet charm.

Generally, poems on ascending to transcendence and traveling in the realms of clarity describe the beauties of heaven and joyful lives of its inhabitants. The adept gains access to this charmed world through appropriate Taoist practices and rituals. Tu Kuang-t'ing and T'ang poets reveal non-esoteric information about pacing the void and the delights awaiting a successful adept in the heavens. They make the Taoist project very attractive. In general the poets are prepared to treat the subject much more playfully and to display more curiosity than the hagiographer, but they share an idea of the Queen Mother's role in ascents to transcendence. She figures in both poetry and sacred biography as the source of techniques for gaining entrance to paradise, guardian of the gates, and registrar of transcendents. She also governs all women in the Tao, those on the path in this world and those who have already attained transcendence, as we shall see in the next chapter.

6

❖❖ *Her Dependents:*
Women of the T'ang

The Queen Mother of the West ruled immortal women. In Tu Kuang-t'ing's *Records of the Assembled Transcendents of the Fortified Walled City*, the Queen Mother appears first as founder of the entire religious lineage. Tu's introduction states that "women transcendents take Metal Mother as most honored" (*YCCHL*, 30324).

As embodiment of ultimate yin, highest goddess, and ruler of female transcendents, the Queen Mother had a special relationship with all women. The opening section of Tu Kuang-t'ing's hagiography lists her most important functions: "In heaven, beneath heaven, in the three worlds, and in the ten directions, all women who ascend to transcendence and attain the Way are her dependents" (*CMYC*, 24158). She cares for women Taoists everywhere in the universe, both perfected and aspirants. T'ang writers frequently refer to her in poems about Taoist women. In accord with the Shang ch'ing vision expressed by Tu, she appears as teacher, judge, registrar, and guardian of female believers. Her forms reflect Tu's definitions, but we shall see how the poetic sensibility subtly alters the content.

Women's lives in medieval China were circumscribed by the family circle; their work bounded by domestic economy. The roles open to them were defined by the all-powerful Chinese family: filial daughter, dutiful wife, self-sacrificing mother, and chaste widow. A woman's duty to the state and to her family decreed that she must marry and bear children to continue the ancestral line. Yet some Shang ch'ing Taoist writers frowned on marriage as an obstacle to transcendence. The woman was caught in a double bind with no way to win: sacrifice social acceptance or sacrifice salvation. One uncharacteristic passage in Tu's introduction to his collection of lives presents marriage as a possible religious vocation for women. The idea recalls the Christian notion of marriage as a sacrament and calling. Tu calls marriage the "way of one yin and one yang" and considers it one road among many to perfection and immortality (*YCCHL*, 30324). He reaches back to earlier ideas of yin-yang cosmology and of divine marriage as the creative force in the universe. He implies that even married women may find the Way.

The Queen Mother nurtured all women in the Tao, but she favored some. A hierarchy of paths to transcendence for women is clearly visible in Tu Kuang-t'ing's writings. Marriage is low on the list. Foremost among female vocations was that of the Taoist religious, practicing Shang ch'ing austerities such as fasting and meditation. Tu revered nuns residing within Taoist orders and recluses outside any institution.[1]

In the visions of T'ang poets, the Queen Mother nurtured all women in Taoism, but she was the special patron of women outside the normal world of family. She protected Taoist nuns and hermits, as well as female artists and prostitutes. Young women who chose not to marry and old ones who found themselves alone could turn to her. She supported women of all ages and walks of life, rich and poor, respectable and despised, lay and religious, in Taoism. But she saved her special patronage for those without advocates within the family system.[2]

Women in Taoism

Together with the Queen Mother, Tu Kuang-t'ing's *Records of the Assembled Transcendents of the Fortified Walled City* contains biographies of twenty-eight mortal women, half of them people of the T'ang, who became Taoist saints. What difference did it make that they were women? In one sense, it made all the difference in the world; in another, it made no difference at all.

Tu himself implies that gender distinctions are significant when he writes a separate book about lives of women and goddess. He also gives them distinctive titles: "The ultimate position for men who attain the Way is realized lord, and the ultimate position for women who attain the Way is primal ruler" (*YCCHL*, 30324). He implies that women's practices are separate when he tells us one of his subjects acquired immortality through "female transcendence" (*YCCHL*, 30333). But different does not mean of lesser value. Taoist authors have traditionally valued the yin or female side of the yin-yang dichotomy as a worthy and essential part of creation.[3] Tu's introduction to his collection of lives asserts that men's and women's paths are equal but separate: "The positions of male realized ones and female transcendents are regulated. . . . The primal father and mysterious mother go along as equals, complementing each other" (*YCCHL*, 30324). Tu seems to make no distinction between male and female adepts when he states in one biography that a person is raised to posthumous celestial office "according to virtue and talent, unrestricted by distinctions between male and female" (*YCCHL*, 30333). In other words it makes no difference in the end whether the practitioner is male or female.

The idea is that the paths are separate, but the goals of practice are identical and the Tao is one. This agrees with Taoist beliefs that yang and yin are both essential, and the Tao itself, resolving all contradictions, does not distinguish between genders. As Tu states in his introduction: "Although the Way is one, its practice reveals distinctions. Therefore they say that the ways of the transcendents number in the hundreds. We are not limited by a single route; there is not just a single method to grasp" (*YCCHL*, 30324). Tu's biographies describe the religious practice of women masters. They start with mental attitudes of faith and inner resolution. Early acts include good works such as caring for the sick or hungry, burying the dead, restoring shrines, and defending the faith. Good works deepen their compassion and resolve, creating the virtue necessary for women to go on to the next stage of specific Shang ch'ing practice, which includes fasting and sexual abstinence. These preliminaries for study and meditation lead in turn to the desired fruits of the faith: terrestrial and astral travel, visits from deities, the ability to teach and transmit texts, miraculous powers, gifts of the elixir of immortality, and finally the ultimate reward of eternal life and divine office.

The ideal life of the Taoist woman religious, with its pleasures and rewards, is certainly different from the norms of medieval Chinese

society. Parents would not wish it for their daughters. The religious
life was strict and rigorous. And yet, as we shall see, Tu Kuang-
t'ing's version of Shang ch'ing Taoism had tremendous appeal to
some women of the time.

Nuns

Why would a medieval Chinese woman become a Taoist nun? She
might take holy orders for various reasons: as a means of refuge or
retreat at the death of a husband, as a purifying intermission between husbands (two famous cases of this strategy involve the T'ang
empress Wu Ts'e-t'ien and Hsüan tsung's beloved consort Yang
Kuei-fei), as a survival tactic for members of the imperial harem
dismissed during anti-luxury campaigns, as a means of escaping
palace intrigue and danger, as a method of avoiding marriage and
living an independent life outside the family, and as a way of obtaining an education. Some parents sent sick daughters to a convent in
the hopes of curing them; in times of famine, parents might hand
over starving daughters so they might survive. These motives exist
in addition, of course, to genuine religious vocation, which is hard
to measure.

Pursuit of an education was probably a major attraction for
women entering the Taoist convent. This was clearly true in the
parallel case of the Buddhist monastic orders for women.[4] Monastic
life, since it allowed some women to acquire literacy in the interests
of reading the scriptures, provided one way for women to gain an
education and access to information and techniques that led to independence and power. Taoist nuns and high-ranking priestesses
might acquire considerable power and prestige in their own right,
and move among the highest circles of T'ang society.

Most nuns we know about were members of the elite. Some
Taoist nuns belonged to the T'ang royal family. Three poems in the
Complete T'ang Poetry honor Jade Verity, a T'ang princess who was
granddaughter of the emperor whose posthumous title was Kao
tsung (r. 649–84), daughter of Jui tsung (r. 684–90 and 710–12), and
sister of Hsüan tsung (r. 712–56), all devotees of Taoism. Jade Verity
took the vows of a Taoist nun in 711, along with her sister, Princess
Golden Transcendent. Jui tsung built Jade Verity a lavish temple in

the northwest section of Ch'ang an, near the imperial harem. This is one example of the T'ang royal family's committed and generous patronage of Taoism.[5]

Poems to Jade Verity resemble hymns in praise of high-ranking Taoist priestesses. The poems link her with the Queen Mother. In "Song of the Transcendent Person Jade Verity," Li Po describes her residence on Mount Hua, the holy mountain of the west, where there was a T'ang shrine to the goddess. Jade Verity worshiped her there and at her shrine on Mount Sung. As in poems on refined masters, Li stresses her successful Taoist practice. She wanders at will to holy mountains and to heavenly constellations such as the Celestial Drum. Not only does she have divine powers, but her charisma is enough to ensure the Queen Mother's personal welcome, a sign of legitimacy and status.

> The transcendent person Jade Verity
> Oftentimes goes to the peaks of grand Mount Hua.
> At pure dawn she sounds the Celestial Drum;
> A whirlwind arising, she soars upward on paired dragons.
> She plays with lightning, without resting her hands,
> Traverses the clouds, without leaving a trace.
> Whenever she enters the Minor Apartment Peak,
> The Queen Mother will certainly be there to meet her.
> (CTS, 948)

Kao Shih (716–65) wrote a pair of poems on Jade Verity that flatter both nun and imperial clan. For a T'ang dynasty princess to enter a Taoist convent is only natural, according to Kao, for the virtue of the royal Li clan derives from its primal ancestor Lao-tzu, known as the Mysterious Primordial, deified author of *The Way and its Power* and high god of Shang ch'ing Taoism. Common lore held that Jade Verity's brother Hsüan tsung, often referred to as a dragon, who was on the throne when Kao Shih wrote these poems, was really an immortal in disguise. The clan itself will benefit from the princess's merit:

> It's often said the dragon's virtue was originally that of a
>   heavenly transcendent,
> And who claims transcendent people have all studied
>   transcendence?

> I'd rather say, as the Mysterious Primordial pointed out, that the
> days of the Li clan
> Are more numerous than years of the peach planted by the
> Queen Mother.
>
> (CTS, 1213, no. 1)

In Kao's second poem, the princess as guardian of the convent
library refuses to transmit Taoist esoterica to the narrator:

> In transcendent archives of the transcendent palace, there is a
> realized transcendent.
> But celestial treasures and celestial transcendence are secrets that
> must never be revealed.
> Even if we ask about Hsüan the Illustrious One's three hundred
> years,
> How can that compare to a thousand years of the great Way?
>
> (CTS, 1213, no. 2)

We might note as a stylistic aside Kao's repetition in both poems
of the word *hsien,* "transcendent." Repetition was supposed to be
taboo in short poems, but Kao uses it effectively, producing both
emphasis and hypnotic rhythm.

Jade Verity is a transcendent librarian, guarding secrets for initi-
ated eyes only. The Taoist arts of long life she knows would make
the three-hundred-year lifespan of the Yellow Thearch look small
by comparison. The goddess's clients, unlike most women of their
era, might read and collect important texts. In fact, the opportunity
for education and access to the doors literacy could open were one of
the most attractive features of the life of female religious, both
Buddhist and Taoist, in medieval China. The chance to acquire
literacy was attracting women to the convent in Europe at the same
time. In his pair of poems on the princess, Kao Shih calls on the
Queen Mother of the West as an image of longevity for the dynasty,
protection for secret Taoist teachings, and nurture for the female
faithful.

Novices

One group of poems concerning the Queen Mother's associations
with women in Taoism describes how these female masters and
eminent nuns came to be. This group takes as its subject a palace

lady entering religious life. Their typical plot traces the lady's departure from the palace, evidence of her calling, rites and signs of her change in status, and entry into the new community. Such verses often have titles like "Sending off a Person from the Han Palace to Enter the Way." Although the poems concern contemporary women, they are ostensibly set in the Han dynasty; in consequence, details such as names of palaces and people refer to that era. Such poems may depict a novice's feelings as she allows her hair to be shorn, gives up her court finery for monastic garb, and changes her secular name for a religious one. A note of joy sounds in music as she joins her new peers. The joy mingles with resignation and with regrets of those left behind.

Many poets wrote moving poems on this subject of an aristocratic lady taking holy orders. Let Yin Yao-fan's (fl. 813) "A Person from the Palace Enters the Way" introduce them:

> She takes off and discards her palace makeup, her embroidered robes of multi-colored damask,
> And dons a golden crown and plain white garments, cut to suit her.
> Having been given a name, she's recently offered up her resignation to the lord her king's decree;
> Register hanging at her belt, for the first time she consults her master, an aged lady scholar.
> At white daybreak, she passes over the jade staircase;
> In the pure empyrean, she dreams of pacing the Turquoise Pond.
> Her girl companions with their green-glinting topknots repress sorrow at separation;
> Her release from those years of envy over favors and private affairs is now complete.
>   (*CTS*, 2956)

Religious visions and dreams prefigure the novice's vocation. T'ai Shu-lun (732–89), in a poem called "A Person from the Han Palace Enters the Way," writes:

> Wind sighing and soughing in her white hair, she exits the palace gates;
> Feathered clothes and a starry crown—intentions toward the Way fixed in her mind.

> By the Empyrean Han's nine tiers, she parts from phoenix
>   watchtowers;
> In cloudy mountains, where will she go search for the peach tree
>   spring?
> Under the drunken moon of the Turquoise Pond, wearied by
>   dreams of transcendence,
> Her jade carriage riding upon spring, she declines her thearch's
>   mercy.
> Turning her head back, she blows her syrinx to companions
>   above heaven;
> At the Supreme Yang Palace, when flowers fall, with whom will
>   he discuss it?
>
> (CTS, 1647)

An older female companion of the emperor leaves the palace to fulfill a lifelong goal when she retires to the convent. There she puts on her new clothes and readies herself for meditative flights to the Milky Way. The emperor will miss her conversation. Her dreams of the Turquoise Pond foreshadow a visit to Mount K'un-lun, where the nun, at the end of her life on earth, will register with the Queen Mother as a new immortal. Preregistration with the goddess, as special guardian of women in Taoism and as heavenly registrar, may have formed part of the ordination ceremony for nuns during the T'ang dynasty.

A vow before the Queen Mother is an essential step in the process of becoming a Taoist nun and devoting one's life to seeking transcendence. Sometimes the poet merely mentions a visit to the Turquoise Pond, which the reader understands as including a vow. In "Sending off a Person from the Palace to Enter the Way," on the other hand, Hsiang Ssu (fl. 836) reports the contents of a vow in which the novice swears to imitate the jade girl Tung Shuang-ch'eng. In Tu Kuang-t'ing's account of the Queen Mother's visit to Han Wu-ti, Tung is a member of the goddess's entourage.

> "I vow to follow the transcendent woman Tung Shuang-ch'eng
> Before the Queen Mother, to act as her companion and make
>   progress."
> When she first wore the jade crown, it often impeded her
>   greetings;
> Departing the Metal Basilica, she took a separate name.

Picking up a baton, she strikes the lithophone for the new fast
  by the cyan drop-off,
Then approaches the zither given in former days in the
  Shimmering Yang Basilica.
From dawn to dusk, burning incense circles the altar top;
Pacing the void, she still sounds a repressed song.
                              (*CTS*, 3370)

Putting on her awkward new cap, the novice visits the goddess
in her Metal Basilica where she tends to immortal business. Receiving her new name in religion, she sets out to emulate the celestial musician Tung Shuang-ch'eng in earnest, playing ceremonial
sounding stones and a zither that the Queen Mother gave to Han
Wu-ti in his palace when she descended long ago. Incense carries her
prayers to heaven, while the ritual songs linger in her throat as she
begins to walk the heavens in meditation.

Wang Chien, at the end of his poem "Sending off a Person from
the Han Palace to Enter the Way," quotes a slightly different vow:

She leaves off combing her thicket of side-locks and washes off
  her rouge;
On her head she wears a lotus blossom crown as she emerges
  from the Palace of Never-Ending Life.
As other disciples fetch away the verses and repetitives she sang,
Other palace women separate and distribute her dancing cloaks
  and chemises.
Inquiring of the master, she obtains a graph from the classics.
Entering quietude, she still burns incense from inside the palace.
She professes a vow to have an audience at P'eng-lai with the
  Queen Mother,
Then return to the human world to bestow transcendent
  formulas.
                              (*CTS*, 1802)

Where Hsiang Ssu emphasizes the spiritual progress the female
adept intends to make on the path to transcendence, Wang Chien
stresses the new nun's compassionate intention to use her esoteric
knowledge to save all living creatures. The two vows reveal two
paths of female religious devotion in the T'ang: solitary individual
salvation and good works. Both paths require obedience, a virtue

considered as appropriate to female religious in T'ang China as in medieval Europe. The oath of compassion may show the influence on Taoism of the bodhisattva vow of Mahayana Buddhism, in which the Buddhist believer swears to save all living beings before entering nirvana. Shang ch'ing Taoism agrees with Mahayana Buddhism in valuing good works, but such acts mark only the beginning of a path the believer must continue with correct practice. The Shang ch'ing school shares with Theravadan Buddhism the notion that only a few may enter the kingdom of heaven, and only then through difficult practice. In form, the Taoist nuns' oath reveals Buddhist influence, but their goals—immortality and celestial office—are distinctively Taoist.

Fragments of novices' vows appear in poems by Hsiang Ch'i and Wang Chien. The words of one entire vow, deriving perhaps from a T'ang ceremony of entrance to the novitiate, survives separately in a poem entitled "Song" attributed to the female Taoist adept Ch'i Hsiao-yao:

> I look laughingly at the glaucous sea, about to turn to dust,
> As I part from gathered realized ones, before the Queen
>   Mother's flowers.
> It will be a thousand years before I return home, departing to
>   the realm above the heavens,
> Meanwhile I'll treasure and give consideration to people in this
>   world.
>
> (CTS, 4998)

This nun's oath replicates the vow of a "banished transcendent," Taoism's answer to the bodhisattva vow of Buddhism. A banished transcendent is an immortal punished for some heavenly crime by exile to the human world. While in our world, the immortal can earn a shorter term by practicing good works among humans. Extraordinarily talented people, including the T'ang poet Li Po, were sometimes termed banished transcendents by their contemporaries. The new nuns swear to aspire to conduct themselves like transcendents on earth.

Li Shang-yin writes an original variation on the theme of a palace lady taking holy orders. Li's poem responds to a work by his friend, Mr. Han, entitled "Sending off a Person from the Palace to Enter the Way." Instead of proceeding directly through the usual scenario of a poem on the subject, Li describes Han's despondency over losing his lover to her calling.

> A star emissary is dispatched and returns, not of his own accord.
> Paired lads hold it up with both hands: her green and rose-gem chariot.
> Beneath a nine-branched lamp, she'll attend court at the Metal Basilica;
> Amid clouds of the Three Simplicities, she'll serve at the Jade Storied Building.
> Wild and unrestrained, she completes a long-term separation with Phoenix Girl;
> She wants to wander together with the moon goddess, also widowed and alone.
> At that former time it seemed she loved the Worthy Han;
> Buried bones may become ash, but regrets will never cease.
> (CTS, 3260)

It seems that Han, a secretary in the imperial bureaucracy, has been carrying on an affair with one of the emperor's consorts. Li depicts that lady's departure from the royal harem and entry into the convent, apparently on the death of the emperor, as a visit to the Queen Mother. The star messenger comes from the heavens to call home Han's widowed mistress. Blue lads carry off her bejeweled vehicle to a meeting in the goddess's official business hall, the Metal Basilica. In the future she will serve in cosmic rather than imperial courts. She leaves human companions to join the moon goddess, Ch'ang Oh, another intimate of the Queen Mother. Her earthly relationships become a thing of the past. Her lover of former days, a minor bureaucrat who has no power to keep her with him, is inconsolable and mourns her as if she were dead.

Female Taoist Masters

Many poets wrote verses to high-ranking Taoist priestesses. These resemble their counterparts presented to male Taoist masters. Such works describe the subject's practice and accomplishments, much as Tu details them in his individual biographies, concluding with a request for instruction. The Queen Mother arrives to bear witness to the adept's manifest virtue and certify her as a transcendent. Hymns honoring priestesses are distinguished from those

presented to priests by more or less explicit sexual attraction between the narrator and the subject; she casts a spell over him. The
line between sensual and religious allure is fine indeed. The usually
sublimated sexual chemistry suggests the Shang ch'ing ideal of
sacred marriage between goddess and adept.

One category of poems is hymns in praise of female refined
masters, holders of the highest title in a Taoist cloistered community. Refined masters had no administrative tasks, but brought prestige and blessings to a temple through their charisma and practice.

Both Wang Wei and Li Po address poems to a Refined Master
Chiao who lived at Marchmount Sung, holy mountain of the center.[6] In "Given to the Eastern Mountain Refined Master Chiao,"
Wang Wei, addressing her respectfully as his senior, delights in her
great age and abilities. He credits her with the ability to transcend
limitations of space by flying to all the holy mountains of China.
Nor can time oppress her; she has lived continuously since at least
the Warring States period when she witnessed the gift of a ritual
vessel to a feudal lord. She has just made the ritual visit to the Queen
Mother that certifies her status as one of the chosen. Now her
eventual ascent is assured.

> The prior-born, for a thousand years and more,
> Has dwelt in every one of the Five Marchmounts.
> In the far distant past, you recognized the Ch'i feudal lord's tripod;
> You've newly passed by the Queen Mother's hut.
> You cannot take Confucius or Mo-tzu for a master,
> And what's the use of inquiring about Chang Chü?
> When the time is right, your jade tubes bring the phoenix;
> In bronze bowls, then, you can hook fish.
> With body held erect, you talk in the void;
> With brilliant eyes, you write in the middle of the night.
> Spontaneously you possess the art of refining cinnabar;
> From time to time you discuss the beginning of Grand
>   Simplicity.
> You incessantly receive printed summons revealed by high gods;
> Sometimes the gods descend in soft-wheeled chariots.
> Mountains become still, springs exceedingly resonant,
> Pines lofty, their branches revolve and spread out.
> You prop up your chin and inquire of a woodcutting sojourner,
> "What's it like again in the world?"
>   (CTS, 707)

Master Chiao has no further use for the teachings of Confucius or Mo-tzu and has surpassed the accomplishments of even the lofty hermit Chang Chü. Her divine music attracts heavenly birds; she catches fish in elixir basins. She lifts her body to take off; her eyes emit light for holy writing. She refines alchemical elixirs and propounds Taoist wisdom. A familiar of deities who write and even visit in silent carriages, she has become unaccustomed to the ways of the world, prompting her final question to the woodcutter.

Like Wang Wei, Li Po notes Refined Master Chiao's great age and Taoist cultivation. He too wishes to beg her teachings. Li pays her a visit, then honors her with "Given to Refined Master Chiao from Mount Sung," which begins with a preface:

On Sung hill there is a divine person: Chiao the Refined Master. I do not know where she comes from. Also it is said that she lived in Ch'i and Liang times. Her age, by appearance, I might estimate at fifty or sixty. She regularly does embryonic breathing; she has stopped eating the five grains. She lives on Minor Apartment Peak. When she wanders, she proceeds as if flying. In a flash, she suddenly goes a myriad *li*. In the present generation, some people pass it down that she has entered the Eastern Sea and climbed Mount P'eng-lai. In the end, no one can fathom her comings and goings. I enquired about the Way at Minor Apartment Peak, then climbed all thirty-six peaks. I heard a message in the wind, so I sprinkle my quill and make an indirect gift.

> Two apartments skim the blue heavens;
> Thrice-flowering trees contain purple mist.
> In their midst is a stranger from the P'eng-lai seas;
> I think I recognize a resemblance to the transcendent Ma Ku.
> The Way resides within her; our babble never influences her.
> Her traces are eminent, her visions already continuous.
> Occasionally she dines on golden goose stamens;
> Repeatedly she reads aloud from green moss tablets.
> To the far points of the eight directions, she enjoys roaming and
>   relaxation;
> To the Nine Far Marches, she extends her all-inclusive circuit.
> Bringing down the calabash, she ladles out Ying River water;
> Dancing cranes come to Yi River.
> Returning home to the top of the uninhabited mountain,
> Alone, she brushes away autumn auroral clouds and sleeps.
> A star-glory vine moon is suspended as her morning mirror;
> A pine wind seems to cause evening strings to call out.

To hide her brilliance, she dwells in seclusion on Mount Sung;
To rarefy her earth-soul, she perches in a tent of clouds.
Her rainbow chemise, how it flutters and tosses,
As phoenix airs become more and more attenuated!
I wish that you, as Queen Mother of the West,
Would look down upon me as upon Tung-fang Shuo.
Purple writs—if only they could be transmitted,
I'd inscribe them on my bones and vow to practice them.

(CTS, 954)

Li confirms Wang Wei's statement that Refined Master Chiao goes back at least to the Warring States era and possesses the ability to fly from her home on the holy mountain of the center to other sacred spots. The transcendent can travel in time or space to reach any era or location she wishes. Li compares her to a banished transcendent from the Isles of the Blessed in the Eastern Sea and to a Taoist goddess, Ma Ku (Ms. Hemp), associated with that ocean. Having attained the Way, she rests in a state of constant meditation. She fasts or dines on elixir plants, reading numinous texts. She travels to the ends of the universe, now using a ladle of stars to serve holy water from one river, now directing cranes in a sacred dance beside another. She returns to the seclusion of her mountain hut, where the poet finds her. Dressed like a goddess, surrounded with faint heavenly music, she awakens in him a desire to be her disciple. He vows to incise her teachings on his very bones and follow them faithfully if only she will transmit them. In his final lines the narrator likens Refined Master Chiao to the Queen Mother of the West, suggesting the woman who has impressed Li Po so deeply partakes of the qualities of her patron deity.

A number of shorter poems addressed to Refined Masters reveal their intimacy with the Queen Mother. Such verses often have a light, humorous tone. They may address the goddess as "Amah" or "wetnurse": nursemaid or nanny to the priestesses. The informal tone emphasizes their closeness. In such poems, the formality and respect due from human worshipers to a high deity are sacrificed in favor of familiarity. Feelings and terms of address appropriate to members of the same family replace those used in a religious or bureaucratic hierarchy. And the poet often identifies the priestess as the Queen Mother's daughter or girl attendant: a member of her household. As in a medieval Chinese convent or house of prostitution, members' relationships with their superior are governed by the terms of fictive kinship. Showing the power of the family as a model of social order in medieval China, convent, brothel, and goddess's entourage are constructed as artificial families.

Po Chü-i appends a pair of quatrains to a scroll of ten poems on pacing the void he has sent Refined Master Hsiao. One quatrain suggests the priestess's reliance on the Queen Mother: Po submits his poems to that goddess for approval and then borrows her jade girl Tung Shuang-ch'eng to carry his scroll. Here the goddess, both mother and mother superior of female adepts, plays divine censor.

> Flowered paper, turquoise wrapper, pine-black graphs:
> Taking them above heaven—with whom can I open them?
> I tried submitting them to the Queen Mother—it seemed they
>   might bear chanting,
> Now I dispatch Shuang-ch'eng to bring still more.
> (CTS, 2612, no. 2)

A four-line poem by Ch'üan Te-yü (759–818), "Playfully Given to Refined Master Chang," addresses the goddess as Amah, emphasizing the Refined Master's kinship with her. The priestess reveals herself to the narrator as a transcendent when she dances, beckons seductively from a grotto, and offers him a drink of flowing auroral clouds.

> Moon cape whirling and twirling, she plucks apricot flowers;
> Beckoning me to the grotto's mouth, she urges me to drink
>   flowing auroral clouds.
> When I'm half-intoxicated, she suddenly performs the "Cloud
>   Harmony Tune,"
> Leading me to suspect she's a member of the household of
>   Amah from Tortoise Mountain.
> (CTS, 1913)

Liu Yen-shih (742–813) praises Refined Master Ch'eng by comparing her to one of the Queen Mother's jade girls who attended the ceremonies in Han Wu-ti's palace. The "white swallows," the beautiful Chao sisters of the Han, are gone forever, but thanks to her practice the Shang ch'ing master Ch'eng has only grown more youthful and alluring with the years.

Once you followed Amah to the Han palace fast;
Phoenix-harnessed dragon coaches arrayed on the jade staircase.
Just now the white swallows have disappeared without a trace,
But your cloud hair-coils today display jade pins.
(*CTS*, 2828, no. 4)

Shih Chien-wu (fl. 820) playfully scolds Female Taoist Master Jade Flower Cheng. Warning her not to be an idle nymph but take her studies seriously, he points to the Queen Mother as both teacher and intimate.

Don't pick lotus flowers in the middle of Bright Mirror Lake;
Instead take Amah as your master and study the divine
    transcendents.
A vermilion thread inadvertently fallen into your blue bag:
Now which string from your harp is it?
(*CTS*, 2969, no. 2)

Poets treat refined masters in conflicting fashion, perhaps suggesting the ambivalence T'ang men felt about high-ranking women religious. Some they present as serious leaders or meditators; others behave like coquettes. The authors' combination of reverence, sexual attraction, and sometimes condescension has parallels in male attitudes toward female religious in medieval Europe. But the writers agree that these priestesses, like the jade girls to whom they are compared, have a special intimacy with the Queen Mother.

Recluses and Adepts

Female recluses and adepts lived outside the establishment of temples and convents, but were nevertheless revered and thought to bring blessings to the district where they resided. Would-be disciples were always trying to persuade these women to divulge their holy truths. Poems addressed to them feature the Queen Mother in the role of instructor and protector. As in the case of poems dedicated to high-ranking priestesses, poets compare gifted or lofty hermits and saints to the divine attendants of the Queen Mother. Shih Chien-wu, in "Canto of the Transcendent Woman," a quatrain on an ancient Taoist calligrapher who writes with a brush fashioned of hair from the rabbit in the moon, highlights her age, eminence, and skill by mentioning the goddess.

Among the flock of transcendent women, her name is highest;
She once saw the Queen Mother of the West plant transcendent
    peaches.
The metal slips she takes up in her hands are written in no
    ordinary brush;
They say hers is made from fur of the jade rabbit at heaven's
    side.
                                                    (*CTS*, 2971)

Shih wrote another poem to an aged Taoist recluse, "Given to the
Transcendent Crone Who Skims the Heavens," comparing that old
woman to the Queen Mother herself.

How long has it been since Amah descended from the heavens?
Among previous dynasties, only the Illustrious One of the Han
    knew her.
Her transcendent peaches have ripened no less than three times.
Look! He's full—Tung-fang Shuo, that singular child!
                                                    (*CTS*, 2969)

In the crone's long lifetime, three cycles of the goddess's peaches
have passed. That takes her from the time of King Mu of the Chou
to Emperor Wu of the Han and up to the T'ang. She has obviously
seen it all but still is willing to give some elixir peaches to a mischievous boy, perhaps the narrator himself. The poet often portrays
himself as Tung-fang Shuo, that thief of peaches and symbol of
human imagination and rebellion.

The goddess often figures as special protector of older women.
One strong tradition depicts the Queen Mother herself as a white-
haired crone. Old women are often widowed. By choice or by
accident, they may find themselves unprotected and alone, outside
the bounds of the traditional family circle within which most medieval Chinese women lived and found the meaning of their lives. If
they are childless, older women are especially vulnerable in traditional Chinese society, which defines a mature woman's worth in
terms of her motherhood. Herself immeasurably old and yet possessed of great dignity and authority, childless and yet the mother of
all, the Queen Mother brought respect to the position of the older
woman.

The Queen Mother also protected young women who had chosen
to live alone. Chang Chi addresses "The Maiden Who Does Not

Eat" to a Taoist maiden who dwells in the mountains meditating and doing respiratory exercises. She abstains from normal food, even from herbal drugs. The narrator's admiration for this silent and anorexic maiden shows in his final question.

> How many years have you dwelt in the mountains?
> You've already created a green-downed body.
> Guarding your breath, you regularly thin out your speech;
> Concentrating your thoughts, you yourself see divinities.
> You nourish the tortoise and at the same time do not eat.
> Even herbal drugs you reject, so that they grow dust.
> I must ask the Western Queen Mother,
> What's your rank among the transcendents?
>
> (CTS, 2277)

Chang's poem reveals a connection between women's religious practice and fasting, also found in the West in medieval times.[7] Control of eating, even to the point of fasting to death, and the connection between special foods and spiritual nourishment characterizes Chinese as it does Western female saints. Tu Kuang-t'ing's records of female saints record fasting as an important practice in almost every T'ang life. Abstinence from a normal diet, called "cutting off the five grains," was a precondition to meditation and visualization for both men and women in Shang ch'ing Taoism. By cutting off the five grains, the adept showed herself ready to separate from daily life and this world, to make sacrifices and submit to discipline. Starvation itself might make her more susceptible to visions: Native American religion also involves fasting to the point of becoming sensitive to messages from the other world.

Medieval poems on recluses and adepts assume the Queen Mother's role as protector of women in Taoism, especially female religious and especially those submitting to strenuous regimens. They reveal the goddess's care for older women and take for granted her position as registrar of female transcendents.

Love Life

The Queen Mother governed not only solitary practice but also Taoist love and marriage. Shang ch'ing Taoism generally favors celibacy for both men and women as a requisite to immortality, but older traditions of marriage and sexuality as paths to health and longevity are never really lost. The value Chinese society places on family and lineage acts strongly against any religion that demands celibacy. In Tu Kuang-t'ing's writings, marriage is listed as one path to transcendence. His biography of the goddess includes her consort and his part in creation. Tu also mentions her role in providing the Shang ch'ing founder with a divine bride.

Unconstrained by the rigors of Shang ch'ing beliefs, T'ang poets never did reject sexuality as part of the religious life. According to the poets, love affairs between Taoist priestesses and laymen fell under the Queen Mother's jurisdiction as the deity responsible for arranging liaisons for divine women. Poets also loved to speculate on the love lives of Taoist nuns, much as modern writers imagine sex in the Catholic convent. But the T'ang writers had an additional impetus to consider the affairs of the nuns. If they believed their own figures of speech and equated the nuns with female transcendents, then a love affair with one of them provided a delightful path to immortality.

Li K'ang-cheng (fl. 742–56) wrote his "Song of the Little Jade Floriate Transcendent" in honor of the Refined Master Jade Flower Cheng (also the recipient of a teasing poem by Shih Chien-wu, see above). Comparing her to a divine woman, Li praises her Taoist accomplishments. He describes their encounter in terms of an ascent to transcendence via various celestial points until they finish by breakfasting on elixirs at the Queen Mother's paradise on Mount K'un-lun:

> Little Purple Yang Transcendent—her given name is Jade Flower;
> In a pearl basin she receives dew, then makes cakes of cinnabar.
> Of variable attitude and congealed passions, within five-colored clouds,
> Her delicately beautiful countenance lasts thousands of years: a lotus blossom.
> Among Selected Women in the Purple Yang Palace, the conceited are uncountable,
> But when one sees Jade Flower in the distance, they all seem to hide their beauty.

The sun as it first emerges by the lofty audience hall does not
    have her perfected allure;
Flowing wind from Lo River islands moves spontaneously in
    her wake.
By the Jade Template Staircase—rainbow white damask
    apartments;
By Cyan Inscribed Gates—frosty netted gauze curtains.
Transcendent Ch'ang Oh and her cinnamon tree prolong their
    own springs;
The Queen Mother's peach flowers have never yet fallen.
The Lady of the Supreme Primordial visits the Realm of
    Supreme Clarity.
Passing time in isolation and quiet inside the deep palace, she is
    annoyed with its many-layered city walls.
She undoes her belt pendants, moved in vain by Ch'eng Chiao-fu.
Blowing the syrinx, she does not follow Flying Rose-gem Hsü.
Relaxed and easygoing, she paces the purple courtyard;
Subtle and difficult to perceive, she takes the Ying Platform
    Road.
With the noble scholar from orchid tumulus, she declines a
    mutual encounter,
But toward the young notary from north of the Ch'i, she turns
    back and looks.
A proud emissary from the Glaucous Isle-land loves gold and
    cinnabar;
Purifying his heart, he returns his far-off gaze to the tip of the
    clouds.
Feathered umbrella and rainbow gown: each recognizes the other.
Transmitting passions, we describe our thoughts to each other—
    extended without limit.
Extending without limit,
We will follow one another eternally.
Reaching the empyrean, we pass the Golden Watchtowers;
Playing with images, we descend to the Turquoise Pond.
In the evening we spend the night by mica curtains of the Purple
    Archives;
In the morning we eat K'un-lun mushrooms from the
    Mysterious Orchard.
I did not study orchid incense—the middle way is severed;
But she instructs the blue bird to report our mutual thoughts.

                            (CTS, 1156)

Li describes his encounter with the female Taoist master Cheng in terms of a divine marriage. He compares Cheng to a jade girl who collects dew from heaven and compounds an elixir that has already made her eternally youthful. Her beauty puts other goddesses in the shade; her charisma moves natural forces. Li compares her to the Nymph of the Lo River, a famous divine seductress, portrayed in art and literature skimming the waves and stirring up the wind.

Living in paradise in the company of other eternal creatures such as the goddess of the moon, Jade Flower becomes annoyed at the perfection and immutability of her life. Her palace becomes her prison. In the guise of a Yangtze River goddess, she seduces a mortal lover. (Undoing her belt pendants is a sign of disrobing prior to making love, and the belt pendants themselves are a love token.) Her pity is in vain, however; being immortal, she must eventually leave him.

Leaving, she does not follow the Queen Mother's entourage to the Han palace, and she ignores the pleas of a famous poet, instead turning her attention to the humble narrator. The narrator presents himself as an adept, future divine office holder, and emissary of the gods: someone worthy of Jade Flower's attention. After he purifies himself, they make wedding vows. Their honeymoon journey is a miniature pacing of the void: they wander the heavens, ingesting elixirs and collecting powers. In the end, the narrator, like the Martial Thearch of the Han, fails to practice her teachings and is banished from the Way. The final line provides the consolation that the blue bird, the Queen Mother's messenger, will keep him in communication with the priestess.

In an untitled quatrain, Li Shang-yin longs for the remembered company of a Taoist priestess called Precious Lamp. Picturing her about to drink an elixir on a cold night, he hopes once again to meet her in the Queen Mother's paradise:

> The transcendent person of the Purple Archives is known as
>   Precious Lamp;
> Her cloud broth not yet swallowed, it sets and freezes.
> What would it be like, on a night with snow and moon
>   mingling their radiance,
> To be once again on the twelve stories of the Turquoise Tower?
>
> (CTS, 3245)

Li Shang-yin addresses another poem to sisters who were Taoist nuns; here the Queen Mother figures as the intended victim of a celestial theft. Li calls the poem "On a Moonlit Night, Again I Send a Message to Sung Hua-yang and Her Younger Sister":

> Stealing peaches and snatching drugs: these things are difficult to do simultaneously.
> In the middle of her twelve-layered city walls, we've locked up the multi-colored toad.
> We should taste them together with "thrice blossoming" on the same night,
> Then the jade storied buildings will be nothing but these rock crystal curtains.
>
> (CTS, 3264)

The narrator, like Tung-fang Shuo, plans to steal the goddess's peaches. He urges the Sung sisters to snatch her elixir (the "thrice blossoming"). The moon-toad is locked up in the Queen Mother's palace with its twelve-layered walls. If the lovers eat both divine peaches and elixir, the rock crystal curtains of their bedroom will transform themselves into the jade staircase of the transcendents' palace, and their bedroom will become a microcosmic heaven on earth.

Lay Heroines

In poems that share imagery with works on priestesses and novices, T'ang dynasty writers compared laywomen of great beauty and talent to the goddess's attendants. Also like verses on the priestesses, poets' attitudes toward their subjects vary from awe to lust, reflecting the whole range of dreams and illusions T'ang men had about women. Details of the attendants' clothing, appearance, and attributes match descriptions appearing in Tu Kuang-t'ing's hagiographical account of the goddess, translated in Chapter 2. Portrayals range from reverent to seductive.

Yü Hsüan-chi (844–68) was a T'ang dynasty Taoist nun who had a short and violent life.[8] Known for her literary and sexual relationships with the greatest writers of her day, she was executed at the age of twenty-five on the charge, never satisfactorily proved, of murdering her maidservant. Tu Kuang-t'ing does not include her in his collection of immortals' biographies; perhaps she failed to live up to his standards of self-denying practice or he feared political repercussions.

During her short life Yü Hsüan-chi wrote a number of extraordinary poems, including a lesbian love poem dedicated to three orphaned sisters of refined literary and musical accomplishments who were briefly her neighbors in a guest house. Chinese male poets regularly used male voices to declare their passions for women and female voices to express their conceptions of women's feelings about men. In a departure that must have been shocking in its time, Yü uses a woman's voice to express her own romantic responses to women. She compares the three southern girls to luxurious pet birds in the "Rhapsody on the Parrot" by Ni Heng of the second century A.D. and to famous beauties of old. Little Hsi, whom Yü claims was not as lovely as these three, is Hsi Shih, a famous "state-toppling beauty" credited with causing the downfall of a Warring States kingdom.

Their startling loveliness and apparently supernatural talent make the poet exclaim that they must formerly have been immortal attendants of the Queen Mother. She places them in a spot associated with the Queen Mother's cult: the Lesser Existence Grotto on Mount Wang wu. Yü Hsüan-chi wishes they could tarry to make love: rain and blowing the syrinx are regular metaphors for sexual expressions of love. "Blowing the syrinx" also refers to techniques of ascending to transcendence by means of music as did the ancient immortals Lord Hsiao and Lung Yü. The mixture of divine and worldly love, a commonplace of Shang ch'ing imagery, has a parallel in troubadour songs of medieval Europe. The poet wishes the Queen Mother would serve as a divine matchmaker, as she did in blessed heterosexual unions. As we saw in the case of the priestesses, their comfortable familiarity with the goddess is expressed in the intimate form of address, "Amah," that they use toward her. The four women enjoy an evening of wine, poetry, and music together and then part. As was Yü Hsüan-chi before she took her vows, the orphaned sisters are courtesans, a group especially protected by the Queen Mother. The poem begins with a preface:

K'uang, Wei, and P'ou are three sisters who were orphaned when young. Moreover, they were accomplished from the beginning. Now they have written these poems. The poems are essential and pure; they would be hard to match. How could even the linked verses on snowflakes of the Hsieh household add up to them? There was a stranger who came from the capital city and showed them to me. Consequently I put in order these rhymes.

> Formerly I heard that in the southern nations, flowery faces were few,
> But today my eastern neighbors are three sisters.
> In their dressing room, looking at one another: the "Rhapsody on the Parrot."
> At their cyan window, they must be embroidering phoenix slips.
> Pink fragrant plants fill the courtyard, ragged and jaggedly broken off.
> Green strained wine overflows our cups; one after another we put them to our mouths.
> I suspect that they once acted as girl attendants at the Turquoise Pond;
> Coming in exile to this dusty world, they did not become males.
> I might finally venture to compare them to the appearance possessed by Lady Wen Chi;
> Little Hsi Shih would be speechless before them; I am still more mortified.
> A single tune of ravishing song—the zither seems faraway and indistinct;
> While the four-strings are lightly strummed, they talk, murmuring unclearly.
> Facing the mirror stand, they compete equally with their blue-glinting silk thread hair;
> Opposite the moon, they vie in showing off their white jade hairpins.
> In the midst of the Lesser Existence Grotto, pine dew drops,
> Above the Great Brahma Heavens, willow mist is contained.
> If only they were able to tarry on account of the rain,
> They need not fear that matters of "blowing the syrinx" are not yet understood.
> How many times has the Amah scolded them for talking beneath the flowers?
> Lord Pan once consulted them in a meeting in a dream.
> For a short time I've grasped their pure sentences; it's as if my cloud-soul were cut off.
> If I were looking at their pink faces, even dying would be sweet.

Despondently I look from afar for those delightful people:
   where are they?
Traversing the clouds, I go home to the north, while they return
   home to the south.

                                                        (CTS, 4669)

That the Queen Mother's attendants provided a standard of female skill and beauty for T'ang poets is also clear in Liu Yü-
hsi's poem on a band of dancers, "To Match Lo-t'ien's 'Cudrania
Branch.'" The dance troupe, like the convent and the house of
prostitution, provided a fictive family for the women. They are
compared to jade girls, another group of fictional sisters, who return
home to paradise as soon as their performance ends. The dancers'
departure recalls the upward flight of the Queen Mother's entourage
after the rituals in the Han palace. They have been dancing to a tune
called "Cudrania Branch." Liu's poem was composed in reply to one
by Po Chü-i, a great lover of dance.

> "Cudrania Branch" originally came from the Prince of Ch'u's
>   household;
> Jade faces abundantly sensuous, dancing comportment showy.
> Loosing side-locks, they change hairstyles—simurgh and
>   phoenix topknots;
> New slips woven separately—a fighting-cock patterned gauze.
> Drums urge them forward with fragmented striking—waists
>   and bodies supple;
> Perspiration enhances their netted-gauze cloaks with rain-dot
>   flowers.
> The tune finished, they bid their farewells by painted mats and
>   depart homeward,
> Once again following the Queen Mother to ascend into misty
>   auroral clouds.
>   (CTS, 2148)

Sun Ch'i (fl. 880) addresses a poem to the singing girl Wang Fu-
niang, a flirtatious entertainer in a brothel in the capital. Here the
Queen Mother, patron saint of prostitutes and female musicians,
appears in the guise of a madame, disciplining and watching out for
her charge.

> Transcendent dress of variegated kingfisher along with pink jade
>   skin:
> She makes light of her full years of residing here, since she first
>   smashed the gourd.

> With auroral cloud cups, she drunkenly urges Squire Liu to
>   gamble;
> Her cloud topknots indolently invite Amah's comb.
> She does not fear bitter cold invading the precious ornaments at
>   her hem and belt;
> From time to time, worrying lest wind lift it, she dimples and
>   grasps her jacket.
> Indolently picturing Little Hsi, she does her makeup the same
>   way,
> But Little Hsi never did obtain her likeness.
>
> (CTS, 4324)

"Smashing the gourd" is a visual pun on written Chinese words: the graph for "gourd," broken in half, makes two graphs for the number eight. Twice eight is sixteen: the age of a girl's sexual maturity. "Smashing the gourd" is also a euphemism for a girl's first menstrual period or her first experience of sexual intercourse.

In "Given to the Singing Girl of the Wei Clan," no. 1, Hsüeh Neng (d. 880) associates the unique talent of another singer with the Queen Mother in a novel fashion. First likening her extraordinary voice to a penetrating knife that pierces the listener's chest, he finally compares it to one perfect blossoming peach. Both can break your heart.

> Sounds of tubes and strings freezing, the singing she produces is
>   so lofty;
> How many people conceal a wounding knife near their heart?
> As I think and calculate again—what would bear comparison?
> Just a single tree, newly opened, of the Queen Mother's peaches.
>
> (CTS, 3414)

In "Parting with the Ching chou Singing Girl Tuan Tung-mei," no. 2, Hsüeh I-liao (fl. 845), takes forlorn leave of a singing girl with whom he has passed a happy year. He compares a farewell dinner with his mistress to a feast by the Turquoise Pond, identifying her as one of the Queen Mother's attendants.

> Amah's peach flowers seem just like multi-colored damask;
> Paris grass looks exactly like smoke.
> In an instant I'll be facing the vastness of the Glaucous Sea again,
>   gazing off into the far distance,
> Depressed and despondent. Delighting in passions, we were
>   well matched for a single year.
>
> (CTS, 3315–16)

Dead Women

Attendance by women on the Queen Mother, like visiting the Turquoise Pond, provided a poetic euphemism for death—not only the death to earthly concerns that entering a convent entailed but also the literal death of women. Since she ruled a Taoist paradise inhabited by immortals who had departed from the world, people naturally saw her as queen of the land of the dead.

In "To Match Middle Deputy Wu's 'Sighing over the *Sheng* Artist,'" written by Li Ch'ün-yü (fl. 847) in sympathy for a grieving friend, a dead *sheng* player's spirit has followed the wind upward and disappeared. The *sheng* is a mouth organ, a traditional Chinese instrument often made of clay that produces a haunting and doleful sound. The poet at once celebrates her talents and mourns her death when he compares her to a transcendent musician in the Queen Mother's service, and he likens her long and final journey to the attendant's return trip to Mount K'un-lun. The dance of departing jade girls becomes a final dance of death:

> Her beautiful substance and transcendent bearing have followed
>   the wind just like smoke;
> Phoenix sounds severed, the platform where she blew now
>   stands empty.
> The multitude of passions seem like grasses: resenting the
>   returning green.
> Without being ruled, apricot flowers in spring naturally turn
>   pink.
> The earring she dropped still remains, beneath a fragrant tree;
> The scent she left behind gradually becomes extinguished within
>   jade halls.
> She must have departed only just now, embracing her Cloud
>   Harmony Pipes;
> From here it's a lengthy return to Amah's palace.
>   (*CTS*, 3454)

Liu Ch'ang-ch'ing (fl. 749) uses the Queen Mother's household as a metaphor for death in a poem about the T'ang dynasty emperor Te tsung's (r. 799–805) mother. All trace of the empress dowager had been lost during the An Lu-shan rebellion of 756. After the revolution, officials specially appointed by the emperor searched but never found her. In Liu's poem, bodies of fallen ladies have been buried, and the palaces prepared for the empress dowager's return. Te tsung waits and anxiously looks for her. Liu addresses this poem to one of the investigating officials, Mr. Shen from the judge's office, on the occasion of his arrival to start the search.

> People of the Extended Happiness Palace have swept up the
> fallen flowers;
> The ruling king just now awaits her, with five-colored chariots.
> His vassals and handmaidens together have inspected and looked
> afar in a myriad directions,
> But probably she is in Amah's household with its layered city
> walls.
>
> (CTS, 854)

"In Amah's household" is the medieval Chinese equivalent of the Western expression "gone to a better world."

In life and death, in the family and outside it, the Queen Mother protected and encouraged women. She helped them in their profession and in their personal life. She led them to the Way, happiness, and immortality. The goddess taught and empowered men as well as women, but her relation with women seems more intimate and familial. We only rarely see men refer to her as "Amah," for example.

What sort of models were the Taoist priestesses she protects? How are we to resolve the apparent contradiction of such powerful and prestigious female figures with the limited roles available to actual women in medieval China? Surely Tu is not preaching that all women should imitate the goddess and her jade maidens to the extent of refusing marriage and retreating from society. But in some sense she and the priestesses provide idealized examples of practice for women to emulate, both inside and outside the home. We might look at the example of the priestesses or recluses in terms of stages of a woman's life: a woman might concentrate on devotion and good works during her youth and childbearing years, then move to more extreme methods of fasting, sexual abstinence, continual meditation, and finally ingesting elixirs in old age, when her children might be grateful for her noninterference. A woman thrown outside the family circle by circumstance or strong vocation might start this process earlier, but it was not for everyone.

The function of the female saints whose stories Tu recounts in the

Records of the Assembled Transcendents of the Fortified Walled City and to whom T'ang poets wrote hymns of praise goes beyond that of models. These women are also creators of community, centers of cults, and themselves intermediaries in human relations with divinities. Unlike Western saints who carry the prayers of the faithful to heaven, these intermediaries transmit texts and liturgies as well as blessings and forgiveness from the gods to mortals. Tu intended in his biographies to bring them into the orthodox fold and grant them honor while keeping their cult securely in place below that of the high gods. He intended to glorify and validate the path of Shang ch'ing Taoism, the school of which he was a master, through their lives. Finally they served as living auspicious omens who brought glory to the reigning imperial house.

T'ang poets had many reasons to write about priestesses and saints: to glorify and flatter them, to gain their teachings, to make love to them, to praise the dynasty that harbored them, to badger officials into supporting them. They also wrote with relish about the other women clients of the goddess: courtesans and artists. These might be independent women, worthy of respect, but they are clearly objects of male fantasy as well.

As they appear in T'ang poetry, the Queen Mother's attendants are intermediary model figures. They provide T'ang men with something a high goddess such as the Queen Mother herself denies, an intimate sexual object. Perhaps they provided T'ang women with examples of beautiful and perfect but somehow approachable beings whom they might emulate.

Tu Kuang-t'ing's biography of the goddess and her image in T'ang poetry suggest that medieval Chinese men and women experienced the Queen Mother of the West in different ways, with some degree of convergence. Both male and female Taoists see her in terms of various kinship relations. She provides an ideal maternal figure for both men and women. The goddess is creator, nurturing mother, and supreme ancestress of all. She serves as mediator between the divine and human worlds as well as master who reveals sacred teachings. She is the divine matchmaker who introduces the adept to his or her spiritual spouse.

But she is much more important to women than to men. For women in Taoism, she stands at the origin of the teaching lineage and sanctions the whole structure of institutionalized Taoism seen at the local level in the convent. She is the ultimate abbess, the top authority in the religious family to which they belong. She is also a direct inspiration and role model. Whatever their walk of life, T'ang women turn to her for comfort or instruction.

The central themes of T'ang poems about women in Taoism are precisely those that most deeply concern the Queen Mother as she is presented by Tu: transcendence and divine passion. The Shang ch'ing Taoist adept's project of attaining eternal life in paradise by nurturing an immortal embryo inside himself is joined in her worship with the human need for love and a sense of belonging. Poems to women Taoists figure the adept's bliss on achieving transcendence in the only metaphors most people have to express the highest good in this life: sexual union or maternal love. People of the T'ang united their two greatest longings in worship of the goddess: the wish to transcend death and the desire for perfect love. Tu Kuang-t'ing and the T'ang poets capture these aspirations in separate but mutually complementary manners.

❖ *Conclusion*

The last words in Tu Kuang-t'ing's hagiography of the Queen Mother of the West are "This is not a complete account" (*CMYC*, 24164). It would be impossible to tell all the tales, read all the poems, or interpret all the meanings of the goddess in medieval China. The most we can hope for is to have illuminated a few of the threads that, woven together, constitute her image.

The image of the Queen Mother of the West presented in these pages makes no sense apart from her specific context: that context is T'ang dynasty literati culture. She reflects the tensions as well as the accomplishments of that elite and male-dominated culture. She embodies the fantasies of T'ang men who provide most of our textual material about her—dreams of the perfect mother, perfect lover, and perfect teacher. Yet she also protects T'ang women, especially those embarked on the Taoist religious path, and promises fulfillment of their wishes for education, status, and transcendence.

Some general features of the Queen Mother's image may be considered universal qualities of major deities the world over, such as her characteristic gifts of wisdom, divine union, and immortality. But the details that give meaning to her attributes are specific to the Shang ch'ing school of Taoism and are uniquely Chinese. The wisdom is knowledge of the Tao, the divine union joins the adept with a jade maiden of impeccable credentials, and immortality is gained through Taoist religious practices. The goddess reflects the Chinese tendency to classify the world into a hierarchical order ultimately based on the human family. The supreme example of this tendency on earth is the emperor, son of heaven and father and mother of his people, who stands at the head of the hierarchy of the imperial bureaucracy. The goddess stands at the top of the female line of gods and immortals in the Taoist celestial bureaucracy, which mirrors the earthly imperium; a posthumous position in that system is the highest good a medieval Chinese person could imagine.

Her enormous resilience and hold on the Chinese imagination and faith over the centuries may relate in part to the way in which her image changes in response to basic human needs, assuming guises appropriate to successive historical periods. Her image in the T'ang embodies Shang ch'ing beliefs, which in turn had absorbed an older heritage of legends about meetings between goddesses and kings and a tradition of worshiping a goddess of immortality who lived on a remote mountain in the west. The cult of the goddess reflects the relation of the Taoist religion and the Chinese state in medieval times: the imperial court patronized the Shang ch'ing school and honored its deities and was in turn supported by that school in its claim to possess the mandate of heaven.

Along with the relation between religion and the state, the Queen Mother's image in T'ang poetry shows the intimate connection between religion and literature that was taken for granted in medieval China. Religious and literary texts were not separate genres any more than religion was separate from daily life. The central themes of the T'ang poems are precisely those that religious texts present as concerning the Queen Mother most deeply: transcendence and divine passion. The Shang ch'ing adept's project of attaining eternal life in paradise by nurturing inside himself an immortal embryo is joined in her worship and in poetry with the human need for love. The adept's bliss on achieving transcendence is often expressed in both canonical texts and poetry in terms of sexual union. People of the T'ang united two of the greatest human longings in their worship of the goddess: the wish to conquer death and the desire for perfect love.

Reference Matter

Notes

For complete author names, titles, and publication data for the works cited here in short form, see the Bibliography, pp. 263–80. For the abbreviations used in the Notes, see pp. xiii–xiv.

Introduction

1. For a study of poems on the ascent of Mount T'ai, including Li Po's set of six, see Kroll, "Verses from on High." On the structure, contents, and compilation of the *Ch'üan T'ang shih*, see Kroll, "*Ch'üan T'ang shih*," in Nienhauser, *Indiana Companion*, 364–65.

2. On Shang ch'ing Taoism, see Robinet, *La révélation du Shangqing*; and Strickmann, "The Mao Shan Revelations." On Ling pao Taoism, see C. Bell, "Ritualization of Texts"; and Bokencamp, "Sources."

3. For the history and formation of the Taoist canon, see Ch'en Kuo-fu, *Tao tsang yüan liu k'ao*; and Ōfuchi, "Formation of the Taoist Canon."

4. *CMYC*, HY 782, 30, 24158–64; also appearing with minor changes in *Yün chi ch'i ch'ien*, 30324–30. The same biography appears, abridged, in Li Fang et al., *T'ai p'ing kuang chi*, 56.1a–3a. For a study of Tu Kuang-t'ing's life and work, see Verellen, *Du Guangting*; for a preliminary study of this text, see Cahill, "Reflections of a Metal Mother." For translations of biographies from this collection, see Cahill, "Pien Tung-hsüan"; Köhn, "Mother of the Tao"; and Schafer, "Three Divine Women."

Chapter 1

1. Shima, *Inkyo bokuji sōrui*, 133.3. I am grateful to Professor David Keightley of the Department of History of the University of California

at Berkeley for his help in interpreting possible references to the Queen Mother in the oracle bone inscriptions.

2. Although the translation of *mu* as "mother" is not certain, the alternative translation of *mu* as a simple negative does not fit the grammar or context of the oracle bone inscriptions on sacrifices. There is no reason to believe the character has been written incorrectly or substituted for another. For the connection of the later goddess known as the Queen Mother of the West with *hsi mu* in the oracle bone inscriptions, in addition to her lunar and solar associations, see Ch'en Meng-chia, "Ku wen tzu." See also Akatsuka, *Chūgoku kodai no shūkyo*, 443. For her connection with successful harvests, see Bucksbaum, "The Word *Fang* in the OBI."

3. It is tempting to speculate that the tiger images on ritual vessels of the late Shang and early Chou dynasties represent the western *mu* divinity. These vessels were used in ancestral sacrifices and buried with the dead. The iconography of the tiger image has not yet been fully interpreted, but most art historians believe it signifies death and the afterlife and may also serve an apotropaic function. The tiger sometimes holds a small human in her jaws or in her embrace, suggesting she is an agent of death and transcendence. Going through the tiger's mouth means dying. Chou and later texts attest that the tiger is considered a yin animal, a fierce and powerful embodiment of the dark female force, and is linked with the west, metal, and death, all associations she shares with the Queen Mother. The complementary yang animal is the dragon, connected with the east, wood, and new growth, associations he shares with the goddess's consort. The find in tombs at Puyang of a tiger and a dragon formed by shells may indicate that the tiger of the west occurred much earlier than was previously believed (see *Wenwu* 1988.3 and 1988.11, but see also Hua Xia Kaogu 1988.4). Chou art and religious texts depict the tiger as an envoy of the Queen Mother, confirming their close relationship at a later date. A late Shang or early Chou bronze *yu* vessel in the Sumitomo Museum in Kyoto depicts a tiger embracing a small human who has his head in her open jaws (for an illustration, see *Sekai bijutsu zenshu*, vol. 12 [Kyoto: Kadokawa shōten, 1962], pl. 28). The Musée Cernuschi in Paris has an almost identical bronze. For a late Chou text linking the Queen Mother and tiger, see *SHC*, 2.19a.

4. *Chuang-tzu*, 6.11a. On the gap between the deity of the oracle bones and the deity or deities mentioned by Chuang-tzu and other Warring States authors, see Fracasso, "Holy Mothers."

5. *Hsün-tzu* (ch. 27), 96.13. Karlgren ("Legends and Cults," 271–72) asserts that this passage in the *Hsün-tzu* means that Yü studied under "(the prince of) the Si Wang state." He is led to this conclusion by the substitution of the graph *kuo* (nation or state) for *mu* in the text and his belief that "Yü

would not have had a female teacher." In fact, legendary early emperors regularly received instruction from goddesses, according to Taoist belief and early Chinese tradition. Yet Karlgren may have been right for the wrong reason—the dual tradition of the deity as a person and a place in the early texts is strong.

6. On euhermerization (more precisely reverse euhermerization) in Chinese myth, see Bodde, "Myths of Ancient China." The same essay discusses the nature of early Chinese myth as we have it today as both fragmentary and preserved in hostile sources—another reason for the gaps in our references to the Queen Mother during the early periods.

7. The first five chapters of the *SHC*, edited by Liu Hsin (ca. 50 B.C.–A.D. 23), probably date to the fourth century B.C. The second part, chapters 6–13, probably dates to the early Han; the third part, chapters 14–18, consists of additions made by Kuo P'u, the fourth-century commentator whose notes cover the whole text. On dating and authorship of the *SHC*, see Loewe, *Ways to Paradise*, 148*nn*11–12.

8. Kominami, "Seiōbo." Kominami (42–48) collects early texts and commentaries on the *sheng* and discusses its connection to the goddess. See also Chauncey S. Goodrich, "Hsi Wang Mu's Headdress" (unpublished paper, American Oriental Society national meeting, 1988).

9. *Shih ming*, ch. 15.

10. On shamanism, see Eliade, *Shamanism*; and Blacker, *Catalpa Bow*. For a study of Chinese hymns with shamanistic elements, see Hawkes, *Ch'u Tz'u*.

11. *Erh ya*, 21.9.7; see also 14.4.1. See also *Shih ming*, 3.44. I am indebted to earlier studies of the Queen Mother of the West during the Han dynasty: Dubs, "Ancient Chinese Mystery Cult"; Theresa June Li, "Hsi-wang-mu"; Loewe, *Ways to Paradise*, chap. 4.

12. *SC*, 123.13; *HS*, 28B(1).10a–b; *HHS*, 88.14a, 2.17a, 23.34a. These historical sources quote, misquote, and correct one another, adding to the geographical confusion. For Han literati's understanding of the geographical location of the Queen Mother's land, see also Wang Ch'ung, *Lun heng*, 19.8b; and *HNT*, 4.13a. For Chinese attitudes toward the exotic occident during the T'ang dynasty, see Schafer, *Golden Peaches*.

13. See Girardot, *Myth and Meaning*.

14. *SHC*, 16.3a. The paradise reference in this citation comes from a later part of the text but may contain earlier ideas.

15. See, e.g., Ssu-ma Hsiang-ju, *Ta jen fu* (Rhapsody on the great man), *SC*, 117.3060.

16. For studies of this cult and translations of some passages from the dynastic histories, see Dubs, "Ancient Chinese Mystery Cult"; and Loewe,

Ways to Paradise, chap. 4. I am indebted to both Dubs and Loewe, although my approach differs somewhat from theirs. A reference to earlier cultic activity involving the Queen Mother may appear in Po Chü-i's work (see *Po shih liu chan*, 27.25b). Under the heading "Queen Mother's Tallies," Po reports that in the reign of Ch'eng-ti (36–6 B.C.), people east of the passes were moving in procession holding tallies of the Queen Mother inscribed with a message about longevity.

17. For the connection between the star and the cult, see Hou, "Chinese Belief in Baleful Stars." On portents, see Bielenstein, "Interpretation."

18. For example, the Han essayist Wang Ch'ung (*Lun heng* 2.10b) identifies the Queen Mother as an immortal and associates her with the cult of immortality.

19. Chao Yeh, *Wu Yüeh ch'un ch'iu*.

20. On Han pictorial images of the Queen Mother of the West, see Theresa June Li, "Hsi-wang-mu"; and Loewe, *Ways to Paradise*. On the Queen Mother in Chinese pictorial art from the Han through the Sung dynasties, see Cahill, "Images of Transcendence and Divine Passion."

21. For a study of the iconography of the murals in the Western Han tomb of Po Ch'ien-ch'iu, in which the Queen Mother may be depicted welcoming the soul of the occupant to the next world, see Sun, "Western Han Murals."

22. On the Queen Mother in the Wu Liang shrine reliefs, see Wu Hung, *Wu Liang Shrine*, chap. 4. On the reliefs from the mausoleums at I nan, see Tseng, *I-nan ku hua hsiang*.

23. On the image of the Queen Mother of the West in relation to Buddhist art, see Wu Hung, "Buddhist Elements." For a history of the textual and doctrinal transmission of Buddhism from India to China, see Zürcher, *Buddhist Conquest of China*; and Robinson, *Early Mādhyamika*.

24. For money trees, see Wu Hung, "Buddhist Elements." For the "jade" carving, see the excavation report *Wang-tu erh hao Han mu*.

25. For the relation of mirror inscriptions to Taoism during the late Han and early Six Dynasties period and the fabrication of mirrors, see Cahill, "The Word Made Bronze."

26. Umehara, *Kan sangoku rikuchō kinen kyō zusetsu*, 14–16 (see also 8). See also Karlgren, "Early Chinese Mirror Inscriptions."

27. Umehara, *Album*, pl. 30. See also Karlgren, "Early Chinese Mirror Inscriptions," 222.

28. The bronze horse of the second century A.D. from a tomb at Lei-t'ai, Kansu, is extensively reproduced; see, e.g., Sullivan, *Arts of China*, pl. 86.

29. Peasants as well as members of the elite commissioned images of the Queen Mother. Pan Ku records in the passage translated above that her

followers carried amulets and manikins; they must have depicted the goddess in images resembling those they saw on mirrors and wall decorations of ancestral shrines. Today we have no Han objects of peasant origin showing the Queen Mother; undoubtedly such images were executed in perishable media such as paper or wood and burned or buried in unprotected tombs, as they are among Chinese peasants even now.

30. On the "Rhapsody of the Sweet Springs," see Knechteges, *Han Rhapsody*, 44–58.

31. See Kaltenmark, "Ideology of the *T'ai p'ing ching*."

32. The history and significance of Shang ch'ing Taoism have been made known in recent years by the work of Michel Strickmann in such articles as "The Mao Shan Revelations"; and by Isabelle Robinet in such works as *La révélation du Shangqing*.

33. The Chinese version of this title is Tzu wei yüan ling pai yü kuei t'ai chiu ling t'ai chen yüan chün. T'ao Hung-ching, *Chen ling wei yeh t'u*, 5b.

34. On the *Chen kao*, see Strickmann, "The Mao Shan Revelations"; Hyland, "Oracles of the True Ones"; and Robinet, *La révélation du Shangqing*.

35. For the process of "nourishing the vital essence" (*yang ch'i*), see Maspero, *Taoism and Chinese Religion*, 443–554.

36. See, e.g., *WSPY*, 22.12, 33446, for a description of the goddess's residence. On this text, see Lagerway, *Wu-shang pi-yao*.

37. *Shang-ch'ing Lao-tzu chung ching*, 3b–4a. See also Schipper, "*Le Calendrier de Jade*"; and idem, *Le corps taoïste*. Another text on nourishing the vital essence is the *Hsi Wang Mu chuan wo ku fa*, which espouses heliotherapy and meditation.

38. See Overmyer, *Folk Buddhist Religion*, for a discussion of the worship of the Queen Mother in millenarian cults, the attitudes of officials of church and state toward popular cults, and an analysis of the methods and mechanisms used to suppress information about such cults. See also Overmyer, "Attitudes Towards Popular Religion"; and the earlier work of Groot, *Sectarianism and Religious Persecution*. The Queen Mother of the West is worshiped today in Taoist and Buddhist temples as well as in family shrines. As high-ranking a Buddhist as the president of the Chinese Buddhist Believers Association in 1981, whom I interviewed on Mount Omei in February of that year, claimed that she was the deity most highly revered by his school of Buddhism. The goddess is popularly known as a bodhisattva (*p'u-sa*, properly a Buddhist deity), and her name-recognition among Chinese people in all walks of life today is remarkably high.

39. The *SHC* continues the paradise theme, calling her realm the Wilderness of Satisfaction because of its abundant supply of exotic and delicious food and drink, such as phoenix eggs and sweet dew. Gems grow on trees,

divine creatures play music, and elixir drugs are readily available (*SHC*, 15.5b, 16.3a). The *Shui ching chu* (1.22a) continues the world pillar theme in a section stating that K'un-lun stands at the center of the earth, is 11,000 *li* in height, and the source of the Yellow River.

40. *Shih chou chi*, 5a.

41. *Shen i ching*, 6a. Another reference to the meetings of the Queen Mother and her consort appears, almost buried in anecdotal detail, in the *Tung ming chi* (2.3a). When Tung-fang Shuo appeared in court one day with a divine horse, Han Wu-ti asked about its origins. Tung-fang replied: "Formerly the Queen Mother of the West rode in a carriage of numinous radiance to pay a visit to the dwelling of the King Sire of the East. She haltered this horse and let it wander in the fungus fields. The King Sire of the East became angry and cast off the horse at the celestial banks near the Clear Ford."

42. For the *Lieh hsien chuan*, see Kaltenmark, *Le lie-sien tchouan*, 35–36. Kan Pao of the Chin dynasty tells substantially the same tale in *Sou shen chi*, 1.1a.

43. Fang et al., *Chin shu*, 3197–98. A similar episode appears in Wei Cheng et al., *Sui shu*, 1657. General Hsiang, crushing a rebellion, laid seige to a walled city in the northwest. As he stood on the ramparts watching the city burn, he saw a temple to the Queen Mother and prayed to that goddess to bring rain to extinguish the fires and save the masses. The rain did indeed come. On the shrine of the Queen Mother of the West, see Cahill, "Beside the Turquoise Pond."

44. Fang et al., *Chin shu*, 3197–98.

45. See Han K'ung-yüeh and Lo Feng, "Discovery of a Northern Wei Tomb."

46. Illustrated in Tun-huang wen wu yen chiu so, *Tun-huang mo kao k'u*, vol. 1, pls. 98 & 100 (Cave 249, Western Wei); vol. 2, pl. 84 (Cave 419, Sui).

47. See *YCCHL* 38, 30330–31 for a biography of the Mysterious Woman of the Nine Heavens. For a translation and study of this account, see Cahill, "Sublimation in Medieval China."

48. *Chu shu chi nien*, 6. On the *Chu shu chi nien*, see Shaughnessy, "The Authenticity of the *Bamboo Annals*."

49. *Ta Tai li chi*, 11.7b. The *Shang shu ta chuan* (Great transmissions concerning the *Book of Shang*) clarifies the nature of her gift: "In the time of Shun, the Queen Mother of the West came and submitted as tribute a white jade musical tube" (quoted *HS* 21A.3a–b).

50. Huang-fu Mi, *Ti wang shih chi*, 13. A first-century A.D. scholar is said to have found a white musical tube under Shun's ancestral hall that may have been the white tube in question (*FSTI*, 6.45). The white jade circlet

makes its appearance in Han rhetoric. In A.D. 115, Ma Jung sent Han An-ti a memorial arguing in favor of increased militarization. General Ma lists auspicious events that can be expected if the ruler follows his advice. Among other supernatural benefits, the emperor will surely receive the Queen Mother's white jade circlet, making him Shun's equal (*HHS*, 50A.1969–70).

51. See note 5 to this chapter.

52. *Chu shu chi nien*, 45. (The entry on the thirteenth year is cited as a variant in a note on the seventeenth year.)

53. Liu Tsung-yüan, *T'ien wen t'ien tui chu*, 21, 27, 66. Liu Tsung-yüan's commentary shows that one T'ang poet answered the questions as I suggest here. For a translation of the passage discussed here, see Hawkes, *Ch'u Tz'u*, 73.

54. *Lieh-tzu*, ch. 3. For a translation of the *Lieh-tzu*, see Graham, *Book of Lieh-tzu*; Graham dates the text to around A.D. 300. That details of the story were already known in the Han dynasty is clear from an incidental note in *SC*, 43.1779. A chapter tracing the genealogy of the Chao clan records that Father Ts'ao, a clan ancestor, gave the king eight excellent horses. King Mu later appointed Father Ts'ao charioteer on his hunting expedition to the far west, where the Queen Mother received the king in audience. Delighting in her, he abandoned all thoughts of returning home. When a vassal ruler suddenly rebelled, Mu sped off to attack him, covering a thousand *li* a day, thanks to his fine steeds. Later King Mu awarded Father Ts'ao the city called Chao, from which the clan took its name. A shorter version of the story, perhaps condensed from the *Historical Records*, appears in *FSTI* 1.5, demonstrating its popularity during the Han.

55. In dating the *Transmissions Concerning Mu* as a third-century work incorporating earlier materials, I disagree with Mathieu (*Le Mu tianzi zhuan*), who accepts the traditional early date.

56. A graph is missing from the text at this point. In the variant of the same text preserved in Kuo P'u's commentary to the *Classic of Mountains and Seas* (*SHC* 3.19b), the passage reads "one hundred multi-colored damask cords and one hundred catties of gold and jade."

57. For information on modern revelations of the goddess, see Jordan and Overmyer, *Flying Phoenix*.

58. T'ao Ch'ien, "Tu *Shan hai Ching*"; trans. Hightower, *Poetry of T'ao Ch'ien*, 229–48.

59. On medicinal and magical uses of peaches in early China, see Bodde, *Festivals*, 127–38.

60. The *Tung ming chi* (1.2a) refers to a little-known foretelling of the meeting in an anecdote that underlines the importance of music and elixir

drugs in divine rites. Between 134 and 128 B.C., after the emperor had constructed the Longevity and Numina Altar and displayed his religious devotion, he ordered a certain Tung Ko to ascend the altar riding a chariot of clouds and auroral nimbi: "When the third watch of the night arrived, he heard wild fowl cry out; suddenly all was as if brilliantly lit. Then the Queen Mother of the West came, reining in mysterious simurghs as she sang 'The Drug That Makes Spring Return.' Ko could just hear the sound of the Queen Mother's song; he could not see her form. The sound of the song circled around three times and then ceased. As for the branches and leaves of the grasses and trees by the altar, some flew and some shook: they were moved by the song." The next major treatment of the tale after the "Monograph on Broad Phenomena" appears in *Han Wu ku shih* (Old stories about the Martial One of the Han Dynasty). At least two works of this name existed in the Six Dynasties period, one attributed to Ko Hsüan and one to Wang Chien. In the early twentieth century, Lu Hsün made what remains the authoritative edition of the text by joining extracts quoted in T'ang and Sung sources, including manuscripts found in the Buddhist cave temples at Tun Huang on the Silk Route in Chinese Central Asia. The tale recorded in *Old Stories About the Martial One of the Han Dynasty* adds detail to that found in the earlier encyclopedia. The new details bring the story in line with Shang ch'ing Taoism and the cult of the transcendents of the Six Dynasties. The meeting night, the festival of Double Seven, is also Han Wu-ti's birthday. Instead of a white deer, the goddess sends a blue bird as her messenger. Tung-fang Shuo interprets this as an omen indicating the Queen Mother will soon arrive. A ninefold floriate lamp, regularly featured in Shang ch'ing Taoist epiphanies, illuminates the meeting, which now takes place in the Basilica for Receiving Efflorescence. Thunder precedes the goddess's arrival. She descends, accompanied by jade girls and two blue birds, wearing a sevenfold *sheng* headdress and shoes of dark rose-gem with phoenix patterned-soles. At her waist a sword hangs from a long belt. She begins to take on her canonical appearance. When Han Wu-ti requests the elixir of immortality, she supplies him with a list of drugs from the Realm of Grand Clarity, the heaven of Shang ch'ing Taoism. But she predicts that the thearch will prove unworthy of immortality, for his heart still leans toward sensuality and war. She gives him five peaches to eat. When he hides their seeds in his robe, she tells him firmly that these divine fruits cannot grow on earth. She stays until the fifth watch, discussing affairs of this world but refusing to speak of ghosts or divinities. Tung-fang Shuo appears and she identifies him as a mischievous transcendent. As usual in cases of men visited by goddesses, the emperor feels melancholy for a long time after her departure (see Lu Hsün, *Ku hsiao shuo kou ch'en*, 463). The *Pao p'u-tzu* by Ko

Hung, a staunch fourth-century defender of the transcendent cult, refers to the meeting. In Ko's version, the Queen Mother gives the emperor a text she carries rolled up in a purple silk sack; it is the *Wu yüeh chen hsing t'u* (Chart of the veritable forms of the Five Marchmounts), an important text for Shang ch'ing Taoists. Ko Hung and later literati Taoists found the significance of the encounter in the transmission of texts (cited in Chavannes, *Le T'ai-chan,* 431n3).

61. Lu Hsün assumed that this work and other versions of the tale together with various renditions of the story of King Mu are the forerunners of the novel when he explicated them in his lectures on the history of fiction at Peking University (published in *Ku hsiao shuo kou ch'en*). For a study and annotated translation into French of the *Han Wu-ti nei chuan,* see Schipper, *L'empereur Wou.*

62. See Schipper, Introduction, *L'empereur Wou.*

63. See ibid.

64. *(Hsi yüeh) Hua shan chih.*

65. On Mount T'ai and the ceremony of "tossing the dragons and tallies," see Chavannes, "Le jet des dragons." On worship of the Queen Mother during the T'ang and on poems concerning a visit to her shrine, see Cahill, "Beside the Turquoise Pond."

66. See Chavannes, "Le jet des dragons," 118–26, for his visits to Mount T'ai and Mount Wang wu.

67. Tu Kuang-t'ing, *Tung t'ien fu.*

68. See, e.g., Yü Hsüan-chi, *CTS,* 4669.

69. *(Hsi yüeh) Hua shan chih* states that a belvedere of the Queen Mother was moved to Mount Hua from a mountain in Chekiang province during the period 627–50.

70. See Schafer, *Divine Woman,* for a study of archaic goddesses in T'ang literature.

71. On the quest of the goddess in Chinese literature, see Hawkes, "Quest of the Goddess." On the quest theme in one group of poems, see Cahill, "Sex and the Supernatural."

Chapter 2

1. For the life and works of Tu Kuang-t'ing, see Imaeda, "To Kōtei shōkō"; and Verellen, *Du Guangting.* For studies and translations from this text, see Schafer, "Three Divine Women"; Köhn, "Mother of the Tao"; and Cahill, "Reflections of a Metal Mother," "Pien Tung-hsüan," and "Primordial Ruler, Metal Mother."

2. The names Queen Mother of the West, Queen Mother, and Amah

occur too frequently to cite. Many examples of each will appear in the course of this work. One example apiece for her other names in poetry follow. The goddess is called Western Mother in the seventh of Li Ho's "Twenty-three Poems on Horses" (*CTS*, 2328); she is Metal Mother in Wei Ch'ü-mo's "Canto on Pacing the Void," no. 15 of 19 (*CTS*, 1865–66); Ts'ao T'ang calls her Queen Mother of the Nine Heavens in the ninety-third of his ninety-eight "Lesser Wanderings in Transcendence" (*CTS*, 3836); and Wei Ying-wu names her Divine Mother in "The Jade Girls' Song" (*CTS*, 1090).

3. For studies of related deities, see Kroll, "In the Halls of the Azure Lad"; and Riegel, "Kou-mang and Ju-shou."

4. See the story of the metal and the metalsmith in ch. 6 of the *Chuang-tzu* (trans. Watson, *Chuang-tzu*, 85), and the Tao as Mysterious Female in ch. 6 of the *Tao te ching* (trans. Waley, *Way and Its Power*, 149).

5. See, e.g., *WSPY* and *HWTNC*.

6. Shen Pin, in his "Rhymes Recollecting Transcendence" (*CTS*, 4388), refers to both the nine heavens and the Realm of Supreme Clarity. Li Po refers to the Realm of Grand Clarity in his "Flying Dragon Conductus," no. 1 (*CTS*, 924).

7. The Heavenly Barrier Pass appears in connection with the Queen Mother in Li Po's "Flying Dragon Conductus," no. 2 (*CTS*, 924); the Mysterious Barrier Pass in Ting Tse's "On the Supreme Prime Day, I Dream of the Queen Mother Submitting a Jade Bracelet" (*CTS*, 1698); the Milky Way in examples too numerous to cite; the four wildernesses and eight extremities are mentioned in Po Chü-i's "A Picture of the Eight Chargers" (*CTS*, 2497); the Boundless Abyss and Realm of Utter Silence in Li Ch'ün-yü's "Mu, the Son of Heaven" (*CTS*, 3448).

8. Jade Mountain appears in Li Po's "Lodged in Words," no. 2; (*CTS*, 1024); Tortoise Mountain in Ch'üan Te-yü's "Playfully Given to Refined Master Chang" (*CTS*, 1913); Sea Turtle Mountain in Ts'ao T'ang's "The Martial Thearch of the Han Gives a Feast in the Palace for the Queen Mother of the West" (*CTS*, 3827). Mount K'un-lun appears in poems too numerous to cite here. It takes the name Highgate in Li Ho's "Turquoise Pond Music" (*CTS*, 2339–40), and the name Triple Mountain in Wei Ying-wu's "Song of the White Mynah Who Presides over the Precious Belvedere" (*CTS*, 1091). K'un-lun's peaks are named in T'ang poetry: Lofty Hunting Park in Li Shang-yin's "The Nine Times Perfected Palace" (*CTS*, 3243); Mysterious Orchard in Li K'ang-cheng's "Song of the Little Jade Floriate Transcendent" (*CTS*, 1156); and Lofty Whirlwind Palace in Wu Yün's "Wandering in Transcendence," no. 20 (*CTS*, 4942).

9. On Taoism in the work of Ts'ao T'ang, see Schafer, *Mirages on the Sea of Time*.

10. The Queen Mother appears at Mount Hua in Li Po's "Song of the Transcendent Person Jade Verity" (*CTS*, 948); at Mount T'ai in Li Po's "Wandering on Mount T'ai" (*CTS*, 1003); at Mount Wang wu in Yü Hsüan-chi's rhymes on three sisters (*CTS*, 4669); at Mount Sung in Li Po's "Given to the Refined Master Chiao from Mount Sung" (*CTS*, 954); and on Mount Mao in Pao Jung's "Song of the Transcendents' Meeting" (*CTS*, 2918).

11. The nine turquoise watchtowers are mentioned in Ch'en T'ao's "Flying Dragon Conductus" (*CTS*, 4396); the Turquoise Platform in Pao Jung's "Song of the Transcendents' Meeting" (*CTS*, 2918); the Metal Basilica in Hsiang Ch'i's "Sending off a Person from the Palace to Enter the Way" (*CTS*, 3370); the Blue-gem Palace in Wu Yün's "Wandering in Transcendence," no. 20 (*CTS*, 4942).

12. Tu Kuang-t'ing says he quotes the *Erh ya*, a Han glossary on the classics, but in fact he cites Kuo P'u's commentary to the *SHC*, 2.23b and 16.7b.

13. See Schipper, *L'empereur Wou*, 93–94, for a translation into French of the corresponding passage in the *HWTNC*.

14. The goddess's white and frost-like figure appears in Ting Tse's "On the Supreme Prime Day, I Dream of the Queen Mother Submitting a Jade Bracelet" (*CTS*, 1698); the nine-starred crown in Li Ch'i's "Song of the Queen Mother" (*CTS*, 750); her rainbow chemise and moon-colored jacket in Po Chü-i's "Rainbow Chemise and Feathered Jacket" (*CTS*, 2644–45); jade belt pendents and rings in Lu Kuei-meng's "The Square Resonators" (*CTS*, 3770); the sword and letters of appointment in Ts'ao T'ang's "The Martial Thearch of the Han Gives a Feast in the Palace for the Queen Mother of the West" (*CTS*, 3827). The gifts she carries include territorial charts in Pao Jung's "Remembering the Suburban Sacrifice to Heaven" (*CTS*, 2932); tallies and a bag in Wei Ying-wu's "Assorted Songs on the Martial Thearch of the Han," nos. 1–2 (*CTS*, 1093) and texts in cases too numerous to cite.

15. See Schipper, Introduction, *L'empereur Wou*, for the Lady and her role in the *HWTNC* and a lost biography of the Mao brothers. Tu's accounts of the Lady in the stories of the Martial Thearch and Lord Mao, in both *CMYC* and her biography in the *YCCHL*, derive from the *HWTNC*, which in turn derives from Shang ch'ing texts, including a lost biography of the Mao brothers.

16. The names mentioned in Tu's account refer not to texts extant in the present canon but to holy scriptures mentioned in other Shang ch'ing texts such as the *Declarations of the Realized Ones* and in texts considered canonical by Shang ch'ing Taoists such as the *WSPY*.

17. For more Taoist love songs in T'ang poetry by goddesses, see Cahill, "Marriages Made in Heaven."

18. Ko Hung, *Pao p'u-tzu.*

19. *Yü jen* (feathered person) was an old term, derived from the cult of immortality, for a transcendent. The phrase *pai jih sheng t'ien* (to ascend to heaven in broad daylight) derives from the same source. Tu Kuang-t'ing uses it twice in *YCCHL* to describe women who achieve the highest state of transcendence.

20. The commentary in Li Po, *Li T'ai-po ch'üan chi*, 1106–7, interprets the birds as female members of the royal household.

21. For the poem from the "Nineteen Old Songs" of the Han dynasty that this echoes, see Shen Te-ch'ien, *Ku shih yüan*, 88.

22. In Tu Kuang-t'ing's *Tung t'ien fu*, Chang's grotto is the fifty-eighth lucky place he identifies. On the deification of Lao-tzu in Han Taoism, see Seidel, *La divinisation de Lao tseu.*

23. The Lesser Existence Grotto-heaven is one of the thirty-six grotto-heavens mentioned in Tu Kuang-t'ing's *Tung t'ien fu.*

24. A chariot drawn by *ch'i-lin* appears in Li Ch'i's "Song of the Queen Mother" (*CTS*, 750); six dragons in harness with the sun holding the reins pull the vehicle in Pao Jung's "Remembering the Suburban Sacrifice to Heaven" (*CTS*, 2932); Li Yü-chung mentions a five-colored cloud chariot in "When the Sun First Illuminates the Phoenix Storied Building" (*CTS*, 2889); Ts'ao T'ang has the goddess riding a five-colored dragon in "The Martial Thearch Waits for the Queen Mother of the West to Descend" (*CTS*, 3827).

25. *CTS* titles this poem "The Queen Mother's Song"; I follow an alternative title suggested by the editors' notes.

Chapter 3

1. For pre-Ch'in sources on the Yellow Thearch, see Karlgren, "Legends and Cults," 199–365. For a discussion of Ch'ih Yu, see Bodde, *Festivals*, chap. 4. On concealing the *chia* and calculating the six *jen*, as well as pacing the Dipper and the Five Talismans, see Robinet, "Study of the Relationship." Extant texts in the *Tao tsang* explicate all these techniques, which had become part of the Shang ch'ing teachings.

2. On the Mysterious Woman of the Nine Heavens, see Gulik, *Sexual Life*, 75–76, 121, 122n, 123, 139–41. For her biography, see *YCCHL*, 24199–200. For a translation and study of this biography, see Cahill, "Sublimation in Medieval China."

3. Compare to poems of the *Ch'u tz'u*: see *Tung chün* (Lord of the East), trans. Hawkes, *Ch'u Tz'u*, 41–42.

4. For pre-Ch'in sources on Yü Shun, see Karlgren, "Legends and Cults."

5. For hagiographical accounts of Lao-tzu and Yin-tzu, see *Lieh hsien chuan* (trans. Kaltenmark, *Le lie-sien tchouan*), as well as an account of Huang ti. The "Scripture of Constant Purity and Quiet" is the same as the "Grand Supreme Marvelous Scripture of Constant Purity and Quiet as Explicated by Lord Lao" in the current *Tao tsang* (HY 620), which has a commentary by Tu Kuang-t'ing (HY 758). On the cult of Lao-tzu, see Seidel, *La divinisation de Lao tseu*.

6. On the poem by Lu Kuei-meng, the painting by Han Kan, and the horse called Night-Shining White; see Cahill, "Night-Shining White."

7. For an analysis of the poems by Liu Ch'a, Yüan Chen, and Po Chü-i on paintings of the horses of King Mu, see Cahill, "Reflections, Disputes, and Warnings."

8. Chi Yu-kung, *T'ang shih chi shih*, 122.

9. The same poem is attributed to three different authors: to Li Ch'iao (*CTS*, 425); with the title "Composed on Imperial Command: We Encounter Snow in the Imperial Hunting Park" to Hsü Yen-po (*CTS*, 472); and to Chao Yen-po (*CTS*, 612).

10. On the image of the white clouds in T'ang poetry, see Cahill, "A White Clouds Appointment."

Chapter 4

1. On the song of the child, see T'ao Hung-ching, *Chen kao*, ch. 5. For a biography of Chang Tzu-fang, see *SC*, ch. 55.

2. On the Great Wall, see Waldron, *Great Wall*. The present Great Wall dates from the Ming and features much reconstruction.

3. For the religious practices discussed in this passage, see Maspero, "Methods of 'Nourishing the Vital Principle' in the Ancient Taoist religion," in *Taoism and Chinese Religion*; on liberation by means of the corpse (*chieh shih*), see Robinet, "Metamorphosis and Deliverance."

4. On the "Esoteric Transmissions Concerning the Martial Thearch of the Han," its textual history and affiliations, see Schipper, Introduction, *L'empereur Wou*. For a study of the story of the Martial Thearch in early Chinese fiction, including several early versions of the story of his meeting with the Queen Mother, see Lu Hsün, *Ku hsiao shuo kou ch'en* (his comments on *Han Wu ku shih* appear on p. 463).

5. On the *chiao* ritual, see Saso, *Taoism*; and Lagerway, *Taoist Ritual*.

6. Trans. Watson, *Courtier and Commoner*, 79–106.

7. For the circumstances surrounding the composition of the poem, see Waley, *Life and Times*, 154–55. See also Schafer, *Golden Peaches*, 114–15.

8. On the tubes, see Bodde, "Chinese Cosmic Magic."

9. The deified Lao-tzu was venerated at the Floriate Clear Palace under the name of Hsüan Yüan (Mysterious Primordial). A long description of that palace in Ch'eng Yü's "Poem on the Gate Fording the Yang" (*CTS*, 3439) mentions the altar. Other poems by Tu Fu, Wang Chien (*CTS*, 1785), and Li Shang-yin also refer to this altar and indicate that the imperial palace in Ch'ang an also contained one of the same name. On the Floriate Clear Palace (*Hua ch'ing kung*), see Schafer, "Development of Bathing Customs."

10. The poem is entitled "Together with Supervisor of Affairs Yen, I Heard That a Transcendent Passed Close to the Jade Stamens at T'ang Prosperity Belvedere; Accordingly I Composed Two Regulated Quatrains," no. 1.

11. For studies of the evolution of the text, see Schipper, Introduction, *L'empereur Wou*; and Cahill, "Reflections of a Metal Mother." The account of the goddesses' visit to the Mao brothers follows closely the text preserved in the *Mao shan chih* (HY 304).

12. Lady Wei, who appears frequently in Shang ch'ing texts such as the *Chen kao*, was second only to the Queen Mother in importance. For her biography, see *YCCHL*.

13. On the song, see Schipper, *L'empereur Wou*, 54–55. For the "Song of the Metal Mother Flying in the Void," attributed to Meng Chiao, see *CTS*, 2253.

Chapter 5

1. On the use of Buddhist terminology and teachings in Taoist contexts, see Zürcher, "Buddhist Influences."

2. On aspects astronomical, Taoist, and literary of pacing the void in medieval China, see Schafer, *Pacing the Void*; and idem, "Wu Yün's 'Cantos on Pacing the Void.'"

Chapter 6

1. On Taoist practices, see Maspero, "Methods of 'Nourishing the Vital Principle' in the Ancient Taoist Religion," in *Taoism and Chinese Religion*, 443–554. On Shang ch'ing practice in the T'ang, see Köhn, *Seven Steps*. On hierarchies of practice for women, see Cahill, "Practice Makes Perfect."

2. On the special relationship between the Queen Mother and women during the T'ang, see Cahill, "Performers."

3. See Ames, "Taoism and the Androgynous Ideal."

4. On the Buddhist monastic orders for women in medieval China, see Tsai, "Chinese Buddhist Monastic Orders for Women." On women in

T'ang Taoism, see Despeux, "L'ordination des femmes Taoistes." For poems on Taoist nuns and priestesses, see Schafer, "Capeline Cantos."

5. On Jade Verity, see Schafer, "The Princess Realized in Jade."

6. On Refined Mistress Chiao, see Kroll, "Notes on Three Taoist Figures."

7. On fasting as a practice for women religious in medieval Catholicism, see R. Bell, *Holy Anorexia*; and Bynum, *Holy Feast*.

8. For Yü Hsüan-chi, see Walls, "The Poetry of Yü Hsüan-chi."

Bibliography

For the abbreviations used here, see pp. xiii–xiv.

Works in Western Languages

Acker, William. *Some T'ang and Pre-T'ang Texts on Chinese Paintings.* Leiden: Brill, 1974.

Ames, Roger T. "Taoism and the Androgynous Ideal." *Historical Reflections: Women in China* 8.3 (1981): 21–46.

Baldrian-Hussein, Farzeen. "Inner Alchemy: Notes on the Origin and Use of the Term *neidan*." *Cahiers d'Extrême Asie* 5 (1989–90): 163–90.

Bell, Catherine. "Medieval Taoist Ritual Mastery: A Study in Practice, Text, and Rite." Ph.D. dissertation, University of Chicago Divinity School, 1983.

———. "Ritualization of Texts and Textualization of Ritual in the Codification of Taoist Liturgy." *History of Religions* 27.4 (1988): 366–92.

Bell, Rudolph. *Holy Anorexia.* Chicago: University of Chicago Press, 1985.

Benn, Charles. "Religious Aspects of Emperor Hsüan-tsung's Taoist Ideology." In D. Chappell, ed., *Buddhist and Taoist Practice in Medieval Chinese Society.* Honolulu: University of Hawaii Press, 1987, 127–45.

Bielenstein, Hans. "An Interpretation of the Portents in the *Ts'ien Han-shu*." *Bulletin of the Museum of Far Eastern Antiquities* 22 (1950): 127–43.

Bilsky, Lester James. *The State Religion of Ancient China.* Taipei: Tung fang wen hua, 1975.

Blacker, Carmen. *The Catalpa Bow: A Study of Shamanistic Practices in Japan.* London: George Allen & Unwin, 1975.

Bodde, Derk. "The Chinese Cosmic Magic Known as Watching for the Ethers." In idem, *Essays on Chinese Civilization*, ed. Charles Le Blanc and Dorothy Borei. Princeton: Princeton University Press, 1981, 351–72.

———. *Festivals in Classical China*. Princeton: Princeton University Press, 1975.

———. "Myths of Ancient China." In idem, *Essays on Chinese Civilization*, ed. Charles Le Blanc and Dorothy Borei. Princeton: Princeton University Press, 1981, 45–84.

———. "Some Chinese Tales of the Supernatural: Kan Pao and His *Sou-shen chi*." In idem, *Essays on Chinese Civilization*, ed. Charles Le Blanc and Dorothy Borei. Princeton: Princeton University Press, 1981, 331–50.

Bokencamp, Stephen R. "Sources of the Ling-pao Scriptures." *Mélanges chinoises et bouddhiques* (Special issue: Tantric and Taoist Studies in Honour of R. A. Stein, vol. 2, ed. Michel Strickmann) 21 (1983): 434–86.

Boodberg, Peter A. *Selected Works of Peter A. Boodberg*. Ed. Alvin P. Cohen. Berkeley: University of California Press, 1979.

Bucksbaum, Dessa. "A Study of the Word *fang* in the OBI." Seminar paper, University of California, Berkeley, 1978.

Bulling, Annaliese. *The Decoration of Mirrors of the Han Period*. Ascona, Switz.: Artibus Asiae, 1960.

Bynum, Caroline Walker. *Holy Feast and Holy Fast: The Religious Significance of Food to Medieval Women*. Berkeley: University of California Press, 1987.

Cahill, Suzanne E. "Beside the Turquoise Pond: The Shrine of the Queen Mother of the West in Medieval Chinese Poetry and Religious Practice." *Journal of Chinese Religions* 12 (1984): 19–32.

———. "The Image of the Goddess Hsi Wang Mu in Medieval Chinese Literature." Ph.D. dissertation, University of California, Berkeley, 1982.

———. "Images of Transcendence and Divine Passion." *Ars Orientalis*, forthcoming.

———. "Marriages Made in Heaven." *T'ang Studies*, forthcoming.

———. "Night-Shining White: Traces of a T'ang Dynasty Horse in Two Media." *T'ang Studies* 4 (1986): 91–94.

———. "Performers and Female Taoist Adepts: Hsi Wang Mu as the Patron Saint of Women in Medieval China." *Journal of the American Oriental Society* 106 (1986): 155–68.

———. "Pien Tung-hsüan: A Taoist Woman Saint of the T'ang Dynasty." In Arvind Sharma, ed., *Women in World Religions: Biographies*. Forthcoming.

———. "Practice Makes Perfect: Paths to Transcendence for Women in Medieval China." *Taoist Resources* 2.2 (1990): 23–42.

———. "The Primordial Ruler, Metal Mother." *Taoist Resources*, forthcoming.

———. "Reflections, Disputes, and Warnings: Three Medieval Chinese Poems About Paintings of the Eight Horses of King Mu." *T'ang Studies* 5 (1987): 87–94.

———. "Reflections of a Metal Mother: Tu Kuang-t'ing's Biography of Hsi Wang Mu." *Journal of Chinese Religions* 13–14 (1985–86): 127–42.

———. "Sex and the Supernatural in Medieval China: Cantos on the Transcendent Who Presides Over the River." *Journal of the American Oriental Society* 105 (1985): 197–220.

———. "Sublimation in Medieval China: The Case of the Mysterious Woman of the Nine Heavens." *Journal of Chinese Religions* 20 (1992): 91–102.

———. "A White Clouds Appointment with the Queen Mother of the West." *Journal of Chinese Religions* 16 (1988): 43–53.

———. "The Word Made Bronze: Inscriptions on Medieval Chinese Bronze Mirrors." *Archives of Asian Art* 39 (1986): 62–70.

Chapin, Helen. "Toward the Study of the Sword as Dynastic Talisman: The Feng-ch'eng Pair and the Sword of Han Kao-tsu." Ph.D. dissertation, University of California, Berkeley, 1940.

Chavannes, Edouard. "Le jet des dragons." Paris: *Mémoires concernant l'Asie orientale*, 3 (1919): 53–126.

———. *Le T'ai-chan: Essai de monographie d'un culte chinois*. Annales de Musée Guimet, 28. Paris, 1910.

Chavannes, Edouard, trans. *Les mémoires historiques de Se-ma Ts'ian*. 6 vols. Paris: E. Leroux, 1895–1905.

Cheng Te-k'un. "Travels of Emperor Mu." *Journal of the North China Branch of the Royal Asiatic Society* 64 (1933): 124–42.

Despeux, Catherine. "L'ordination des femmes Taoïstes sous les T'ang." *Etudes chinoises* 5.1-2 (1986): 53–100.

DeWoskin, Kenneth J. *Doctors, Diviners, and Magicians of Ancient China: Biographies of Fang-shih*. New York: Columbia University Press, 1983.

Doré, Henri. *Récherches sur les superstitions en Chine*. 18 vols. Shanghai: T'usewei Printing Press, 1914–38.

Dubs, Homer. "An Ancient Chinese Mystery Cult." *Harvard Theological Review* 35.4 (1942): 221–40.

Dubs, Homer, trans. *History of the Former Han Dynasty*. 3 vols. Baltimore: Waverly Press, 1944.

Duyvendak, J. J. L. "The Dreams of Emperor Hsüan-tsung." *India Antiqua* 1947: 102–8.

Eberhard, Wolfram. *Lokalculturen im alten China*, vols. 1–2. Leiden: T'oung Pao, 1942.

Eliade, Mircea. *Myth and Reality*. New York: Harper, 1963.

————. *Shamanism: Archaic Techniques of Ecstasy*. Princeton: Princeton University Press, 1964.

Fairbank, Wilma. *Adventures in Retrieval*. Harvard-Yenching Institute Series, 28. Cambridge, Mass.: Harvard University Press, 1972.

Ferrand, Gabriel. "Le K'ouen-louen et les anciennes navigations interocéaniques dans les mers du sud." *Journal asiatique*, ser. 11, vol. 13 (1919): 239–492.

Finsterbusch, Kate. *Verzeichnis und Motivindex der Han-Darstellungen*, vols. 1–2. Wiesbaden: Otto Harrassowitz, 1966, 1971.

Fish, Michael B. "Yang Kuei-fei as the Hsi Wang Mu: Secondary Narrative in Two T'ang Poems." *Monumenta Serica* 32 (1976): 337–54.

Forke, Von A. "Mu Wang und die Königen von Saba." *Mitteilungen des Seminars für Orientalische Sprachen zu Berlin* 7, (1904): 117–72. (See review by Edouard Huber, *Bulletin de l'Ecole Française d'Extrême Orient* 4 [1904]: 1127–31; and response by Forke, "Se Wang Mu," *Mitteilungen* 7: 409–17.)

Fracasso, Riccardo. "Holy Mothers of Ancient China: A New Approach to the Hsi-wang-mu Problem." *T'oung Pao* 74 (1988): 1–46.

Frodsham, J. D. *The Poems of Li Ho (791–817)*. Oxford: Clarendon Press, 1970.

Giles, Herbert A. "Who Was Si Wang Mu?" *Adversaria Sinica* (Shanghai) 1905: 1–19. (See review by Paul Pelliot, *Bulletin de l'Ecole Française d'Extrême Orient* 5 [1905]: 416–21.)

Girardot, Norman. *Myth and Meaning in Early Taoism: The Theme of Chaos (huntun)*. Berkeley: University of California Press, 1983.

Graham, A. C. *The Book of Lieh-tzu: A Classic of Tao*. New York: Columbia University Press, 1990.

Groot, J. J. M. de. *Sectarianism and Religious Persecution in China*, vols. 1–2. Leiden: Brill, 1901. Reprinted—Taipei: Literature House, 1963.

Guisso, R. W. L. *Wu Tse-t'ien and the Politics of Legitimation in T'ang China*. Bellingham: Western Washington State University Press, 1978.

Gulik, Robert Hans van. *Sexual Life in Ancient China*. Leiden: Brill, 1974.

Harper, Donald J. "The Han Cosmic Board." *Early China* 4 (1978–79): 1–10.

Hartman, Charles. *Han Yü and the T'ang Search for Unity*. Princeton: Princeton University Press, 1986.

Hawkes, David. *Ch'u Tz'u: The Songs of the South*. Boston: Beacon, 1962.

————. "The Quest of the Goddess." In Cyril Birch, ed., *Studies in Chinese Literary Genres*. Berkeley: University of California Press, 1974, 42–68.

Henricks, Robert G. *The Poetry of Han-shan*. Albany: State University of New York Press, 1990.

Hightower, James. *The Poetry of T'ao Ch'ien*. Oxford: Clarendon Press, 1970.

Ho Peng Yoke. "Alchemy on Stones and Minerals in Chinese Pharmacopoeias." *Chung Chi Journal* 7 (1967–68): 155–70.

———. *The Astronomical Chapters of the Chin Shu, with Amendments, Full Translation, and Annotations*. Paris and the Hague: Mouton, 1966.

Ho Peng Yoke and Joseph Needham. "Elixir Poisoning in Medieval China." *Janus* 48 (1959): 221–51.

Homann, Rolf. *Pai Wen P'ien or The Hundred Questions: A Dialogue Between Two Taoists on the Macrocosmic and Microcosmic System of Correspondences*. Leiden: Brill, 1976.

———. *Die wichtigsten Körpergottheiten im Huang-t'ing ching*. Göppingen: Göppinger Akademische Beiträge, Verlag Alfred Kummerle, 1971.

Hou Ching-lang. "The Chinese Belief in Baleful Stars." In Holmes Welch and Anna Seidel, eds., *Facets of Taoism*. New Haven: Yale University Press, 1979, 193–228.

Hung, William. *Tu Fu: China's Greatest Poet*. New York: Russell & Russell, 1952.

Hurvitz, Leon. *Scripture of the Lotus Blossom of the Fine Dharma (The Lotus Sutra)*. New York: Columbia University Press, 1976.

Hyland, Elizabeth Watts. "Oracle of the True Ones: Scroll One." Ph.D. dissertation, University of California, Berkeley, 1984.

Jordan, David, and Daniel L. Overmyer. *The Flying Phoenix: Aspects of Chinese Sectarianism in Taiwan*. Princeton: Princeton University Press, 1986.

Kaltenmark, Maxime. "The Ideology of the *T'ai p'ing ching*." In Holmes Welch and Anna Seidel, eds., *Facets of Taoism*. New Haven: Yale University Press, 1979, 19–52.

———. *Le lie-sien tchouan*. Peking: Université de Paris, Centre d'Etudes sinologiques de Pekin, 1953. Reprinted—Paris: Collège de France, Institut des Hautes Etudes Chinoises, 1987.

Kaplan, Harry. "Lyrics on Pacing the Void." *Phi Theta Papers* (Berkeley, Calif.) 14 (1977): 51–60.

Karlgren, Bernard. "Early Chinese Mirror Inscriptions." *Bulletin of the Museum of Far Eastern Antiquities* 6 (1934): 9–74.

———. "Legends and Cults in Ancient China." *Bulletin of the Museum of Far Eastern Antiquities* 18 (1946): 199–465.

Kazetsky, Patricia Eichenbaum, and Alexander Soper. "A Northern Wei Painted Coffin." *Artibus Asiae* 51.1–2 (1991): 5–28.

Kinsley, David. *Hindu Goddesses: Visions of the Divine Feminine in the Hindu Religious Tradition*. Berkeley: University of California Press, 1986.

Kirkland, J. Russell. "The Last Taoist Grand Master at the T'ang Imperial Court: Li Han-kuang and T'ang Hsüan-tsung." *T'ang Studies* 4 (1986): 43–67.

Knechtges, David R. *The Han Rhapsody.* Cambridge, Eng.: Cambridge University Press, 1976.

Knechtges, David R., trans. *Wen Hsüan or Selections of Refined Literature.* 2 vols. Princeton: Princeton University Press, 1982, 1987.

Köhn, Livia. "The Mother of the Tao." *Taoist Resources* 1.2 (1989): 37–113.

———. *Seven Steps to the Tao: Sima Chengzhen's "Zuowang lun."* Monumenta Serica Monographs, 20. Nettetal: Steyler Verlag, 1987.

Köhn, Livia, and Y. Sakade, eds. *Taoist Meditation and Longevity Techniques.* Ann Arbor: University of Michigan Press, 1989.

Kroll, Paul W. "In the Halls of the Azure Lad." *Journal of the American Oriental Society* 105 (1985): 75–94.

———. "Li Po's Transcendent Diction." *Journal of the American Oriental Society* 106 (1986): 99–117.

———. "Notes on Three Taoist Figures of the T'ang Dynasty" [1. Szu-ma Ch'eng-chen; 2. Refined Mistress Chiao; 3. The Lady of the Highest Prime]. *Society for the Study of Chinese Religions Bulletin* 9 (1981): 19–41.

———. "Ssu-ma Ch'eng-chen in T'ang Verse." *Society for the Study of Chinese Religions Bulletin* 6 (1978): 16–30.

———. "The True Dates of the Reigns and Reign-periods of the T'ang." *T'ang Studies* 2 (1984): 25–30.

———. "Verses from on High: The Ascent of T'ai Shan." *T'oung Pao* 69 (1983): 223–60.

Lagerway, John. *Taoist Ritual in Chinese Society and History.* New York: Macmillan, 1987.

———. *Wu-shang pi-yao: somme taoïste du VIe siècle.* Paris: Ecole Française d'Extrême Orient, 1981.

Laufer, Berthold. *Jade: A Study in Chinese Archaeology and Religion.* Chicago: Field Museum of Natural History, 1912.

Legge, James, trans. *The Chinese Classics,* 5 vols. Hong Kong: Hong Kong University Press, 1961.

Levi, Jean. "L'abstinence des céréales chez les taoïstes." *Etudes chinoises* 1983.1: 3–47.

———. "Les fonctionnaires et le divins: Luttes de pouvoir entre divinités et administrateurs dans les contes des Six Dynasties et des T'ang." *Cahiers d'Extrême Asie* 2 (1986): 81–110.

Li, Theresa June. "Hsi-wang-mu: A Study of Early Textual and Visual Evidence." M.A. thesis, University of Pennsylvania, 1978.

Liu, James J. Y. *The Poetry of Li Shang-yin.* Chicago: University of Chicago Press, 1969.

Loewe, Michael. *Chinese Ideas of Life and Death: Faith, Myth, and Reason in the Han Period.* London: George Allen & Unwin, 1982.

———. *Ways to Paradise: The Chinese Quest for Immortality.* London: George Allen & Unwin, 1979.

Lu Hsün. *A Brief History of Chinese Fiction.* Trans. Yang Hsien-yi and Gladys Yang. Peking: Foreign Languages Press, 1964.

Maspero, Henri. "Légendes mythologiques dans le *Chou King.*" *Journale asiatique* 102 (1924): 1–100.

———. "Les procédés de 'Nourrir le principe vital' dans la religion taoïste ancienne." In idem, *Le taoïsme et les religions chinoises.* Paris: Gallimard, 1971, 479–589. Trans. Frank A. Kierman, Jr., *Taoism and Chinese Religion.* Amherst: University of Massachusetts Press, 1981, 443–554.

———. "Le taoïsme." In idem, *Le taoïsme et les religions chinoises.* Paris: Gallimard, 1971, 293–466. Trans. Frank A. Kierman, Jr., *Taoism and Chinese Religion.* Amherst: University of Massachusetts Press, 1981, 263–430.

Mather, Richard, trans. *Shih-shuo Hsin-yü: A New Account of Tales of the World.* Minneapolis: University of Minnesota Press, 1976.

Mathieu, Remi, trans. *Le Mu tianzi zhuan: Traduction annotée, étude critique.* Paris: Institut des Hautes Etudes Chinoises, 1978.

Needham, Joseph. *Clerks and Craftsmen in China and the West.* Cambridge, Eng.: Cambridge University Press, 1970.

Needham, Joseph, and collaborators. *Science and Civilisation in China,* vols. 1–6.1. Cambridge, Eng.: Cambridge University Press, 1956–83.

Nienhauser, William H., Jr., ed. and comp. *The Indiana Companion to Traditional Chinese Literature.* Bloomington: Indiana University Press, 1986.

O'Flaherty, Wendy D. *Women, Androgynes, and Other Mythical Beasts.* Chicago: University of Chicago Press, 1980.

Ōfuchi, Ninji. "The Formation of the Taoist Canon." In Holmes Welch and Anna Seidel, eds., *Facets of Taoism.* New Haven: Yale University Press, 1979, 253–67.

Overmyer, Daniel L. "Attitudes Toward Popular Religion in Ritual Texts of the Chinese State: *The Collected Statutes of the Great Ming.*" *Cahiers d'Extrême Asie* 5 (1989–90): 199–221.

———. *Folk Buddhist Religion: Dissenting Sects in Late Traditional China.* Princeton: Princeton University Press, 1976.

Owen, Stephen. *The Poetry of the Early T'ang.* New Haven: Yale University Press, 1977.

Porkert, Manfred. *The Theoretical Foundations of Chinese Medicine: Systems of Correspondence.* Cambridge, Mass.: MIT Press, 1974.

Read, B. E. *Chinese Medicinal Plants from the Pen Ts'ao Kang Mu, AD 1597.* Peking, 1936.

———. "A Compendium of Minerals and Stones Used in Chinese Medicines from the *Pen Ts'ao Kang Mu*, Li Shih-chen, 1597 AD." *Peking Society of Natural History Bulletin* (special issue) 3 (1928).

Riegel, Jeffrey. "Kuo-mang and Ju-shou." *Cahiers d'Extrême Asie* 5 (1989–90): 55–83.

Robinet, Isabelle. *Meditation taoïste.* Paris: Dervy-Livres, 1977.

———. "Metamorphosis and Deliverance from the Corpse in Taoism." *History of Religions* 19 (1979): 37–70.

———. "Randonnées extatiques des taoïstes dans les astres." *Monumenta Serica* 32 (1976): 159–273.

———. *La révélation du Shangqing dans l'histoire du taoïsme.* 2 vols. Paris: Ecole Française d'Extrême Orient, 1984.

———. "A Study of the Relationship Between the *Shang-ch'ing* Movement and the *Fang-shih* and the Seekers of Immortality." Paper presented at the Third International Conference on Taoist Studies, Unterägeri, 1979.

Robinson, Richard. *Early Mādhyamika in India and China.* Madison: University of Wisconsin Press, 1967.

Saso, Michael. *Taoism and the Rite of Cosmic Renewal.* Bellingham: Western Washington State University Press, 1972.

Schafer, Edward H. "The Capeline Cantos: Verses on the Divine Loves of Taoist Priestesses." *Asiatische Studien* 32 (1978): 5–65.

———. "The Development of Bathing Customs in Ancient and Medieval China and the History of the Floriate Clear Palace." *Journal of the American Oriental Society* 76 (1956): 57–82.

———. *The Divine Woman: Dragon Ladies and Rain Maidens in T'ang Literature.* Berkeley: University of California Press, 1973.

———. *The Golden Peaches of Samarkand.* Berkeley: University of California Press, 1963.

———. *Mao Shan in T'ang Times.* Society for the Study of Chinese Religions, Monograph 1. Boulder, Colo., 1980.

———. *Mirages on the Sea of Time: The Taoist Poetry of Ts'ao T'ang.* Berkeley: University of California Press, 1985.

———. "Mineral Imagery in the Paradise Poems of Kuan Hsiu." *Asia Major* 10 (1963): 73–102.

———. *Pacing the Void: T'ang Approaches to the Stars.* Berkeley: University of California Press, 1977.

———. "The Princess Realized in Jade." *T'ang Studies* 3 (1985): 1–23.

———. "Three Divine Women of South China." *Chinese Literature: Essays, Articles, Reviews* 1 (1979): 31–42.

———. "The Transcendent Vitamin: Efflorescence of *Lang-kan*." *Chinese Science* 3 (1978): 27–38.

———. "Wu Yün's 'Cantos on Pacing the Void.' " *Harvard Journal of Asiatic Studies* 41 (1981): 377–415.

Schipper, Kristofer M. "*Le Calendrier de Jade*: Note sur le *Laozi zhongjing*." *Nachrichten der Gesellschaft für Natur- und Völkerkunde Ostasiens* 125 (1979): 75–80.

———. *Le corps taoïste—corps physique—corps social.* Paris: Fayard, 1982.

———. *L'empereur Wou des Han dans la legende taoïste.* Paris: Ecole Française d'Extrême Orient, 1965.

———. "The Taoist Body." *History of Religions* 17 (1978): 355–86.

Seidel, Anna. *La divinisation de Lao tseu dans le taoïsme des Han.* Paris: Ecole Française d'Extrême Orient, 1969.

———. "Imperial Treasures and Taoist Sacraments." *Mélanges chinoises et bouddhiques* (Special issue: Tantric and Taoist Studies in Honour of R. A. Stein, vol. 2, ed. Michel Strickmann) 21 (1983): 291–371.

———. "Tokens of Immortality in Han Graves." *Numen* 24 (1982): 79–122.

Sharma, Arvind, ed. *Women in World Religions.* Albany: State University of New York Press, 1987.

Shaughnessy, Edward L. "On the Authenticity of the *Bamboo Annals*." *Harvard Journal of Asiatic Studies* 46 (1986): 149–80.

Sivin, Nathan. *Chinese Alchemy: Preliminary Studies.* Cambridge, Mass.: Harvard University Press, 1968.

———. "The Theoretical Background of Elixir Alchemy." In Joseph Needham and collaborators, *Science and Civilisation in China*, vol. 5.4. Cambridge, Eng.: Cambridge University Press, 1980, 210–323.

Soothill, William. *The Hall of Light.* London: Lutterworth Press, 1951.

Stein, Rolf A. "Jardins en miniature d'Extrême Orient." *Bulletin de l'Ecole Française d'Extrême Orient* 42 (1943): 1–104. Rev. ed. of 1987 trans. Phyllis Brooks, *The World in Miniature: Container Gardens and Dwellings in Far Eastern Religious Thought.* Stanford: Stanford University Press, 1990, 1–119.

———. "Religious Taoism and Popular Religion from the Second to the Seventh Centuries." In Holmes Welch and Anna Seidel, eds., *Facets of Taoism.* New Haven: Yale University Press, 1979, 53–81.

Strickmann, Michel. "The Longest Taoist Scripture." *History of Religions* 17 (1978): 331–54.

———. "The Mao Shan Revelations: Taoism and the Aristocracy." *T'oung Pao* 63 (1977): 1–64.

————. "On the Alchemy of T'ao Hung-ching." In Holmes Welch and Anna Seidel, eds., *Facets of Taoism*. New Haven: Yale University Press, 1979, 123–92.

Sullivan, Michael. *The Arts of China*. 3rd ed. Berkeley: University of California Press, 1986.

Sun Tso-yün. "An Analysis of the Western Han Murals in the Luoyang Tomb of Bo Qianqiu." Trans. Suzanne E. Cahill. *Chinese Studies in Archaeology* 1.2 (1979): 44–78.

Tanakh: The Holy Scriptures. New York: Jewish Publication Society, 1988.

Tate, G. H. H. *Mammals of Eastern Asia*. New York: Macmillan, 1947.

Tsai, Kathryn A. "The Chinese Buddhist Monastic Order for Women: The First Two Centuries." In Richard W. Guisso and Stanley Johanesen, eds., *Women in China: Current Directions in Historical Scholarship. Historical Reflections / Reflexions Historiques*. New York: Philo Press, 1981, 1–20.

Twitchett, Dennis, ed. *Sui and T'ang China*. The Cambridge History of China, vol. 3, pt. 1. Cambridge, Eng.: Cambridge University Press, 1979.

Umehara Sueji. *Album of the Moriya Kōzō Collection*. Tokyo, n.d.

————. "The Late Mr. Moriya's Collection of Ancient Chinese Mirrors." *Artibus Asiae* 18 (1955): 238–56.

Verellen, Franciscus. *Du Guangting (850–933): Taoïste de cour à la fin de la Chine médiévale*. Memoires de l'Institut des Hautes Etudes Chinoises, 30. Paris: Collège de France, 1989.

Von Sach, Erwin. *Han Yü's poetische Werke*. Harvard-Yenching Institute Series 7. Cambridge, Mass.: Harvard University Press, 1952.

Wagner, Rudolph G. "Lebenstil und Drogen im Chinesischen Mittelalter." *T'oung Pao* 59 (1973): 79–178.

Waldron, Arthur. *The Great Wall of China: From History to Myth*. Cambridge, Eng.: Cambridge University Press, 1990.

Waley, Arthur. *The Life and Times of Po Chü-yi, 772-846 AD*. London: Allen & Unwin, 1949.

————. *The Way and Its Power*. London, 1934. Reprinted—New York: Grove Press, 1958.

Walls, Jan W. "The Poetry of Yü Hsüan-chi: A Translation, Annotation, Commentary, and Critique." Ph.D. dissertation, Indiana University, 1972.

Ware, James. *Alchemy, Medicine, and Religion in the China of AD 320: The Nei-P'ien of Ko Hung*. Cambridge, Mass.: MIT Press, 1966.

Watson, Burton. *Courtier and Commoner*. New York: Columbia University Press, 1974.

Watson, Burton, trans. *The Complete Works of Chuang-tzu.* New York: Columbia University Press, 1968.

———. *Records of the Grand Historian of China.* 2 vols. New York: Columbia University Press, 1961.

Wechsler, Howard. *Offerings of Jade and Silk: Ritual and Symbol in the Legitimation of the T'ang Dynasty.* New Haven: Yale University Press, 1985.

Welch, Holmes. *The Parting of the Way: Lao Tzu and the Taoist Movement.* Boston: Beacon, 1957.

Welch, Holmes, and Anna Seidel, eds. *Facets of Taoism.* New Haven: Yale University Press, 1979.

Wolf, Arthur P., ed. *Religion and Ritual in Chinese Society.* Stanford: Stanford University Press, 1974.

Wu Hung. "Buddhist Elements in Early Chinese Art (2nd and 3rd Centuries AD)." *Artibus Asiae* 47 (1986): 263–352.

———. *The Wu Liang Shrine: The Ideology of Early Chinese Pictorial Art.* Stanford: Stanford University Press, 1989.

Yu Fei-an. *Chinese Painting Colors: Studies of Their Preparation and Application in Traditional and Modern Times.* Trans. Jerome Silbergeld and Amy McNair. Seattle: University of Washington Press, 1988.

Zürcher, Eric. *The Buddhist Conquest of China.* 2 vols. Leiden: Brill, 1959.

———. "Buddhist Influences on Early Taoism: A Survey of Scriptural Evidence." *T'oung Pao* 66 (1980): 84–147.

Works in Chinese and Japanese

Akatsuka Kiyoshi 赤塚忠. *Chūgoku kodai no shūkyō to bunka* 中國古代の宗教と文化 (Ancient Chinese religion and culture). Tokyo, 1977.

Chang Hua 張華. *Po wu chih* 博物志 (Monograph on broad phenomena). TSCC. Shanghai, 1939.

Chang Hung-chao 張鴻釗, ed. *Shih ya (Shih yao erh ya)* 石雅(石藥爾雅) (The *Erh ya* of mineral medicines). *Ti chih chuan pao* 地質傳報, ser. B, no. 2. Peking, 1921.

Chao Yeh 趙曄. *Wu Yüeh ch'un ch'iu* 吳越春秋 (Springs and autumns of Wu and Yüeh). TSCC. Shanghai, 1937.

Ch'en I-hsin 陳貽焮. *T'ang shih lun ts'ung* 唐詩論叢 (Collection of essays on T'ang poetry). Hunan: Jen min, 1960.

Ch'en Kuo-fu 陳國符. *Tao tsang yüan liu k'ao* 道藏源流考 (Examination of the origin and development of the Taoist canon). Hong Kong: Chung Hua, 1963.

Ch'en Meng-chia 陳蒙家. "Ku wen tzu chung chih Shang Chou chi ssu" 古文字中之商周祭祀 (The sacrificial system of the Shang and Chou found in ancient inscriptions). *Yen ching hsüeh pao* 燕京學報 19 (1936): 91–155.

Ch'en Yin-k'o 陳寅恪. *Yüan Po shih chien cheng kao* 元白詩箋證稿 (Commentaries and textual research on the poetry of Yüan Chen and Po Chü-i). Shanghai: Ku chi, 1958.

Chi Yu-kung 計有功. *T'ang shih chi shih* 唐詩紀事 (Recorded anecdotes concerning T'ang poetry). Hong Kong: Chung Hua, 1962.

Chou li yin te fu chu su yin shu yin te 周禮引得附注疏引書引得 (Index to the *Rites of Chou* and to the titles quoted in its commentaries). Peking: Harvard-Yenching Institute, 1940.

Chu shu chi nien 竹書紀年 (Bamboo annals). Ed. Wang Kuo-wei 王國維. TSCC. Shanghai, 1936.

Ch'ü Yüan 屈原, attributed. *Ch'u tz'u* (Lyrics of Ch'u). *Ch'u tz'u pu chu* 楚辭補註 ed. Hong Kong: Chung Hua, 1963.

Ch'üan T'ang shih 全唐詩 (Complete T'ang poetry). Taipei: Fu hsing, 1967.

Chuang-tzu yin te 莊子引得 (Index to *Chuang-tzu*). Peking: Harvard-Yenching Institute, 1947.

Erh-ya yin te 爾雅引得 (Index to the *Erh ya*). Peking: Harvard-Yenching Institute, 1941.

Fan Yeh 范曄 et al. *Hou Han shu* 後漢書 (Book of the Latter Han). Peking: Chung Hua, 1963.

Fang Hsüan-ling 房玄齡 et al. *Chin shu* 晉書 (Book of Chin). Peking: Chung Hua, 1973.

Han Fei-tzu 韓非子. *Han Fei-tzu chi shih* 韓非子集釋 (Collected explications of Han Fei-tzu). Ed. Ch'en Ch'i-you 陳奇猷. Shanghai: Chung Hua, 1958.

Han K'ung-yüan and Lo Feng. "The Discovery of a Northern Wei Tomb with a Lacquered Coffin in the Central Plain" (in Chinese). *Mei shu yen chiu* 1984.2: 3–16.

Han Wu-ti nei chuan 漢武帝內傳 (Esoteric transmissions concerning the Martial Thearch of the Han). TSCC. Shanghai, 1937.

Hayashi Minao 林巳奈夫. *Kandai no kagami* 漢代の鏡 (Han mirrors). Kyoto, 1990.

———. "Kan kyō no zuhyō ni, san ni tsuite" 漢鏡の圖柄二, 三について (Two or three points about the design of Han mirrors). *Tōhō gakuhō* 東方學報 44 (1973): 1–65.

Hsi Wang Mu chuan wo ku fa 西王母傳握固法 (Transmission of the method of grasping the firmness taught by the Queen Mother of the West). HY 263.

Hsi Wang Mu pao shen ch'i chü ching 西王母寶神起居經 (Scripture on the activities and rest of the precious deities from the Queen Mother of the West). HY 1308.

(Hsi yüeh) Hua shan chih (西嶽)華山志 (Monograph on [the Western Marchmount] Mount Hua). HY 307.

Hsiao T'ung 蕭統. *Wen hsüan* 文選 (Literary selections). Hong Kong: Shang wu, 1973.

Hsü Chien 徐堅. *Ch'u hsüeh chi* 初學記 (Record of beginning studies). Peking: Chung Hua, 1962.

Hsün-tzu yin te 荀子引得 (Index to the *Hsün-tzu*). Peking: Harvard-Yenching Institute, 1950.

Huai nan-tzu hung lieh chi chieh 淮南子鴻烈集解 (*Huai Nan-tzu* with a broad and eminent collection of commentaries). Ed. Liu Wen-tien 劉文典. Shanghai: Shang wu, 1926.

Huang ti chiu ting shen tan ching 黃帝九鼎神丹經 (Scripture concerning the divine elixir of the nine tripods of the Yellow Thearch). HY 884.

Huang ti yin fu ching 黃帝陰符經 (Scripture concerning the Yellow Thearch's yin talismans). HY 31.

Huang t'ing ching 黃庭經. Ed. Kristofer M. Schipper. *Concordance du Houang-t'ing king*. Paris: Ecole Française d'Extrême Orient, 1975.

Huang t'ing nei ching ching 黃庭內景經 (Scripture of inner phosphors from the yellow courtyard). In *Yün chi ch'i ch'ien* 雲笈七籤 (Seven slips from a bookbag of clouds). HY 1026, ch. 11–12.

Huang t'ing tun chia yüan shen ching 黃庭遁甲緣身經 (Scripture from the yellow courtyard on concealing the *chia* and on the predestined body). HY 872.

Huang-fu Mi 皇甫謐. *Ti wang shih chi* 帝王世紀 (Record of generations of thearchs and kings). TSCC. Shanghai, 1937.

I ching 易經 (Classic of Changes). Ed. Yeh Shao-chün 葉紹鈞. *Shih san ching so yin* 十三經索引. Shanghai: K'ai ming, 1934.

Imaeda Jirō 今田次郎. "To Kōtei shōkō" 杜光庭小考 (An investigation of Tu Kuang-t'ing). In *Yoshioka hakase kanreki kinen: Dōkyō kenkyū ronshu* 吉岡博士還曆紀念:道教研究論集 (Collected essays in Taoist thought and culture: Festschrift for Yoshioka Yoshitoyo). Tokyo: Kokusho kankōkai, 1977.

Inshū senkoku 殷周戰國 (Yin, Chou, and Warring States periods). Sekai bijutsu zenzhu 世界美術全集 (Complete collection of fine arts of the world), vol. 12. Tokyo: Kadokawa shoten, 1962.

Kan Pao 干寶. *Sou shen chi* 搜神記 (Record that gathers up deities). Peking: Chung Hua, 1981.

Ko Hung 葛洪. *Pao p'u-tzu* 抱朴子 (The master who embraces the uncarved block). Ed. Wang Ming 王明. *Pao p'u-tzu nei p'ien chiao shih* 抱朴子內篇校釋 (Comparative explications of the inner chapters of the *Pao p'u-tzu*). Peking: Chung Hua, 1980.

Ko Hung 葛洪, attributed. *Shen hsien chuan* 神仙傳 (Transmissions concerning the divine transcendents). Shanghai: Shuo k'u, 1914.

Komai Kikutani 駒井和愛. *Chūgoku kokyō no kenkyū* 中國古鏡の研究 (Research on ancient Chinese mirrors). Tokyo, 1953.

Kominami Ichirō 小南一郎. "Seiōbo to shichi seki denshō" 西王母と七夕傳承 (The Queen Mother of the West and traditions about the seventh night). *Tōhō gakuhō* 東方學報 46 (1974): 33–81.

Kuo Mao 郭茂. *Yüeh fu shih chi* 樂府詩集 (Collection of music bureau poetry). Peking: Chung Hua, 1979.

Li chi yin te 禮記引得 (Index to the *Record of Rites*). Peking: Harvard-Yenching Institute, 1937.

Li Fang 李昉 et al. *T'ai p'ing kuang chi* 太平廣記 (A broad record of the era of great peace). Peking: Jen min wen hsüeh, 1959.

———. *T'ai p'ing yü lan* 太平御覽 (The era of great peace, for imperial scrutiny). Shanghai: Chung Hua, 1960.

Li Ho 李賀. *Li Ho shih ko chi chu* 李賀詩歌集注 (Poems and songs of Li Ho, collected with commentaries). Shanghai: Ku chi, 1977.

Li Po 李白. *Li T'ai-po ch'üan chi* 李太白全集 (Complete collected works of Li T'ai-po). Peking: Chung Hua, 1977.

Li Shang-yin 李商隱. *Li I-shan shih chi* 李義山詩集 (Collected poems of Li I-shan). Hong Kong: Chung Hua, 1978.

Li Shih-chen 李時珍. *Pen ts'ao kang mu* 本草綱目 (Materia medica). Hong Kong: Shang wu, 1974.

Lieh hsien chuan 列仙傳 (Transmissions concerning the arrayed transcendents). HY 294.

Lieh-tzu chi shih 列子集釋 (Collected explications of the *Lieh-tzu*). Ed. Yang Po-chün 楊伯峻. Peking: Chung Hua, 1979.

Liu Hsü 劉昫 et al. *T'ang shu* 唐書 (Book of T'ang). Peking: Chung Hua, 1975.

Liu I-ch'ing 劉義慶. *Shih shuo hsin yü* 世說新語 (A new telling of tales of the world). *Shih shuo hsin yü yin te* 世說新語引得. Peking: Harvard-Yenching Institute, 1933.

Liu Ta-pin 劉大彬. *Mao shan chih* 茅山誌 (Monograph on Mount Mao). HY 304.

Liu Tsung-yüan 柳宗元. *T'ien wen t'ien tui chu* 天問天對註 (Heavenly questions and heavenly responses, with commentary). Peking: Chung Hua, 1975.

Lu Hsün 魯迅. *Ku hsiao shuo kou chen* 古小說鈎沈 (Fishing in the depths of old fiction). In *Lu Hsün ch'üan chi* 魯迅全集 (Lu Hsün's complete collected works), vol. 8. Shanghai: Jen min wen hsüeh, 1938.

Meng-tzu yin te 孟子引得 (Index to the *Meng-tzu*). Peking: Harvard-Yenching Institute, 1940.

Mu T'ien-tzu chuan 穆天子傳 (Transmissions concerning Mu, the son of heaven). TSCC, Shanghai, 1937.

Ou-yang Hsiu 歐陽修 et al. *Hsin T'ang shu* 新唐書 (The new book of T'ang). Shanghai: Chung Hua, 1975.

Ou-yang Hsün 歐陽詢. *I wen lei chü* 藝文類聚. Shanghai: Chung Hua, 1965.

Pan Ku 班固 et al. *Han shu* 漢書 (Book of Han). Peking: Chung Hua, 1962.

Po Chü-i 白居易. *Po Chü-i chi* 白居易集 (Collected works of Po Chü-i). Peking: Chung Hua, 1979.

———. *Po shih liu t'ieh shih lei chi* 白氏六帖事類集. Taipei: Hsin hsing, 1975.

San tung chu nang 三洞珠囊 (A beaded satchel from the three grottoes). HY 1131.

Shan hai ching chiao chu 山海經校註 (The *Classic of Mountains and Seas* with comparative commentaries). Ed. Yüan Ho. Shanghai: Ku chi, 1979.

Shang ch'ing Lao-tzu chung ching 上清老子中經 (The central classic of Lao-tzu from the realm of supreme clarity). HY 1160.

Shang ch'ing liu jen ming chien fu yin ching 上清六壬明鑑符隱經 (The yin scripture concerning the bright mirror talisman of the six *jen* from the Realm of Supreme Clarity). HY 860.

Shang ch'ing yüan shih pien hua pao chen shang ching chiu ling t'ai miao kuei shan hsüan lu 上清元始變化寶眞上經九靈太妙龜山玄錄 (The mysterious register from Tortoise Mountain of the nine numina and the grand verity derived from the treasured and veritable supreme scripture concerning transformation and changes of the primordial commencement from the Realm of Supreme Clarity). HY 1382.

Shang shu ta chuan 尚書大傳 (Great transmissions concerning the *Book of Documents*). TSCC, Shanghai, 1936.

Shen i ching 神異經 (Classic of deities and oddities). Shuo k'u. Shanghai, 1914.

Shen Te-ch'ien 沈德潛. *Ku shih yüan* 古詩源 (A spring of ancient poetry). Peking: Chung Hua, 1963.

Shen Ts'ung-wen 沈從文. *Chung kuo ku tai fu shih yen chiu* 中國古代服飾研究 (Research on ancient Chinese clothing and ornamentation). Hong Kong: Shang wu, 1981.

Shih chou chi 十洲記 (Record of ten isle-lands). Shuo k'u. Shanghai, 1914.

Shih ming 釋名 (Explaining terms). *Shih ming shu cheng p'u* 釋名疏証補 ed. Shanghai: Shang wu, 1938.

Shima Kunio 島邦男. *Inkyo bokuji sōrui* 殷墟卜辭綜類 (Classification of divination terms from the wastes of Yin). Taipei: T'ai hsün, 1969.

Shu ching 書經 (Classic of history). *The Chinese Classics*, vol. 3. Trans. James Legge. Reprinted—Hong Kong: Hong Kong University Press, 1960.

Shu ching: Shih san ching so yin 書經:十三經索引 (Index to the thirteen classics). Ed. Yeh Shao-chün 葉紹鈞. Shanghai: K'ai ming, 1934.

Shu i chi 述異記 (Record that narrates oddities). Shuo k'u. Shanghai, 1914.

Shui ching chu yin te 水經注引得 (Index to the *Classic of the Waterways with Commentary*). Peking: Harvard-Yenching Institute, 1934.

Shuo wen chieh tzu ku lin 說文解字詁林 (A forest of commentaries on the *Shuo wen chieh tzu* dictionary). Ed. Ting Fu-pao 丁福保. Shanghai: I hsüeh shu chü, 1928.

Ssu-ma Ch'ien 司馬遷. *Shih chi* 史記 (Records of the historian). Peking: Chung Hua, 1962.

Ssu-ma Kuang 司馬光. *Tz'u chih t'ung chien* 資治通鑑 (A comprehensive mirror for the aid of government). Peking: Chung Hua, 1963.

Su Hsüeh-lin 蘇雪林. *T'ien wen cheng chien* 天問正簡 (Explication of the "Heavenly Questions"). Taipei: Kuang tung, 1973.

Sun Tso-yün 孫作雲. "Lo yang Hsi Han Po Ch'ien-ch'iu mu pi hua kao shih" 洛陽西漢卜千秋墓壁畫考釋 (An analysis of the Western Han murals in the Lo yang tomb of Po Ch'ien-ch'iu). *Wen wu* 文物 1977.6: 17–22.

Ta Tai li chi 大戴禮記 (Record of the rites according to the Elder Tai). TSCC. Shanghai, 1937.

Ta T'ang liu tien 大唐六典 (Six standards of the great T'ang dynasty). Taipei: Wen hai, 1962.

Ta tung chen ching 大洞眞經 (Veritable scripture of the great grotto). In *Yün chi ch'i ch'ien* 雲笈七籤 (Seven slips from a bookbag of clouds). HY 1026, ch. 8.

T'ai ch'ing shang kao kuei shan hsüan lu 太清上高龜山玄錄 (The mysterious register of the supreme and lofty Tortoise Mountain from the Realm of Grand Clarity). HY 1383.

T'ai shang Lao chün shuo ch'ang ch'ing ching miao ching 太上老君說常清靜妙經 (The marvelous scripture of constant purity and quiet as explicated by Lord Lao of the Grand Supreme). HY 620. Commentary by Tu Kuang-t'ing. HY 758.

T'ai shang ling pao wu fu ching 太上靈寶五符經 (Scripture of the five talismans of the numinous treasure from the Grand Supreme). HY 388.

T'ai shang san t'ien (t'ien) cheng fa ching 太上三田(天)正法經 (Scripture of the rectified method of the three fields [heavens] from the Grand Supreme). HY 1194.

T'ai shang yüan pao chin t'ing wu wei miao ching 太上元寶金庭無爲妙經 (Marvelous scripture on non-action from the metal courtyard of the primordial treasure from the Grand Supreme). HY 1388.

T'ang hui yao 唐會要 (Assembled essentials of the T'ang). Taipei: Shih chieh, 1960.

Tao tsang 道藏 (Treasure house of the way). *Cheng t'ung* 正統 ed. First printed 1444. Reprinted—Taipei: I wen, 1976. 60 vols.

T'ao Hung-ching 陶弘景. *Hsüan tung ling pao chen ling wei yeh t'u* 玄洞靈寶眞靈位業圖 (Chart of the ranks and functions of the realized ones and the numina of the numinous treasures from the mysterious grotto). HY 167.

T'ao Hung-ching 陶弘景, ed. *Chen kao* 眞誥 (Declarations of the realized ones). HY 1010.

T'ao Yüan-ming 陶淵明. *T'ao Yüan-ming chi* 陶淵明集 (Collected works of T'ao Yüan-ming). Peking: Tso chia, 1956.

Tseng Chao-yü 曾昭燏. *I nan ku hua hsiang shih mu fa chüeh pao kao* 沂南古畫像石墓發掘報告 (Report on the excavation of an ancient carved stone tomb at I nan). Shanghai: Wen hua kuan li chü, 1956.

Tso chuan 左傳. *Ch'un-ch'iu ching yin te* 春秋經引得 (Index to the *Spring and Autumn Annals*). Peking: Harvard-Yenching Institute, 1937.

Tu Fu 杜甫. *Tu Shao-ling chi hsiang chu* 杜少陵集詳註 (The poetry of Tu Shao-ling with detailed commentary). Ed. Ch'iu T'ao-ao 仇兆鰲. Peking: Chung Hua, 1974.

————. *Tu shih hsiang chu* 杜詩詳注 (Tu's poetry with detailed commentary). Peking: Chung Hua, 1979.

————. *Tu shih yin te* 杜詩引得 (Index to Tu's poetry). Ed. William Hung. Peking: Harvard-Yenching Institute, 1940.

Tu jen ching 度人經 (Scripture on ferrying human beings across to salvation). HY 1.

Tu Kuang-t'ing 杜光庭. *Tu kuang ch'eng chi* 杜廣成集 (Collected works of Tu, master of broad completion). HY 616.

————. *Tung t'ien fu ti yüeh tu ming shan chi* 洞天福地嶽瀆名山記 (A record of grotto-heavens, beneficent locations, marchmounts, conduits, and famous mountains). HY 599.

————. *Yung ch'eng chi hsien lu* 墉城集仙錄 (Record of the assembled transcendents of the fortified walled city). HY 782. For another version, see *Yün chi ch'i ch'ien* 雲笈七籤 (Seven slips from a bookbag of clouds). HY 1026, ch. 114.

Tun chia chen ching 通甲眞經 (Veritable scripture on concealing the *chia*). HY 856.

Tun-huang wen wu yen chiu so 敦煌文物研究所 (Tun-huang Cultural Research Institute). *Tun-huang mo kao k'u* 敦煌莫高窟 (Grottoes at Tun-huang). Chung kuo shi k'u 中國石窟 (Stone caves of China), vols. 1–2. Peking: Wen wu, 1982.

Tung chen t'ai wei chin hu chen fu 洞眞太微金虎眞符 (Veritable talisman of the metal tiger from the grand tenuity, from the grotto verified division of the canon). HY 1326.

Tung ming chi 洞冥記 (Record of grotto-underworlds). Shuo k'u. Shanghai, 1914.

Tung t'ien shang ch'ing ching yao tzu shu chin yin hsiang ching 洞天上清精要

紫書金銀象經 (Gold and silver scripture of images in the purple text of essential requirements from the Realm of Supreme Clarity hidden in the grotto-heavens). HY 1304.

Tzu yang chen jen nei chuan 紫陽眞人內傳 (Inner transmissions concerning the realized person of the purple yang). HY 303.

Umehara Sueji 梅原末治. *Kan sangoku rikuchō kinen kyō zusetsu* 漢三國六朝紀年鏡圖說 (An illustrated discussion of dated mirrors from the Han, Three Kingdoms, and Six Dynasties periods). Kyoto, 1943.

Wang Ch'ung 王充. *Lun heng* 論衡 (Discussions weighed in the balance). Peking: Chung Hua, 1979.

Wang Ming 王明. *T'ai p'ing ching ho chiao* 太平經合校 (Comparative edition of the *Classic of Great Peace*). Peking: Chung Hua, 1960.

Wang-tu erh hao Han mu 望都二號漢墓 (Han tomb number two at Wang-tu). Peking: Wen wu, 1959.

Wei Cheng 魏徵 et al. *Sui shu* 隋書 (Book of Sui). Peking: Chung Hua, 1973.

Wen I-tuo 聞一多. *Shen hua yü shih* 神話與詩 (Myth and poetry). Hong Kong: Chung Hua, 1956.

Weng Tu-chien 翁獨健. *Tao tsang tzu mu yin te* 道藏子目引得 (Combined indexes to the authors and titles of books in two collections of Taoist literature). Peking: Harvard-Yenching Institute, 1935.

Wu shang pi yao 無上秘要 (Compendium of insurpassable essentials). HY 1130.

Ying Shao 雁劭. *Feng su t'ung i* 風俗通義 (Comprehensive meanings of airs and customs). *Feng su t'ung i chiao shih* 風俗通義校釋 (Comprehensive meanings of airs and customs, with comparisons and commentary). Tientsin: Jen min, 1980.

Yün chi ch'i ch'ien 雲笈七籤 (Seven slips from a bookbag of clouds). HY 1026. Taipei: Tzu-yu, 1973.

Chinese Character List

Ah mu (Amah) 阿母
Ai ti 哀帝
An Fa-ying 安法嬰
An Lu-shan 安祿山
An ti 安帝
Chang Chi 張籍
Chang Chü 長沮
Chang Hua 張華
Chang I-chih 張易之
Chang Jen-t'an 張仁亶
Chang Pi 張碧
Chang Tao-ling 張道陵
Chang Tzu-fang 張子房
Ch'ang an 長安
Ch'ang Oh 嫦娥
Chao Yen-chao 趙彥昭
Chao Yen-po 趙彥伯
chen fei 眞妃
chen jen 眞人
Chen kao 眞誥
Chen ling wei yeh t'u 眞靈位業圖
Ch'en T'ao 陳陶
Ch'en Tzu-ang 陳子昂
Ch'en Yü 陳羽
Ch'eng ti 成帝
Ch'eng tu 成都
Ch'eng Yü 鄭嵎
ch'i 氣

Ch'i Chi 齊己
Ch'i Hsiao-yao 戚逍遙
ch'i-lin (= Japanese *kirin*) 麒麟
chia 甲
chia tzu 甲子
chiao 醮
Chiao Lien-shih 焦鍊師
chieh shih 解尸
Ch'ih Sung-tzu 赤松子
Ch'ih Yu 蚩尤
Chin mu yüan chün 金母元君
chin shih 進士
Chin shu 晉書
Ch'in shih huang ti 秦始皇帝
Ching ch'eng shan 青城山
Ching shan 荊山
Chou Chao wang 周昭王
Chou Wu ti 周武帝
Chu shu chi nien 竹書紀年
Ch'u Kuang-hsi 儲光羲
Ch'u tz'u 楚辭
chüan 卷
Ch'üan T'ang shih 全唐詩
Ch'üan Te-yü 權德輿
Chuang Chi 莊忌
Chuang Nan-chieh 莊南傑
Chuang-tzu 莊子
Ch'un ch'iu 春秋

Chung tsung 中宗
Erh ya 爾雅
Fa Chen 法振
Fan Ch'eng-chün 范成君
fang shih 方士
feng (phoenix) 鳳
feng (sacrifice) 封
Feng Pu 封陟
"Feng shan shu" 封禪書
fu 賦
fu sang 扶桑
Han Kan 韓幹
Han shu 漢書
Han Wu ku shih 漢武古事
Han Wu-ti 漢武帝
Han Wu-ti nei chuan 漢武帝內傳
Han Yü 韓愈
Hang chou 杭州
Hsi Mu 西母
Hsi Shih 西施
Hsi Wang Mu 西王母
Hsiang chün 湘君
Hsiang fu jen 湘夫人
Hsiang Ssu 項斯
Hsiao Lang 蕭郎
Hsiao Shih 蕭士
Hsien Men-tzu 羨門子
Hsien yang 咸陽
hsien jen 仙人
Hsü Fei-ch'iung 許飛瓊
Hsü Hsüan 徐鉉
Hsü Neng 徐能
Hsü Yen-po 徐彥伯
Hsü Yin 徐夤
Hsüan nü 玄女
Hsüan tsung 玄宗
Hsüan-yüan 軒轅
Hsüeh I-liao 薛宜僚
Hsüeh Neng 薛能
Hsün Hsü 荀勗
Hsün-tzu 荀子

Hu Tseng 胡曾
Hua ch'ing kung 華清宮
Hua shan chih 華山志
Huai nan-tzu 淮南子
huang chin 黃金
Huang-fu Jan 皇甫冉
Huang-Lao 黃老
Huang ti 黃帝
hun t'un (chaos) 渾沌
i ch'iu 乙酉
I nan 沂南
I ch'uan 伊川
jen 壬
Jen Sheng 任生
Jui tsung 睿宗
Kao Shih 高適
Kao tsung 高宗
Ko Hsüan 葛玄
Ko Hung 葛洪
Ku Huan 顧歡
Ku K'uang 雇況
Kuan Hsiu 貫休
Kuan Hsiu-t'iao 管修條
Kuan yin 觀音
K'un-lun shan (Mount K'un-lun) 崑崙山
K'un-lun ch'iu (K'un-lun Hill) 崑崙丘
kuo 國
Kuo P'u 敦璞
lang kan 琅玕
Lao-tzu 老子
li 里
Li chi 禮記
Li Ch'i 李頎
Li Ch'iao 李嶠
Li Ch'ing-sun 李慶孫
Li Chiu-ling 李九齡
Li Ch'ün-yü 李羣玉
Li Fu-jen 李夫人
Li Ho 李賀

Li Hsien 李賢
Li Hsien (Chung tsung)
   李顯(中宗)
Li Hsien-yung 李咸用
Li Hua 李華
Li I 李益
Li K'ang-ch'eng 李康成
Li Lung-chi 李隆基
Li Shang-yin 李商隱
Li Shao-chün 李少君
Li Shun-hsien 李舜弦
Li Po 李白
Li Yü-chung 李虞仲
Liang Kuang 梁廣
Lieh hsien chuan 列仙傳
Lieh tzu 列子
Lin Hsiang-ju 藺相如
Ling Kuang-tzu Ch'i 冷廣子期
Ling Pao 靈寶
Liu Ch'ang-ch'ing 劉長卿
Liu Ch'a 劉叉
Liu Ch'e (= Han Wu-ti)
   劉徹(漢武帝)
Liu Fan 劉蕃
Liu Fu 劉復
Liu Hsien 劉憲
Liu Hsin 劉歆
Liu Kang 劉綱
Liu Pei 劉備
Liu Pi 劉泌
Liu Yen-shih 劉言史
Liu Ts'ang 劉滄
Liu Yü-hsi 劉禹錫
Lo lang 樂浪
Lo yang 洛陽
Lu Ching 陸敬
Lu Kuei-meng 陸龜蒙
luan 鸞
Lung Yü (= Ying Nü-erh)
   弄玉(嬴女兒)
Ma Jung 馬融

Ma Ku 麻姑
Mao Chung 茅衷
Mao Hsien-weng 毛仙翁
Mao Ku 茅固
Mao shan 茅山
Mao Ying (= Mao chün)
   茅盈(茅君)
Meng Chiao 孟郊
Ming Huang 明皇
Mo-tzu 墨子
mu (mother) 母
mu (wood) 木
Mu Kung 木公
Mu T'ien-tzu 穆天子
Mu T'ien-tzu chuan 穆天子傳
nei tan 內丹
Nü Wa 女媧
Pai jih sheng t'ien 白日昇天
pai yün 白雲
Pan Ku 班固
Pao Jung 鮑溶
Pao p'u-tzu 抱朴子
P'eng-lai (= P'eng-hu) 蓬萊(蓬壺)
pi 碧
Pien Ho 卞和
Po Ch'ien-ch'iu 白千秋
Po Chü-i 白居易
Po wu chih 博物志
Shan hai ching 山海經
shang (tuning) 商
Shang ch'ing 上清
Shang ch'ing Lao-tzu chung ching
   上清老子中經
Shang ti 上帝
Shang yüan fu jen (= San yüan fu
   jen?) 上元夫人(三元夫人)
Shao kuang 少廣
Shen Ch'üan-ch'i 沈佺期
Shen i ching 神異經
Shen Nung 神農
Shen Pin 沈彬

Shen Shu-an (Master Shen) 沈叔安
sheng 勝
Sheng Chi fu jen 盛姬夫人
Shih chi 史紀
Shih Chien-wu 施肩吾
Shih chou chi 十洲記
Shih Kung-tzu 石公子
Shih Shu-men 石叔門
Shu 蜀
Shun (= Yü Shun) 舜(虞舜)
Ssu-k'ung T'u 司空圖
Ssu-ma Ch'ien 司馬遷
Ssu-ma Hsiang-ju 司馬相如
Su nü 素女
Sun Ch'i 孫桼
Sung Chih-wen 宋之問
Sung Ling-pin 宋靈賓
Sung shan 嵩山
Ta Tai Li chi 大戴禮記
Tai Shu-lun 戴叔倫
T'ai p'ing ching 太平經
T'ai p'ing tao 太平道
T'ai shan = T'ai yüeh 泰山(泰嶽)
T'ang shih chi shih 唐詩紀事
T'ang Yen-ch'ien 唐彥謙
T'ao Hung-ching 陶弘景
Tao te ching 道德經
Tao tsang 道藏
T'ao Ch'ien (= T'ao Yüan-ming)
    陶潛(陶淵明)
Te tsung 德宗
ti 帝
Ti wang shih chi 帝王世紀
T'ien shih tao 天師道
T'ien t'ai shan 天台山
ting 鼎
Ting Tse 丁澤
Tso chuan 左傳
Ts'ao T'ang 曹唐
Ts'ui Huan 崔渙
Ts'ui Kuo-fu 崔國輔
Tu Fu 杜甫

Tu Kuang-t'ing 杜光庭
Tu Yeh 杜業
Tuan An-hsiang 叚安香
Tung Chung-shu 董仲舒
Tung-fang Shuo 東方朔
tung mu 東母
Tung Shuang-ch'eng 董雙成
tung t'ien 洞天
Tung Wang Kung 東王公
Tung Wang Fu 東王父
t'ung 童
Tzu hsien 紫仙
Tzu wei yüan ling pai yü kuei t'ai
    chiu ling t'ai chen yüan chün
    紫微元靈白玉龜臺九靈太眞元君
Wan Ling-hua 婉淩華
Wang Chien 王建
Wang Chün-feng 王君風
wang fu 王父
Wang Fu-niang 王福娘
Wang Han 王翰
Wang Mang 王莽
wang mu 王母
Wang Tzu-ch'iao 王子喬
Wang Tzu-teng 王子登
Wang Wei 王維
Wang wu shan 王屋山
Wei Ch'ü-mo 韋渠牟
Wei Chuang 韋莊
Wei Hua-ts'un 魏華存
Wei Wen ti 魏文帝
Wei Ying-wu 韋應物
Wen T'ing-yün 溫庭筠
wu ch'en 戊辰
wu ssu 戊巳
Wu Jung 吳融
Wu Liang 武梁
Wu shang pi yao 無上祕要
Wu Tse-t'ien 武則天
Wu yüeh (Five marchmounts)
    五嶽
Wu yüeh chen hsing t'u 五嶽眞形圖

Wu Yüeh ch'un ch'iu 吳越春秋
Wu Yün 吳筠
yang ch'i 養氣
Yang Chiung 楊烱
Yang Hsi 楊羲
Yang Hsiung 楊雄
Yang Kuei-fei 楊貴妃
Yang Ssu-fu 楊嗣復
yao ch'ih 瑤池
Yao Ch'ung 姚崇
Yen ti 炎帝
yin 引
Yin Hsi 尹喜
Yin Yao-fan 殷堯藩
yu 卣

Yü Hsiung 有熊
Yü 禹
Yü Chen 玉眞
Yü Fu 喻鳧
Yü Hang 餘杭
Yü Hsüan-chi 魚玄機
Yü jen 羽人
Yü Shun 虞舜
Yü Wang 榆罔
Yüan Chen 元稹
Yüan Chieh 元結
Yüan shih t'ien tsun 元始天尊
Yüan shih t'ien wang 元始天王
Yung ch'eng chi hsien lu 墉城集仙錄
Yung T'ai 永泰

Index

In this index an "f" after a number indicates a separate reference on the next page, and an "ff" indicates separate references on the next two pages. A continuous discussion over two or more pages is indicated by a span of page numbers, e.g., "57–59." *Passim* is used for a cluster of references in close but not consecutive sequence. Entries are alphabetized letter by letter, ignoring word breaks, hyphens, and accents.

Library of Congress Cataloging-in-Publication Data

Cahill, Suzanne Elizabeth.
   Transcendence and divine passion : the Queen Mother
of the West in medieval China / Suzanne E. Cahill.
      p.   cm.
   Includes bibliographical references and index.
   ISBN 0-8047-2112-2 (cl.) : ISBN 0-8047-2584-5 (pbk.)
   1. Hsi Wang Mu (Taoist deity)   1. Title.
BL1942.H75C34   1993
299'.5142114—dc20   92-26835
                                              CIP

∞ This book is printed on acid-free paper.